Vader, Voldemort and Other Villains

Vader, Voldemort and Other Villains

Essays on Evil in Popular Media

EDITED BY JAMEY HEIT

15 - April - 2011

I hope you find
something good, here or
in the world.

McFarland & Company, Inc., Publishers

Jefferson, North Carolina, and London

LIBRARY OF CONGRESS CATALOGUING-IN-PUBLICATION DATA

Vader, Voldemort and other villains : essays on evil in
  popular media / edited by Jamey Heit.
        p.   cm.
  Includes bibliographical references and index.

  ISBN 978-0-7864-5845-5
  softcover : 50# alkaline paper ∞

    1. Evil in motion pictures.   2. Villains in motion pictures.
  3. Evil in literature.   4. Villains in literature.   5. American
  literature — History and criticism.   6. English literature —
  History and criticism.   I. Heit, Jamey, 1979–
  PN1995.9.E93V33   2011
  791.43'655 — dc22   2011002048

BRITISH LIBRARY CATALOGUING DATA ARE AVAILABLE

Front cover: *top* poster art featuring Ralph Fiennes as Lord Voldemort in *Harry Potter and the Order of the Phoenix*, 2007; bottom
from left Mark Hamill as Luke Skywalker, David Prowse as Darth
Vader in *Star Wars Episode V: The Empire Strikes Back*, 1980 (both
Photofest); background © 2011 Shutterstock

Manufactured in the United States of America

McFarland & Company, Inc., Publishers
  Box 611, Jefferson, North Carolina 28640
  www.mcfarlandpub.com

for Henry, John, and Oliver —
may you grow up in a good world

Acknowledgments

At the outset, I would like to extend my sincere thanks to the brilliant women and men who contributed to this project. They brought a sharp intellectual eye to bear on their respective topics, which resulted in essays that were more than worth reading. It was my pleasure and privilege to work with each of them.

To my friends and colleagues at Glasgow, West Chester, and Princeton, I offer my thanks for your contributions to this project, many of which I am sure remain invisible but are no less significant to the way in which this project came together.

My parents and siblings have spent many (perhaps too many!) hours watching and reading together. I am without a doubt better off for the time that we have spent together reading and re-reading, watching and re-watching, and, of course, quoting so many of the stories that appear in this volume.

Finally, to my wonderful wife Amy, who continues to offer her support to each of my crazy ideas: you are a paragon of what is good in this world.

Contents

Preface

This book emerged out of some simple questions I asked in an introductory philosophy course: What is evil? How do we understand it in our culture? And what do these understandings reveal about our values?

In the discussion that followed, students frequently appealed to prominent figures from within popular culture as answers to the first question. Tellingly, they tied their examples clearly to a range of philosophical concepts. Several students mentioned, for example, that evil is that which good must overcome to restore social order — a task we know well because Harry Potter must defeat Voldemort. Some claimed that evil is merely the absence of good, which suggests that evil is not an ontological category so much as a condition that can be overcome. We know this, one student argued stringently, because Darth Vader turns out to be good in the end.

These are just two of the answers that bridged with ease a supposed gap between our culture's intellectual history and the narratives that are etched in our contemporary social identity. What becomes clear in the essays that follow is that traditional ideas about evil are still present and in fact deeply embedded in the contemporary texts that my students cited. The narratives have been altered, of course, by our ever-shifting cultural values and the different media through which we speak of and to these values; yet throughout the initial discussion and this book, similar notes sound again and again.

After the term ended, I found myself returning to this discussion (always a good sign that the course was not offered in vain!). Philosophy in popular culture has proven to be a legitimate academic concern, but many of the projects in this field speak to a particular series in some depth. What this project seeks to do is thread a rigorous discussion concerning popular culture's narratives through a purposefully wide variety of its constituent parts. The results will, I hope, surprise the reader again and again. Each of the authors in this volume approaches a particular figure, story, or genre from her or his own academic perspective, yet a harmony lingers from one chapter to the next.

1

We understand evil in a particular way, a fact evident in the way that we conceptualize and privilege that which we value, namely evil's constant foe: what is good. The contributors to this project come to a variety of conclusions to the second and third questions above, but share a consistent concern with the implications of how we understand evil and situate it against our overarching commitment to what is good. Evil's presence as a crucial element in our cultural fabric frequently implicates us as a receptive audience for the various media that this project explores. I hope, then, that the project encourages a critical and cultural introspection.

Introduction

In "The Generous Gambler," an unexpected and seemingly inexplicable encounter entices Baudelaire's narrator to descend into a luxurious, subterranean dwelling that could well be paradise. Feeling himself "jostled by a mysterious being whom I had always wanted to meet and whom I recognized immediately, although I had never seen him before,"[1] the narrator does not mind the strange, opium-esque sensations that overwhelm his senses. Beneath typical Parisian cafés, the narrator describes a space that could be heaven: "an enchanted island lit by the glow of an eternal afternoon."[2] It is within this context that the narrator sits down with a mysterious other: "My host and I by the time we were sitting down had become good and longtime friends. We ate, we drank excessively all sorts of extraordinary wines, and, no less extraordinary, it seemed to me I got no more drunk than he."[3]

After the narrator drinks with this strangely familiar stranger, his tale shifts in a way that subverts completely the almost sacramental tone that pervades the story at the outset. An offhanded remark brings the story sharply into focus as it lays bare what is at stake amidst the empty wine bottles: "I should note that I had staked, and (in two-out-of-three) lost, my soul, with nonchalance, with heroic indifference. The soul is a thing so impalpable, often so useless, occasionally annoying, that its loss cost me just a little less emotional disturbance than if I had, on a walk, lost my calling cards."[4] This is a strange thing indeed. The narrator loses his soul over some cards and some good cabernet, yet the consequences of so doing, like the entire story, remain hazy. By the time the reader realizes what is at stake in this story, the damage has been done. A mere glance on the street ends up stripping the narrator of his soul, but the result barely registers within the text. The devil's persona does not fit the stereotype of a horned, muscular maleficent hell-bent on tormenting the narrator with a pitchfork. No, this is a sly devil, one who lures the narrator into a mysterious sense of friendship.

Despite the devil's unflappable nature in this story, Baudelaire does indicate that even the devil has a weakness. The narrator recounts that the devil was "only once ... ever in doubt of his power — the time a preacher, more subtle than most, declared from the pulpit: 'Never, my brethren, forget, when you hear enlightenment vaunted, that the neatest trick of the devil is to persuade you that he does not exist.'"[5] The preacher's words suggest a dual threat to the devil. Obviously, he exposes the devil's strategy within a paradigm defined by good versus evil. The latter, which the devil embodies, succeeds best when treated as though it does not exist. Baudelaire cautions through his preacher against naively labeling a progressive world to be free of (and over) evil. The preacher realizes the tendency of his faith — and by extension, the West — to characterize evil as an obvious presence, readily apparent to anyone who takes time to look. Baudelaire's devil seduces the narrator in a way that characterizes evil's ability to thrive. However, as the preacher points out, the devil's success depends on his ability to *avoid* detection ... until it is too late.

The second threat conveyed in the memory that the devil shares echoes the story's beginning; the devil's strength is his deception, a point reiterated as the story's conclusion. As the night ends, the narrator's consolation comes when the devil promises what the good and, by extension, God, should provide. The narrator initially expresses embarrassment at releasing his soul to the devil, but the devil is, as they say, in the details. While ruminating that what would otherwise be perceived as good things — worldly success, beautiful bodies and the like — is at its core evil, the narrator asserts that he "did not dare believe in such prodigious good fortune."[6] The devil's deception relies on its stealth, which is precisely why the preacher's exposure frightens the devil. In the end, however, the threat has passed. After the devil departs, he still manages to seep into the most intimate of good spaces, the narrator's final prayer, which cries out to God: "My God! O my Lord God! make the devil keep his promise!"[7]

A nineteenth-century French short story might seem like an odd place to begin this analysis of recent American popular culture. Baudelaire's take on evil, however, articulates clearly a powerful representation of the devil, which in turn indicates how the devil, embodied evil, provides a significant counterweight to the central conflict that informs so many of our traditional and contemporary cultural narratives: good versus evil. Where Baudelaire's story departs from the "typical" story of good and evil is the way in which the devil's deception slowly overwhelms the narrator's allegiance to a good God.

This God, or at least the good that this God personifies, lies behind the kinds of stories we find in our culture. Moreover, this God affords a kind of guarantee: as good, God ensures that good wins. With few exceptions,[8] this standard prevails throughout the different examples treated throughout this volume. Grounded firmly within the Judeo-Christian tradition, the devil (or, more broadly, evil) has his moments, but in the end, good people and their values prevail when facing the devil's challenges.

It is, however, precisely this narrative expectation that Baudelaire refuses. He taps into an unspoken but deeply suggestive vein in order to pose a question: in the end, what if we want evil to triumph? In Baudelaire's correspondence, he articulates precisely this possibility: "In every man, at every time, there are two simultaneous tendencies — one towards God, the other towards Satan. The invocation of God or spirituality is a desire to be promoted; that of Satan, or animality, is the joy of descending."[9] This excerpt recalls the way in which Baudelaire frames "The Generous Gambler." When the narrator decides to descend with the stranger, he makes a choice that values implicitly and thus reveals his capacity to give in to evil's appeal. The story is clear that the narrator also has a godly side, but from the beginning, Baudelaire emphasizes that his narrator and, by extension, his readers, understand why the devil's invitation is so compelling. Sartre understands this alternative as crucially important to Baudelaire's writing, which "served 'no other purpose than to give [the poet] the opportunity of *observing himself*.'"[10] Evil's purpose is not to doom the victim, but to provide a gauge that upsets an established moral order. Baudelaire's narrator speaks from within a particular moral framework, but, if Sartre is correct, "The Generous Gambler" exposes an underlying desire to dismiss that framework. Evil, then, reflects the desires that the narrator knows not to speak — desires which, when the narrator is pricked by the devil, slowly overwhelm what the narrator otherwise knows to be good. Confusion surrounding terms like good and evil, a mixture made clear in the final prayer, is the result after drinking with the devil.

By subverting the Western paradigm that privileges good over evil, Baudelaire suggests a different trajectory, which makes its way into the canon of popular culture in the hit film *The Usual Suspects*. Verbal Kint,[11] the villain who masquerades as a low-level criminal, turns out to be much more than he lets on. As Agent Kujan interviews him, Kint spins a story to pass time until he posts bail. Throughout the exchange, Agent Kujan insists that he — and the "good" values he represents as a law enforcement officer — will expose Kint's lies. The point of conflict is crucial; Kint is not telling the truth and Agent Kujan knows this. What Agent Kujan does not recognize, much like Baudelaire's narrator, is the power of the devil to deceive without realizing fully what is unfolding. When Agent Kujan asks Kint about a criminal mastermind, Kaiser Söze, Kint responds: "He is supposed to be Turkish. Some say his father was German. Nobody believed he was real. Nobody ever saw him or knew anybody that ever worked directly for him, but to hear Kobayashi tell it, anybody could have worked for Söze. You never knew. That was his power. The greatest trick the devil ever pulled was convincing the world he didn't exist."[12] Like those of Baudelaire's devil, Kint's words do not register fully; the devil is pulling his greatest trick and the good person fails to realize as much. The film's now classic ending reveals the truth: the devil was within Agent Kujan's grasp the entire time. He could have locked up one of the most dangerous criminals if he had only seen through the devil's smokescreen. What *The Usual Suspects* lacks is the preacher who will identify the devil's one weakness, which emphasizes the role that deception plays when evil is afoot (and makes a better viewing experience as well). Kint/Söze exudes confidence in revealing who he is. Agent Kujan's oversight, which links this short analysis back to Baudelaire, illuminates just how clever evil can be. The good cop, the audience, and even the other bad guys in the movie have been suckered, a victory for the devil that emphasizes the effectiveness of his greatest skill.

The capacity in which "The Generous Gambler" and *The Usual Suspects* intersect affords a symptomatic example of how deeply evil affects the characters, images, and narratives of our popular culture's icons. Moreover, they affirm Sartre's claim: evil captures our attention by questioning subtly the cultural standard that good will prevail. In the essays that follow, evil's role in contemporary cultural narratives underscores the extent to which evil is a thread that often stitches our stories together. Evil's presence challenges the privileged good in important ways. For example, intent plays an important role in determining what constitutes good, yet evil's intent can, on occasion, seek similar outcomes. Virtues traditionally associated with good are frequently the province of evil, a coherence that suggests, in Bataille's analysis, that "evil, ... if we examine it closely, is not only the dream of the wicked: it is to some extent the dream of the good."[13] When we examine evil in our culture, this possibility warrants analysis. Merely invoking an accepted paradigm runs counter to the complex narrative frameworks throughout popular culture and, more significantly, the extent to which that culture that affirms these representations often appreciates or sympathizes with evil. One can recognize at the outset, then, that evil occupies a central position in our cultural conception of narrative and morality in its capacity to interrogate the moral assumptions underlying a simplified notion of the good. Though consistently the marginalized component of our tradition's moral binary, evil's presence is undeniable and sometimes necessary, a reality that problematizes the tendency to dismiss it out of hand.

In this volume, the examples from popular culture return frequently to deeply rooted ways of understanding evil. Perhaps the most prominent influence on evil in popular culture is the Judeo-Christian narrative in the first chapters of Genesis. Here one finds the outlines of a paradigm that affirms good over evil, but in a way that cannot ignore evil's presence in established good as a guideline. In the first chapter, God creates a world that God deems to be thoroughly good. However, by the third chapter of Genesis, one finds that the narrative will not unfold smoothly, despite the simplicity one might expect based on God's own description. Evil, in its vague personification, makes an appearance that will provide a counterweight to the world's proclaimed goodness. It is this presence that is unspooled in the narrative fibers that follow. Our culture does not embrace good icons in isolation; those icons must confront and overcome evil, a task that characterizes much of the Genesis story post-creation. While one can simply relegate evil to the margins and consider it to be just a prop for good's eventual triumph, the essays that follow make clear that evil is a far more substantive and therefore troublesome component of the binary that informs a variety of examples.

The Eden story establishes many of the issues that will appear frequently throughout this book. This particular vignette unfolds against the backdrop of an absolute sense of good present in the world's beginning. God's ontological character prohibits responsibility for the very clear reality that the world is not totally good. Thus, one has to explain what is widely known as the problem of evil. How can a good God permit evil to enter into the world? Someone must bear responsibility for tarnishing this good world, because God cannot be the culprit by virtue of who God is understood to be. Augustine usually receives credit for a common response in his doctrine of Original Sin. The logic works well: God created a wholly good world, but God also gave humans free will, which they subsequently exercised in Eden to disobey God. Within this paradigm, however, one finds an unexplained remainder. A snake tempts Adam and Eve to eat the apple that God has prohibited them from eating. This snake, which personifies the devil, accepts *some* responsibility for what follows, but the question remains: how did the snake get in the garden in the first place?

Because the snake is evil, answers prove unnecessary. What is important, the stock explanation goes, is that humans did not resist the snake's tempting suggestions. What matters, then, is the consequences that human actions produce. While evil's ability to produce abject horror, suffering, and despair knows few limits, the often visceral images that convey these consequences follow an underlying trajectory that is similar to the devil's temptation in Eden. Deceptive and often unnoticed, the snake disappears into the narrative background, while Adam and Eve get on with lying to God about what happened. At the heart of the story, then, one finds the elusive element of evil that produces enormous consequences. Problematically, the cause remains undefined, both in its identity and its origin.

The ease with which the snake remains obviously present yet ultimately unexplained prompts a question that frames the following chapters: what, exactly, is evil? This inquiry provides a baseline for the essays throughout this book. In the popular culture figures that this volume examines, it is very easy to spot the evil character(s). In fact, the evil characters frequently steal the show, even if they ultimately fail in their various plots to subvert their good foils. Perhaps a clue lies in the relative consistency of popular culture's characterization of evil. Evil figures often possess some inherent quality that predisposes them to evil, a deficiency that inhibits their free choice. Those evil people cannot help what they do, which, in a tradition that emphasizes free will, disrupts how we evaluate the perpetrators in question. This dislocation usually emerges alongside plans to acquire power, or money, or sex. In each of these notions, there exists a culturally accepted guideline for what is appropriate and what is not. Too much of any of these things limits or destroys altogether the evil person's ability to recognize that he or she no longer upholds the accepted standard, the good, that the cultural narrative paradigm demands. What gets lost in the story, however, is an important philosophical, theological, and anthropological question that affects any definition of evil: if the villains cannot help themselves, are we right to call them villains? Affirmative responses again return to the edenic gap mentioned above. The consequences of "evil" actions are so troubling that the cause ceases to be a consideration.

A significant part of the problem, as discussed above, exists because of the deceptive tactics that so frequently inform how we define evil. Behind deception lies a quality that our culture usually holds up as a moral good: honesty. Traveling back to Eden yet again, however, one finds that otherwise good people who make a mistake exhibit in the wake of that mistake a striking lack of honesty. Adam and Eve *both* try to escape responsibility for their actions in answering to God. Oddly, what seems to differentiate their deception from the devil's temptation (did they just learn from the devil quickly?) is that they are not very good at deceiving the good character. Adam and Eve thus exhibit the capacity to be evil. Their actions unfold contrary to their good origin and, moreover, to our cultural preference to privilege our ability to live in accordance with some good standard. This dissonance in turn generates significant questions about how we understand evil, what role it plays in understanding our moral expectations, and how those who aspire to be good should compensate for our capacity to choose evil. Perhaps more troublingly, the way that evil subverts the notion of an objectively good example in our culture marks out space wherein evil is not simply the antitype to good. Often, the clearly evil characters behave in a way that is, apart from the respective desired ends, "better" than the good hero. The result, which the contributors to this volume recognize with keen insight, is that one thing the evil figures within our popular culture do well is expose the fissures of a binary that treats good and evil as simply good and evil.

In a good way, perhaps, evil often serves to remind us of the (potential) problems associated with affirming good people and good ideas. By examining prominent evil figures in our popular culture, the essays that follow identify and explore the consequences not only of our capacity for evil — whatever it might be and wherever it comes from — but also the blind affirmation of goodness for goodness's sake. As will become clear, in fact, sometimes we identify more readily with the evil character, a tendency that at the very least cannot simply be ignored. The problem is not merely that evil is so deceptive, but that the good characters, the heroes, so frequently struggle to resist evil's advances. This is not, of course, to take sides in the good-versus-evil question, but rather to affirm the significance of evil's resilience within a cultural tradition that values good. Bataille suggests that this is a crucial concern when navigating our cultural attitudes toward evil: "A rigorous morality results from complicity in the knowledge of Evil, which is the basis of intense communication."[14] One can easily dismiss evil as an example of how not to live a good life, but it does not follow necessarily that good people reject evil. The contrary is quite often true, at least for a bit, and what becomes clear throughout this project is an important corollary to the question of what evil is: why does our culture embrace in these famous figures something that the narratives and their underlying moral binaries reject? Evil, it would seem, is more than a foil for good; it is, in Bataille's words, "a sovereign value"[15] in its own right. The language here is crucial; evil is not merely present, but it affords specific *value* within our cultural consciousness. How valuable evil can be is a concern that will emerge forcefully in the essays that follow.

The chapters have been grouped together in a way that should encourage the reader to examine evil in popular culture from related but distinct perspectives. Chapter 1 instantiates what follows by asking a question that is crucial to every figure mentioned in this book: why does our culture find itself drawn to characters that are so clearly bad within our generally accepted moral binaries? Chapter 2 examines that question in light of the connection between America's cultural values in the 1960s and 1970s and films from this period that embody changing attitudes toward evil in the frequent appearance of the devil in their narratives. Chapter 3 examines another iconic figure who exemplifies good gone wrong: the mad scientist. This figure invites close analysis of the possible conflict between that which our modern world values — science — and the capacity of this institution to use its resources in ways that do not cohere with the notion that the pursuit of knowledge is a wholly good endeavor.

Chapters 4 through 6 develop further the capacity in which evil emerges within a variety of popular narratives. In Chapter 4, one finds in the *Twilight* novels that evil is, in some respects, sterilized. No longer the embodiment of overt evil, the villains are instead characters whose discord with the narrative's clearly good protagonists serves to affirm author Stephenie Meyer's own moral belief system. Chapter 5 similarly finds a complex portrayal of evil in the Great Mother archetype in several Disney films. Finally, in Chapter 6 the female FBI agent intertwines with a masculine villain in ways that both challenge and subvert the kinds of moral dichotomies that emerge in chapters 3 and 4.

Evil's integral nature — both within the good-versus-evil binary, as well as within the definition of what constitutes evil — occupies the concerns of chapters 7 and 8. The former examines the alluring evil that C.S. Lewis' White Witch embodies and, in light of this analysis, explores the implications of such a portrayal of evil through the lens of reader-response criticism. The latter analyzes Philip Pullman's *His Dark Materials*, which inverts a traditional Christian moral framework in suggesting an understanding of evil that departs from the standard set by Pullman's predecessors.

Two recent developments in our cultural canon receive due attention in the next two chapters. In Chapter 9, the burgeoning world of gaming reveals a significant possibility that emerges when the audience can participate in the conflict between good and evil. The ability not only to be but also to thrive as a specifically evil avatar suggests that our allegiance to good may not be as strong as other narrative forms suggest. In a similarly revealing way, Chapter 10 examines how the television show *24* blurs the lines between good and evil insofar as these supposedly discordant notions reveal noticeable similarities in both their agendas and the tactics used in order to realize these ends.

The final grouping examines some of the most widely known villains from popular culture. Chapter 11 analyzes the tremendous success of *The Dark Knight*, a film in which the key character is not the protagonist, Batman, but rather the clearly evil Joker. The Joker's appeal suggests reasons why evil may not be dismissed easily. Chapter 12 looks at Darth Vader and concludes that even this apparently vile character holds open a powerful possibility: despite the flaws in a moral binary that sometimes blindly believes in the notion of good, there remains hope that good may still triumph in the end. The final essay, Chapter 13, which explores the nuances of J.K. Rowling's Lord Voldemort, similarly questions the cultural default position that we always prefer good and reject evil in search of that good.

In these introductory comments, I have only begun to touch on the important cultural questions raised, and the answers we tend to provide, when discussing the reality that evil is very much part of our intellectual and cultural fabric. If one opens a book, turns on the television, or goes to the theatre, one is likely to realize what comes into focus in this volume's essays: the devil has not tricked us, at least not yet. Evil is pervasive and therefore needs to be taken seriously. In the chapters that follow, ideas hinted at in this introduction will take further shape through the lenses of varied disciplines. Similar notes will sound and rebound between chapters as each essay recognizes our underlying cultural fascination with evil.

NOTES

1. Charles Baudelaire, "The Generous Gambler," *Paris Spleen: Little Poems in Prose*, trans. Keith Waldrop (Middletown, CT: Wesleyan University Press, 2009), 59.
2. Ibid.
3. Ibid.
4. Ibid., 59–60.
5. Ibid., 60.
6. Ibid., 61.
7. Ibid.
8. One is reminded here of Dark Helmet's famous claim to Lone Star: "Evil will always triumph because good is dumb" (*Spaceballs*). While Dark Helmet parodies the narrative structure of *Star Wars* and, by extension, the paradigm at hand, his remark illuminates two salient features in these introductory remarks. First, Dark Helmet's words turn out to be absurd because the opposite—which our culture expects—inevitably proves to be true. Dark Helmet, Colonel Sanders, and President Skroob make plenty of mistakes that lead to their exile. On the other hand, there is a hint of truth to the claim insofar as evil does rely on good's failure to recognize that evil is at hand. The devil in Baudelaire's story claims as much; evil thrives when good is unaware of evil's presence.
9. Quoted in Georges Bataille, *Literature and Evil*, trans. Alastair Hamilton (London: Marion Boyars, 2006), 52. It is important to note that Baudelaire's comments echo two important elements of the West's Christianized anthropology. First, the dichotomy between good and evil is conveyed through the spatial distinction between up and down. These terms' orienting spatial implications reflect an accepted symbolic value: good is up and evil is down. Secondly, a classic dualism, with its privilege of the spiritual, amplifies the value judgments indicated in the different planes established through spatial language. An implicit partiality exists towards the spiritual, while the body's capacity (and desire) for pleasure problematizes spiritual development. This is, of course, a bias accepted within Christianity's intellectual tradition in most orthodox understandings.
10. Quoted in Bataille, 42.
11. Kint's real first name is Roger, which calls attention to the fact that throughout the film, he goes by Verbal. Kint, as the devil disguised, deceives primarily through language.
12. *The Usual Suspects*, directed by Bryan Singer (Los Angeles: MGM, 2000), DVD.
13. Bataille, 21.
14. Ibid., ix.
15. Ibid.

BIBLIOGRAPHY

Bataille, Georges. *Literature and Evil*. Trans. Alastair Hamilton. London: Marion Boyars, 2006.
Baudelaire, Charles. "The Generous Gambler." *Paris Spleen: Little Poems in Prose*. Trans. Keith Waldrop. Middletown, CT: Wesleyan University Press, 2009.
Spaceballs. Directed by Mel Brooks. Los Angeles: MGM, 2000. DVD.
The Usual Suspects. Directed by Bryan Singer. Los Angeles: MGM, 2006. DVD.

1

The Aesthetic of Evil

Daniel A. Forbes

When *Star Wars* first came out I was a kid who loved to play with action figures. But the first action figures I wanted from *Star Wars* were not the heroes Luke Skywalker and Han Solo. I wanted Darth Vader and an Imperial Stormtrooper. I would of course get the good guy (and good gal) action figures later, but the bad guys were the ones that I found the most fascinating and desirable. Part of the reason why, if you had asked me back then, was that I found these characters cool. And they really *looked* cool — much cooler than any of the heroes. Even their spaceships looked cooler — the TIE fighters and Imperial AT-AT walkers were among my favorites.

I'm not alone. When the *Star Wars* prequels were released there were plenty of toys, posters, and other knick-knacks featuring the new bad guys — Darth Maul, Jango Fett, General Grievous, etc. Another generation of young people clearly found the villains very cool.[1] Even now as an adult I continue to find them very appealing — and, when they're at their best, very intriguing.

On the one hand, this seems very strange. The bad guys are, well, *bad* — we shouldn't idolize or identify with them, should we? We are supposed to reject them for their villainy. Moreover, identifying with the bad guys amounts to picking the losers. They are fated to be defeated in the vast majority of movie and television plots — the bad guys are simply not supposed to win. Why should anyone gravitate toward these characters? On the other hand we recognize that often in the real world the boundaries between good and bad are not so clear — perhaps because these labels represent not so much the intrinsic characters of persons and their actions, but our own judgments about them, judgments shaped by differences in perspective and personal bias. So our interest in evil may not be so strange — it may simply be an interest in a different perspective. Then again, my interest in Darth Vader as a youngster really seemed focused on the fact that he was a *bad* guy — not that I thought his goals or his methods were something I might consider emulating!

The allure of the villain is puzzling. If good and evil have intrinsic natures that oppose one another, and we understand that there are compelling reasons to favor good over evil, evil shouldn't seem so intriguing. Or if good and evil are not intrinsic characters, but simply a way of depicting difference and opposition, then it's not clear why the bad guys should be any more cool than the good guys — it should just be a matter of preference.

The presentation in popular culture of some villains as "cool," which I refer to here as the aesthetic of evil, does not have a simple explanation. Here I will explore one aspect of this phenomenon: the role of the villain in popular narrative and its relation to our perception of narrative meaning. The distinction between good and evil is most readily apparent in the narrative tradition that has its roots in cultural mythology, and continues today in narratives of futuristic and fantastic adventure. The *Star Wars* movies, for example, exemplify the continuation of traditional mythological themes in contemporary popular culture; their creator, George Lucas, was strongly influenced by the work of mythology scholar Joseph Campbell.[2] It is in cinema and television where we can see the shiny black armor and hear the deep voice and mechanical breathing of Darth Vader — and fully appreciate just how appealing he is. So for the most part I will consider examples from fantastic narratives in these media. I will argue that the "cool" appearance and intriguing persona of a villain like Vader reflects the importance of his role in generating meaning in a certain kind of fictional narrative. By contrast there are other sorts of villains who are repellent rather than intriguing, and they reflect a different kind of narrative that serves a different purpose and has a different meaning. But before we can examine the narrative role of the villain in detail, we must first examine how evil is understood as a problem for philosophical thought in general.

The Problem of Evil

Many philosophers regard evil as a problematic feature of the world that requires some sort of explanation. Frequently evil is conceived as a theological problem: if there exists a God (or other supreme being) who is unlimitedly good and powerful, then such a being would eliminate evil wherever it might appear — or even make it impossible for evil to arise in the first place. But the persistent reality of evil in our world seems to show that the existence of this being is in fact impossible: if a being with unlimited power and uncompromising benevolence truly existed, evil would simply never appear in our experience. Hence many attempts have been made to explain the presence of evil in such a way that it does not rule out the possibility of a supremely good and powerful being.[3]

But, as Susan Neiman argues, to conceive of the existence of evil as a problem does not require that we think of it in terms of belief in God. The problem of evil can be framed as a more fundamental existential problem: why do we have the sense that things ought to be otherwise than they are?[4] This problem can be articulated in religious *and* secular ways, and seems equally a problem for both perspectives. The problem demands a solution that in some way makes sense of the reality of evil.

Philosophers and theologians have proposed many solutions to the problem of evil, but finding an explanation for evil often seems to imply that ultimately there's nothing *wrong* with it — that it's in some sense supposed to be here. But if this is so, this contradicts our feeling that evil ought not to exist, even though it does.[5] But perhaps evil simply cannot be explained — and this inexplicability may be what defines evil itself. Perhaps only what is good may be capable of genuine explanation or justification. Hence evil by its very definition should not make sense; it is in fact our frustration with its inexplicability and nonsensicality that incites us to struggle against it in an effort to eliminate it. However, this sort of answer seems paradoxical: if we can say that evil is simply whatever is inexplicable, then doesn't this amount to a sort of explanation? And does it seem right to judge that something we cannot explain must not be good? In any case this approach will not help with the question of why villains are such enticing characters. There are reasons why we find darkly evil characters enticing — and if there are reasons, then there must be an explanation.

Our cultural interest in villains suggests we perceive evil as in some way important; we have a sense that we need the bad guys. But this points directly to the core of the problem: we recognize that evil is somehow indispensable, yet we conceive of it as something that we are obligated to eliminate! Our understanding of evil thus seems deeply contradictory. To undertake the project of making sense of evil is tantamount to judging that it must have some genuine value in our world — but if it has genuine value, it seems to amount to classifying it as a variety of good rather than as something opposed to good by its very nature! What we are called upon to do, then, is explain how evil could be important — without simply converting it into a disguised form of good.

Are Evil and Good Merely Different?

This seemingly inescapable contradiction at the heart of the problem of evil suggests there is perhaps something wrong with our understanding of the problem. If proposed answers regularly lead to contradiction, then maybe the trouble is in our conception of the problem and not in our attempts to solve it. The problem of evil may be what philosophers call a "pseudoproblem"— a puzzle that superficially appears to be a real problem but is really just the effect of ignorance or confusion. Pseudoproblems are corrected not by a direct attack on what we conceive as a problem but instead by showing that there is no real problem in the first place.

The fact that there are villains whose choices we understand, even if we do not agree with them, suggests that the distinction between good and evil is not as clear-cut as we sometimes think. We may take for granted that it is a simple matter to identify who is good and who is evil, as though these labels identify intrinsic qualities of an individual (or at least of his or her actions). We usually take the familiar distinction between good and evil to be a particular instance of opposition, like heat and cold, or light and dark. But perhaps good and evil are simply labels for *opposition itself* when it comes to human motivations — that is, perhaps they identify incompatible differences in perspective or purpose. We label as "good" the perspective we should prefer, and as "evil" any perspective opposed to it. Since different individuals choose differently according to their perspective, perhaps "good" and "evil" are relative: what is "good" for one individual is "evil" for another. We value our own perspective over those of others simply because that is the perspective we happen to hold — and labeling our own perspective "good" turns out to be a way of excusing ourselves from taking the perspectives of others seriously.

So perhaps we can "solve" the problem of evil by simply defusing it: we can say that evil isn't really evil in any absolute sense. It is simply a *different* value rather than an intrinsically *negative* value. So long as we presume that good and evil are inherent characteristics of persons or their actions, we remain trapped by the problem — but as soon as we accept that evil and good are really matters of perspective the problem dissolves. In this way neither good nor evil needs any special explanation — they only require the ordinary explanations of the opponents' motives and how they come into conflict.

Will this solution work? When we examine the actions of heroes and villains closely, we find that both resort to similar methods for achieving their goals. This suggests that perhaps they are simply at odds with one another because their goals are different and incompatible. Sometimes we characterize acts of force, violence, and deception as evil, but frequently both good and evil characters will resort to these methods. Indeed, the use of force often seems necessary in order to defeat the forces of evil, and characters who attempt to negotiate peacefully with villains are frequently depicted as woefully naïve. And we find the hero almost invariably confronts the villain with the same sorts of deception and violence that the villain wields. In the *Star Wars* movies the Galactic Empire is willing to pursue its goals by waylaying small starships, lying to a princess in order to obtain the location of a hidden rebel base, and obliterating planets — but the Rebellion employs spies to obtain the plans to gigantic Death Star battle stations housing thousands of people, and then sends fleets of ships to destroy them. Even the noble Jedi knight Obi-Wan Kenobi is willing to deceive Luke Skywalker about what happened to his father, while Darth Vader is eager to reveal the truth.[6] Good and evil thus seem to amount to a difference of perspective; as Anakin Skywalker quips in *Revenge of the Sith*, from the perspective of the villainous Sith it is the Jedi who are evil.

But perhaps it is really the *goals* of their actions and not their methods that differentiate heroes and villains. The bad guys cause injustice and the good guys fight to restore justice, right? But how exactly do we define justice? The Borg, depicted in some of the *Star Trek* series and films, are an "evil" civilization that lives in an orderly collective consciousness with the goal of "assimilating" other civilizations and their technological knowledge. We (and Starfleet) may object to this goal, but are we really in a position to argue that the Borg are objectively unjust or evil? When we reflect on their goals we can see that they make sense on their own terms: the Borg seek order, growth, and knowledge. We may object that the Borg's goals involve imposing their particular vision of order and knowledge upon others who would live differently. But don't the good guys also want to impose their values on the villains by defeating them?

Some narratives explicitly acknowledge the similarities between good and evil and invite us to grapple with defining the difference. For example, the recent reimagining of the *Battlestar Galactica* television series takes advantage of our expectation that the human survivors are good and the robotic (and very cool-looking!) Cylons who attack them are evil. But the series blurs the boundaries between human and robot, thus inviting us to question whether either side can easily be classified as good or evil. The villainous machines in the *Matrix* trilogy establish a stable order for human beings in a virtual reality simulation — and so they institute a sort of law and order that opposes the unpredictability and potential for destructive chaos inherent in human freedom. In the films of the *Matrix* trilogy the machines seem clearly evil — but one of the short films of the *Animatrix*, "The Second Renaissance," reveals that human civilization's treatment of machines as a slave race is part of what led the machines to create the Matrix in the first place. The disregard humans have for machines, and the willingness of humans to take extraordinarily harmful measures in order to maintain their power, suggests that imprisonment of humanity in the Matrix was in fact the realization of a sort of justice.

Is Evil in a Certain Sense Good? The Function of Villainous Evil in Popular Narrative

Even if good and evil could be differences in perspective, we still desire an explanation for why this distinction persists in popular narrative. Heroes and villains usually *look* different, and this indicates the importance of being able to identify characters as good or evil. There is an important difference between hero and villain as defined by the structure of narrative, and this readily suggests an explanation for the special appeal of the dark villain. The villain is characterized by power, whether it is the overt power of the Dark Side of the Force which Darth Vader wields, or the cunning planning of the otherwise ordinarily empowered Joker in *The Dark Knight*. The villain's use of power to achieve his or her own ends initiates the plot of a narrative in which good and evil square off. The villain's actions create a problem, and the hero's story is the process of resolving the problem by thwarting the villain's plans. Since the villain's power generates narrative drama, perhaps we find the villain appealing because *we* would like to enjoy that sort of power.

But is playing the role of the "problem" in the structure of the plot all there is to being a villain? If so, then all there is to heroism is being the character whose story of struggle we happen to follow in the narrative. If *Star Wars* had opened with the destruction of the Death Star, and then followed Darth Vader's efforts to track down the rebels and destroy their base on Hoth to avenge the loss of the battle station and all the lives aboard it, thus ending the Rebellion's threat to the Galactic Empire — would that have been enough to make Darth Vader the good guy? (Would I then have wanted to buy the Luke Skywalker action figure first because he was the bad guy and therefore cool?) Something about this scenario doesn't seem quite right. Perhaps treating good and evil as merely relative is not as plausible a solution as it initially seems.[7]

There remains a tension between evil as something to be rejected and defeated, and evil as nevertheless *important*, and importantly different from good. When we consider the difference between hero and villain we see that deep down we believe there must be some criterion to objectively (or at least non-subjectively) establish a perspective as inadequate or problematically biased. That is, we are not simply choosing sides based on which one we happen to like better. We have the sense that we are supposed to evaluate each side, and find good reasons for identifying with one side or the other.

The philosopher John Dewey examines the mixture of stability and precariousness in our experience and suggests a possible approach to interpreting the importance of evil. Dewey identifies a tension between the comfortably understood and the dangerously mysterious in our experience, and argues that the latter plays a pivotal role: "The visible is set in the invisible; and in the end what is unseen decides what happens in the seen; the tangible rests precariously upon the untouched and ungrasped."[8] Dewey argues that much of religious belief and philosophy focuses on sanitizing our experience by removing the sense of randomness and danger from our interpretations of the world and grounding our sense of reality in what is permanent and unchanging. We want to conceive of the world as predictable and consistent — but our experience inevitably dashes this hope. Dewey argues that our attempts to make sense of the world should reflect both the safety of what we understand and the danger of what is mysterious to us. Without both the stable and the precarious, we would be incapable of intellectual, social, and moral growth — in short, we would be incapable of *constructive progress*.[9]

Dewey's argument suggests that good and evil in narrative reflect the interplay of stability and danger in our experience, for the very nature of plot presupposes the reality and value of some sort of progress. Different sorts of narratives, then, reflect different aspects of this interplay. In a simple good-versus-evil narrative we may be invited to simply acquiesce to the flow of the story: the forces of stability struggle but in the end defeat danger. The villains in this sort of narrative may be bumbling and even comical (common in narratives for children, where we don't really want to scare them — the bad guys in *Power Rangers*, for example), or they can be exaggeratedly unpleasant (more common for adults, who aren't as easily frightened). But either way the evil is representative of the danger and instability that threaten our security, and our existing values are reinforced through the hero's victory. In this sort of narrative, evil has value simply insofar as it provides a problem for the hero to solve — that is, it has value simply as a necessary symbolic component of the plot.

But the hero-versus-villain narrative structure can reflect a different role for evil. A narrative may invite us to examine the evil that is supposed to be rejected, and at the same time invite us to examine the values we take for granted. In these cases the villain may represent an opposing perspective — and by exploring the narrative we take on the danger of examining our values and possibly changing them. In short, the villain may be symbolic of the risk involved in reflecting on our beliefs — which may threaten established values, but is also necessary for adventure and growth. Hence perhaps part of the villain's "cool factor" is that we are supposed to take an opposing perspective seriously as an alternative to the values we already accept. Alternatively, the bad guys may in fact represent the status quo, and the good guys may seek to destabilize that status quo, just as the Rebellion seeks to destabilize the Galactic Empire. But the bottom line is that the villain plays a valuable role in this sort of narrative — the instigator of a challenge to our values — and thus needs to be appealing in order for us to take the challenge seriously.

If the stability we usually associate with good must be countered by the precarious and dangerous — the factors we associate with evil — then there's good reason that we should find evil interesting, fascinating, and important. Our experience regularly involves uncertainty and danger; hence narratives that do not involve danger seem so unrealistic that we find them uninteresting and irrelevant. We sometimes are not entirely conscious of this symbolic resonance of evil, and in some narratives the villains invite us to reflect on the significance of evil itself. In *The Dark Knight* the Joker at times seems quite conscious of the importance of the interplay between the stable and lawful and the dangerous and chaotic, and seems to take precariousness to a new level in order to make his point to Batman — and to us.

The narrative role of evil suggests an explanation for why the villains are so intriguing — and why they look so cool. Characters like Boba Fett and Darth Maul from the *Star Wars* movies are mysterious and hidden from us by helmets and armor, or a disguise of intricate tattoos. We don't know much about them, and so we are left to speculate about how they came to be who they are — and even who they are in the first place. Their mysterious threat to the heroes symbolizes the open-endedness and precariousness that define their role in the narrative space. They symbolize the danger that can threaten our values — or provoke us to reassess them.

Villains Who Are Not Cool: The Banality of Evil

But does this account of the aesthetic of evil do justice to our sense that evil must be rejected? So far we have examined villains whom we find intriguing. Their appeal relates to their expression of power, and to our sense that evil is in some sense necessary to making our lives precarious in a way that is ultimately good for us. In some sense these presentations of evil reveal a culturally ingrained belief that evil in a broad sense is something that we must accept and even at some level celebrate. We all have a dark side that helps make life complex, interesting, and meaningful. But there are other appearances of evil in narrative where the villains are repellent, and even those of us who find evil fascinating are unable to identify with them. These characters and their actions are utterly horrifying. I argue that in these cases the villain does something that derails our sense of narrative. Here I will examine two striking cinematic examples, *Schindler's List* and *Life Is Beautiful*, both of which depict stories that take place in what many would identify as the worst evil committed in the twentieth century, the Holocaust.[10]

In Steven Spielberg's *Schindler's List* many characters commit acts of evil, but the central villain[11] is Amon Göth, the commandant of the forced labor camp at Płaszów, Poland. Göth commits many disturbing acts in the film, but one in particular is especially chilling. After a party, a drunken Göth has a conversation with Oskar Schindler, who knows that Göth regularly murders Jewish laborers — sometimes because they are not working efficiently, sometimes for no apparent reason. Göth commits these atrocities as an expression of arbitrary power. Schindler, hoping to encourage Göth to stop committing these murders, suggests that killing those one regards as wrong may be justice, but it is not an exercise of power; true power is to refrain from killing even where one is justified in doing so. Göth takes Schindler's suggestion seriously, since at some level he recognizes that he is not as powerful (and not as happy) as he would like to be; despite his power Göth is clearly depressed. He experiments with Schindler's suggestion, "pardoning" a Jewish boy for dropping a saddle, and a Jewish girl who is caught not working. Finally the Jewish boy fails to clean a stained bathtub. Göth initially "pardons" him, but seems unable to reconcile himself to the act of forgiveness. Göth "pardons" himself in a mirror, perhaps forgiving himself for what he is about to do, and then murders the boy.

One thing that makes this scene chilling is that Göth has an opportunity to become more humane and yet in the end he consciously chooses not to change. Why? Does he fear he will lose the respect of his men, or his position of power? Does he enjoy the arbitrary exercise of power over life and death too much? The film does not answer this question for us. But it seems clear that whatever his reason, Göth's decision not to change was unquestionably a moral failure, and one that does not make him intriguing as a villain. In fact in our eyes it *diminishes* him.

In Roberto Benigni's *Life Is Beautiful* there is no clear villain. Benigni's film is in its first half a light slapstick or romantic comedy, but in its second half a comedic drama about the Holocaust. While some at the time of the film's release considered the narrative combination of comedy and concentration camp offensive, this film in no way makes light of the Holocaust. In fact, it contains a scene that is one of the most chilling ever seen in any movie, and it powerfully expresses the horror of the Holocaust without a single act of physical violence.

In the first half of the film we are introduced to Dr. Lessing, a German physician living in Italy. The protagonist of the film, Guido Orefice, an Italian Jew, is a waiter at a restaurant Lessing frequents, and there Guido and Lessing enjoy sharing riddles with one another. In the second half of the film, Guido and his son have been taken to a concentration camp, and during a medical inspection we discover that Lessing is the camp physician. Guido's hopes are lifted as he believes his friend will help him and his son escape the camp, and Guido is encouraged by the fact that Lessing manages to obtain work for him

at a dinner party for the German staff. Lessing makes furtive overtures to
Guido at the party, hinting that he has important news. When they finally
are able to speak privately, Lessing appears ready to suggest a plan for Guido's
escape — but instead poses a riddle. Lessing admits he is stumped by the riddle,
and is desperate for Guido's help in solving it. He pleads for his help, saying,
"Help me, Guido ... I can't even sleep." Guido's face falls as he realizes that
not only does Lessing have no intention of helping with an escape, but it
seems the idea never even occurred to Lessing.

What is particularly horrifying about the scene is that Dr. Lessing effec-
tively *makes himself* into a villain. What we have seen of Lessing earlier in the
movie suggests that he considers Guido a friend and respects him as a human
being. The fact that Lessing is a physician suggests that he has a sense of compassion and respect for human life. And the comedic tone of the movie invites
us to expect that Lessing will help Guido in a time of desperate need. But
Lessing does not simply refuse to help; he fails to acknowledge that Guido
needs his help, because he does not recognize Guido's humanity. And not
only are Guido's hopes crushed, but our expectations of the comedic narrative
are devastatingly disappointed.

The characters of Göth and Lessing illustrate what Hannah Arendt calls
"the banality of evil." Popular narrative portrays villains as consciously evil —
as individuals with fiendish intentions. But through her analysis of the war
crimes trial of Adolf Eichmann, a Nazi official, Arendt judges that that this
man was not a malevolent monster with intentions of evil but rather a fairly
ordinary person. Eichmann's evil did not consist in conscious malevolence,
but in a lack of reflective moral concern in his actions; he was focused more
on his own personal advancement than on the moral ramifications of his
choices, and used "I was only following orders" as an excuse to absolve himself
from responsibility for participation in mass murder.[12] The example of Eichmann reveals that any and all of us are capable of active participation in great
evil, even if we do not consciously intend to do evil.

In both Spielberg's and Benigni's films, the villain has a choice between
doing good and doing evil. But in each narrative the villain makes a choice
that derails the narrative. It's not simply a surprise or a "plot twist," but a
feeling that something has gone wrong with the story itself, something that
ought not to have happened. Though it is a matter of history that the real
Amon Göth did not experience any change of heart about his actions, Spielberg presents him within the narrative of *Schindler's List* as someone who had
a choice, and who made the wrong one. If Göth had decided to keep "pardoning" the Jewish prisoners, more lives would have been saved — perhaps
even his own. The story would have been different, and we also have the sense
that it would have been *better* and more uplifting had Göth chosen differently.

Dr. Lessing by all the rules of dramatic comedy should have helped Guido and his family make an exciting escape from the concentration camp — but instead Lessing reveals he is morally bankrupt. These narrative events are jarring, and they rouse us from a sense of complacency. Many narratives reinforce our conceptions of good and evil, or ask us to reflect on our values, but they do not ask any more of us; we are free to enjoy or reflect upon the narrative as a completed picture. But in cases where the narrative is subjected to a jarring event we are provoked to make a moral judgment that involves feeling simultaneous outrage and sorrow. We find these characters and their actions horrifying because they represent deep moral cowardice. These villains commit atrocities against persons who are unable to resist. What's more, they were in a position to do real good. Had they acknowledged the humanity of those they betrayed and made different choices, the plots of their narratives might have been less tragic. These stories are made sadder because of choices that, given our expectations of the narrative, should not have been made.

And this is part of Spielberg's and Benigni's point. While these films celebrate heroism, they also indict failure where failure was not inevitable. Where conventional cinematic plots leave us feeling comfortable about our values, or at best ask us to reflect thoughtfully on those values, the plots of narratives like *Schindler's List* and *Life Is Beautiful* demand that we check to make sure that we really do live up to our deeper values. Would we stand idly by as others suffer and die? We cannot afford to, both for our own sake and for the sake of those who would be harmed if we failed. And so these films leave us unsettled and feeling an obligation to act against injustice. We are exhorted not to acquiesce to the banality of evil. Where conventional cinematic plots do not incite any concrete action, these films urge us to act to right injustices. They make us uncomfortable so that we may recognize the need to take positive action to make changes. And they remind us that each of us is fully capable of contributing to great good or to great evil even through small acts. Our personal flaws are no excuse for not trying. Even the self-serving, womanizing war-profiteer Oskar Schindler — who even after the war continued to suffer misfortune due to the flaws in his character — was capable of doing a great good in a very bad situation.

The Third Player: Meaning

Our examination of two manifestations of evil in cinematic and television narrative — the villain who is intriguing, and the villain who is horrifying — suggests that good and evil are not the entire picture. The philosopher Charles S. Peirce argues that that when we are faced with a duality, a third thing is needed to complete the picture and stabilize it.[13] We found a problem in the duality of good and evil: when we try to make sense of evil it ends up looking like a species of good, but evil seems to be the sort of thing that must be quite different from good. The third piece of the puzzle that will hold good and evil together without making them the same thing concerns the goal of understanding evil in such a way that it *makes sense* to us. We can refer to this as *meaning*.

The word *meaning* is ironically difficult to define. But since we are examining evil in the context of popular narrative, for our purposes we can identify meaning as what we come away with when we have made sense of a story. If we watch a movie or read a book and cannot make sense of its story, we have a feeling that perhaps the movie has no meaning. I, for one, tried to read William S. Burroughs' *Naked Lunch* and couldn't understand much of what was going on, nor did I have the feeling that what was happening made any sense. I felt as though I wasn't getting anything from the novel, and so I felt that the book lacked meaning. (There are many who disagree with me on this one; maybe I will try to read it again some time.) Moreover, if we experience a story and feel like the plot makes a "wrong turn," we may question whether or not the story is genuinely meaningful because it seems to give us the wrong message. I had this very feeling watching Tim Burton's remake of *Planet of the Apes*. I won't spoil the finale of the movie here, but to me it didn't feel as though it brought the plot to an end in way that made sense. Instead, it involved a plot twist that to me didn't seem connected with the rest of the story. And so I experienced that movie as lacking meaning.

Meaning is the common denominator between narratives with intriguing villains and narratives with repellent villains. In narratives where evil is appealing, we perceive the presence of the villain as making sense within the plot. The villain is an essential part in such narratives and hence has a well-defined and important role. It makes sense that evil should have a particular look and style, so that we can readily identify it and understand how it fits into the narrative. And it makes sense that we in some sense *appreciate* the villain and his or her deeds, because without the villain there is nothing to drive the plot of the narrative. This explains how we can reject the villain for his or her evil character and deeds and nevertheless consider the villain important. It is somewhat paradoxical, but the evildoing of the classic villain is part of our enjoyment of the narrative. If the villain *weren't* appealing, we wouldn't find the narrative as meaningful.

But narratives like *Schindler's List* and *Life Is Beautiful* relate to meaning in a different way. Both films deal with the Holocaust, an event in modern history that continues to reverberate in our collective consciousness. Part of the reason for this is our deep-seated sense that it should never have happened in any civilized culture — which invites the justified worry that, if we are not vigilant, it may happen again. Values that we would expect any civilized culture to uphold — respect for human life and dignity, in all of its forms — were trampled. Hence the Holocaust presents a challenge to our complacency.

In this context the characters of Amon Göth and Dr. Lessing are not ordinary villains. Each is presented with a choice where one option leads to a satisfying (but conventional) conclusion to the narrative, whereas the other derails it. Both Göth and Lessing make the wrong choice and frustrate our expectations. As a result their actions threaten the meaningfulness of the narrative. However, there is a way that we as an audience can actively participate in making meaning out of the jarring events in the narrative: we can choose to take positive moral stands that we are ready to carry out in our own lives. That is, these films do not intend to leave the audience entirely satisfied. They intend to provoke some degree of dissatisfaction — dissatisfaction that will, with luck, lead to positive action to enact, rather than simply accept, the moral values expressed.

One of the lessons of the continuing struggle for civil rights has been that individuals need to take positive actions to make change, rather than wait for these changes to occur "naturally."[14] Could a narrative be used to encourage people to take these actions? I argue that narratives can do this, because *Schindler's List* and *Life Is Beautiful* are clear examples. Both of these movies are uplifting in their own way — they remind us of the possibilities of goodness in the human spirit, even for individuals of ordinary character and ability. But at the same time they involve jarring events in their narrative plots that shake us out of complacency, and these events involve the manifestation of evil. They are not grandiose but a banal sort of evil — the sort that ordinary people are capable of, if they so choose. At the same time they are serious evils that our values absolutely prohibit, and that we feel an obligation to prevent. And so these films leave us feeling unsettled — and if we respond by consciously accepting responsibility to respond to such evils, we are able to supply the meaning of the narrative through our actions.

Where does this leave the aesthetic of evil? As we have seen, evil is not always easy to identify. A conventional narrative that ends with the victory of the good guy and the defeat of the bad guy can still ask challenging questions about how we should identify heroism and villainy. A narrative like *The Dark Knight*, while it concludes with the defeat of its villain, nevertheless invites us to contemplate the challenging critique embodied in the actions of the Joker. Are human beings essentially selfish, and must they inevitably abandon their moral values when their lives are at stake? Does human selfishness inevitably lead to the systematic corruption, betrayal, and deception that entangle *all* the characters in *The Dark Knight*? A narrative that takes advantage of the importance of the role of evil to drive narrative can also be used to invite us to reflect on ideas and values that we take for granted. Where our ideas of "good" may need critical analysis, an evil that seems "cool" can help us to see the chinks in the White Knight's armor. In this way such narratives can show that evil is not good, but it is nevertheless meaningful.

Notes

1. At the time of this writing Lucasfilm is celebrating the 30th anniversary of the release of *The Empire Strikes Back*. The anniversary advertising prominently features the now iconic bounty hunter Boba Fett.

2. An accessible introduction to Campbell's thought (and Campbell's influence on George Lucas' development of the original *Star Wars* trilogy) is Joseph Campbell, *The Power of Myth*, with Bill Moyers, ed. Betty Sue Flowers (New York: Anchor, 1991). For a more involved examination of Campbell's theory of the mythic hero, see Joseph Campbell, *The Hero with a Thousand Faces*, 3rd ed. (Novato, CA: New World Library, 2008).

3. For a classic discussion of the problem of evil in theology, see J. L. Mackie, *The Miracle of Theism: Arguments for and against the Existence of God* (Oxford: Oxford University Press, 1982). For a comprehensive collection of historical texts on the problem of evil, see Mark Larrimore, ed., *The Problem of Evil: A Reader* (Malden, MA: Blackwell, 2001).

4. Susan Neiman, *Evil in Modern Thought: An Alternative History of Philosophy* (Princeton, NJ: Princeton University Press, 2002), 5; Susan Neiman, "What's the Problem of Evil?" in María Pía Lara, ed., *Rethinking Evil* (Berkeley: University of California Press, 2001), 34.

5. The relation between what *is* and what *ought to be* is a central issue in ethical and moral philosophy because our conception of how things ought to be is essential to our moral decision-making. David Hume problematizes the distinction at the conclusion of Book 3, Part 1, Section 1 of *A Treatise of Human Nature* (Oxford: Oxford University Press, 2000) by noting that we have no clear sense of how the facts of how things *are* could define how they *ought to be* (302). Immanuel Kant provides an important response to this problem by arguing in *The Groundwork of the Metaphysics of Morals* (in *Practical Philosophy*, trans. and ed. Mary J. Gregor [Cambridge: Cambridge University Press, 1996]) that the correct conception of how things ought to be — that is, the correct understanding of morality — is derived from pure reason, not from experience of how things are (61–5).

6. For a discussion of honesty and deception in the *Star Wars* movies, see Shanti Fader, "A Certain Point of View: Lying Jedi, Honest Sith, and the Viewers Who Love Them," in *Star Wars and Philosophy*, ed. Kevin S. Decker and Jason T. Eberl (Chicago: Open Court, 2005), 192–204.

7. Still, there are some notable exceptions. For example, the "crime caper" plot (such as *Ocean's Eleven*) primarily follows the criminals rather than those who wish to bring them to justice. Since we naturally identify with whomever the narrative follows, we perceive the criminals as "heroes" in the context of the crime caper narrative. Thus, because of the narrative framing, we *do* at least to some extent identify with individuals who in more conventional plots would ordinarily be classified as villains.

8. John Dewey, "Existence as Precarious and Stable," in *The Philosophy of John Dewey*, ed. John J. McDermott (Chicago: University of Chicago Press, 1981), 280.

9. Ibid., 282.

10. Though these narratives relate to a historical rather than a fictional event, and hence evil in these narratives could be argued to have a different meaning because they relate to reality and not the imaginary, there are also fantastic fictional narratives that involve repellent villains who "derail" our plot expectations. For example, the movies *A Clockwork Orange* and *Brazil* exhibit these sorts of derailments, and it is more difficult in these films to find the perspective of the villains compelling. The films I chose to discuss here, *Schindler's List* and *Life Is Beautiful*,

involve derailings that produce a particularly jarring effect and provoke a strong sense of disgust regarding the villains, at least in me. Hence they make very clear examples for this discussion.

11. I hesitate to call Amon Göth a "villain," since we tend to use this term to refer to characters in narratives and not real persons. However, in 2003 the American Film Institute selected the character of Amon Göth as portrayed in *Schindler's List* as #15 of their Top 50 Villains of all time (http://www.afi.com/tvevents/100years/handv.aspx). Since it seems that the film's portrayal of Göth diverges from the historical person, perhaps we can safely refer to the character in the film as a villain and avoid using the term to describe the real historical person Amon Göth.

12. Hannah Arendt, *Eichmann in Jerusalem: A Report on the Banality of Evil* (New York: Penguin, 2006). For a helpful discussion of Arendt's thought with respect to the problem of evil, see Neiman, *Evil in Modern Thought*, 298–304.

13. Charles S. Peirce, "The Principles of Phenomenology," in *Philosophical Writings of Peirce*, ed. Justus Buchler (New York: Dover, 1955), 74–97.

14. For a brilliant and now classic argument for this lesson, see Martin Luther King, Jr.'s "Letter from a Birmingham Jail," in Martin Luther King, Jr., *I Have a Dream: Writings and Speeches that Changed the World*, ed. James Melvin Washington (San Francisco: HarperCollins, 1992).

BIBLIOGRAPHY

"AFI's 100 Years...100 Heroes & Villains." Available at http://www.afi.com/tvevents/100years/handv.aspx. Retrieved 3 June 2010.

Arendt, Hannah. *Eichmann in Jerusalem: A Report on the Banality of Evil.* New York: Penguin, 2006.

Brazil. Directed by Terry Gilliam. Universal City, CA: Universal Studios, 1998. DVD.

Campbell, Joseph. *The Hero with a Thousand Faces.* 3rd ed. Novato, CA: New World Library, 2008.

_____. *The Power of Myth.* With Bill Moyers. Ed. Betty Sue Flowers. New York: Anchor, 1991.

A Clockwork Orange. Directed by Stanley Kubrick. Burbank, CA: Warner Bros., 2001. DVD.

The Dark Knight. Directed by Christopher Nolan. Burbank, CA: Warner Bros., 2008. DVD.

Decker, Kevin S., and Jason T. Eberl, eds. *Star Wars and Philosophy.* Chicago: Open Court, 2005.

Dewey, John. *The Philosophy of John Dewey.* Ed. John J. McDermott. Chicago: University of Chicago Press, 1981.

Hume, David. *A Treatise of Human Nature.* Oxford: Oxford University Press, 2000.

Kant, Immanuel. *Practical Philosophy.* Trans. and ed. Mary J. Gregor. Cambridge: Cambridge University Press, 1996.

King, Martin Luther, Jr. *I Have a Dream: Writings and Speeches that Changed the World.* Ed. James Melvin Washington. San Francisco: HarperCollins, 1992.

Lara, María Pía, ed. *Rethinking Evil.* Berkeley: University of California Press, 2001.

Larrimore, Mark, ed. *The Problem of Evil: A Reader.* Malden, MA: Blackwell, 2001.

Life Is Beautiful. Directed by Roberto Benigni. New York: Miramax, 1999. DVD.

Mackie, J. L. *The Miracle of Theism: Arguments for and against the Existence of God.* Oxford: Oxford University Press, 1982.

Neiman, Susan. *Evil in Modern Thought: An Alternative History of Philosophy.* Princeton, NJ: Princeton University Press, 2002.

Ocean's Eleven. Directed by Steven Soderbergh. Burbank, CA: Warner Home Video, 2007. DVD (Widescreen Edition).

Peirce, Charles S. *Philosophical Writings of Peirce.* Ed. Justus Buchler. New York: Dover, 1955.

Planet of the Apes. Directed by Tim Burton. Los Angeles: 20th Century–Fox, 2001. DVD.

Schindler's List. Directed by Steven Spielberg. Universal City, CA: Universal Studios, 2004. DVD.

Star Wars Prequel Trilogy. Directed by George Lucas. Los Angeles: 20th Century–Fox, 2008. DVD.

Star Wars Trilogy. Directed by George Lucas. Los Angeles: 20th Century–Fox, 2008. DVD.

The Ultimate Matrix Collection. Directed by Andy Jones, Andy Wachowski, Josh Oreck, Kôji Morimoto, and Lana Wachowski. Burbank, CA: Warner Home Video, 2004. DVD.

2

The Devil Made Me Do It! The Devil in 1960s–1970s Horror Film

Antoinette F. Winstead

The 1960s and 1970s were turbulent and troubled times in American history, times marred by four political assassinations; a bloody, senseless war; and a lying, paranoid president. For nearly thirteen years, beginning with the assassination of President John F. Kennedy in 1963 and ending with the resignation of President Richard M. Nixon in 1974 and the fall of Saigon in 1975, images of death, riots, student protests, and police brutality constantly bombarded Americans. Every night, the evening news served up another dose of black body bags, wounded soldiers, youngsters and adults being attacked with fire hoses or vicious dogs, students being tear-gassed or shot down on college campuses. As a result of what seemed to be a daily pageant of inexplicable violence, incivility, and social unrest, "the idea that evil was a real force in the world was being reconsidered more seriously than ever before" in both secular and religious communities. One sees this reconsideration reflected in the horror films produced during this turbulent era.[1]

The horror films, specifically the satanic horror films, produced during the sixties and seventies capitalized on society's growing anxiety over the nation's chaotic state, due to an unpopular war and civil unrest, and increasing paranoia and fear, due to the rise and influence of women and minorities over institutions once dominated by white males. These films therefore reflected the widely held belief of evil run amok, for what else could possibly explain the sudden upheaval of "traditional" morals and values? Films like *Rosemary's Baby*, *The Exorcist*, and *The Omen* serve as prime examples of how horror films of the time helped furnish an explanation for the nation's chaos, while at the same time providing a rationalization for the paranoia; after all, it is not paranoia if someone is actually out to get you. One finds this principle exemplified in all three films, especially *Rosemary's Baby*.

The theme of Roman Polanski's *Rosemary's Baby* might very well be stated as "justified paranoia." The justification lies in the fact that Rosemary is actually being pursued by a coven of witches, although no one seems to believe her, not even her husband. The one person who does believe her ends up dead, thus solidifying her increasing paranoia. With no one to support her, Rosemary begins to believe that she is possibly going crazy, until she discovers the truth: she and her baby are the target and victims of an insidious, demonic cult. The revelation that her instinctive fear and paranoia were justified comes too late to rectify the damage. This message served as a warning to the American public to be ever vigilant for signs of evil, which — as *Rosemary's Baby*, *The Exorcist*, and *The Omen* demonstrate — could manifest itself in any form, from a seemingly harmless elderly couple, to a board game, to a cute little boy. And if evil could come in such innocuous forms, why not in more conspicuous incarnations like political assassinations, war, and riots? The leap to this conclusion proved a short one and thus provided society a justification for its paranoid fear that evil was alive and flourishing in America.

Rosemary's Baby, *The Exorcist*, and *The Omen* also helped to categorize and define a reason for the violence and evil witnessed by Americans (which actually stemmed from decades of oppression and repression), and in many ways these films provided a cathartic avenue by which to explore what was going on in society. And, like the science fiction films of the fifties, the satanic horror films of the sixties and seventies did so by tapping into the national "paranoia, an[d] irrational fear of the insidious Other who corrupts and ... destroy[s] society from within." Instead of alien invaders (aka Communists), however, these films lauded the most insidious of all "Others," the devil — the progenitor of evil in the world and the perfect foil for all America's ills.[2] Why the perfect foil? Because no matter how innocuous or conspicuous the acts of violence or evil, in Judeo-Christian societies there can be only one perpetrator — the devil, who, fairly or unfairly, has served as the scapegoat for humanity's wrongdoings since the infamous incident with Eve and the forbidden tree in the Garden of Eden.

The Devil — The Universal Scapegoat

As illustrated in the Old Testament (or Hebrew Bible), from the beginning of time, man has sought to foist the blame for his sins and wrong doings on others. It is a form of self-preservation that one sees first demonstrated by

Adam in the Book of Genesis. When God admonishes Adam for eating from the tree of the knowledge of good and evil, Adam immediately blames Eve. Eve, in turn, blames the serpent, who, with no one else to blame, becomes the universal symbol for the ultimate scapegoat. While the serpent is never directly called "the devil," the assumption remains that this tempter of innocent Eve is none other than Satan. Because of this assumption, the devil, by default, has become the symbolic scapegoat for society and been "made to bear responsibility for the faults and problems of others."[3] Considering the extent of the social upheaval in America during the sixties and seventies, it is little wonder that many chose to point the finger at Satan and declare him the source of what appeared to be a national madness.

The devil, the iconic image of evil, goes by many names, including Beelzebub and Iblis (Islamic); however, in the Judeo-Christian tradition, he is commonly referred to as Satan or Lucifer. Though used interchangeably, Satan and Lucifer actually represent two different images of the devil. The name Lucifer (Latin for "light bearer") signifies the devil before his fall from grace. Moreover, when the devil is referred to as Lucifer, it is usually in the context of his role as supreme archangel of God's army. Conversely, the Church's use of Satan (Hebrew for "adversary") commonly refers to the devil after his fall from grace and banishment from heaven. In addition, one should note that Lucifer is often perceived as a beautiful, warring angel, while Satan is often cast as a disfigured demon, who forfeited heavenly perfection for dominion over hell. Satan's disfigurement is an outward manifestation of his open rebellion and sin against God and illustrates his transformation from angel to demon. Moreover, his disfigurement marks a change in his status from supreme archangel and protector of God's heavenly realm to the prince of hell and God's ultimate adversary.

Satan, the "Adversary," as portrayed in the Hebrew Bible, serves as "the prosecutor of Yahweh's court" of believers, working to tempt them "to reject the way of life and redemption and to accept the way of death and destruction."[4] Most often depicted in popular culture as an ugly red demon with horns and a pitchfork, Satan embodies evil — all that is "morally reprehensible, wicked, [and] sinful," and which eventually "leads to pain and suffering in the world."[5] As "the prince of evil spirits" and "the inveterate enemy of God and Christ," Satan commands the ability to "take possession of men's bodies, afflicting them or making them diseased."[6] He also, according to tradition, possesses the power to cause famine, disasters, wars, and political upheaval. Armed with such devastating abilities, Satan is, by all accounts, the archenemy of humanity, seeking to inflict as much turmoil and suffering as possible in hopes of turning humankind against God.

In contrast, Lucifer, the fallen angel, cast out of heaven because of his vanity and pride, frequently appears in literary works as a charismatic, elegant creature, "an impressive and admirable figure," capable of compassion for and an appreciation of humanity. As such, he seeks not to destroy humankind, but to offer enlightenment and freedom from the "ignorance" required by God's law, which demands strict, unquestioning obedience.[7] His "heroic" advocacy for humanity's freedom led to his rebellion against God and his ultimate demise. Characterized as this poetic, mythic freedom fighter, Lucifer often heralds the depiction of a lonely misunderstood warrior — a heroic rebel — whose rebellion "lies in his desire to live forever independently of God," outside the restrictive confines of God's repressive mandate of absolute purity and goodness.[8] When portrayed as the heroic rebel who openly opposed God's law, Lucifer is also associated with the concept of free will, the "capacity ... to choose among alternatives or to act in certain situations independently of natural, social, or divine restraints."[9] It is this association with free will, and rebellion against God, that links him to Adam and Eve and their expulsion from the Garden of Eden, for it was Lucifer who opened their eyes to truth and reason and gave to them what had been denied by God: choice.

Romantics, such as William Blake and Lord Byron, embraced Lucifer's rebellious nature "as a symbol of the progressive spirit rebelling against the established forces of repression" and used this imagery of the devil in their works.[10] Because the Romantics viewed Lucifer's rebellion through a heroic lens, they saw him as a representation of good — defined as openness and light. Conversely, they viewed God as controlling and inflexible, thus evil — defined as constrictive and dark, i.e., the antithesis of good. Works of this period tend to characterize Lucifer as a victim of God's heavy-handed authoritarian nature, rather than as a victimizer of humanity. Thus the misunderstood warrior becomes a scapegoat for God's wrath, not for evil, reinforcing the sympathetic image of a heroic rebel.

One finds this imagery of a controlling God and a heroic Lucifer played out in Blake's *The Book of Urizen* (1794), a retelling of the creation story. In this retelling, Urizen represents God, a tyrannical creator and ruler, who proclaims himself the "One King, one God, one Law."[11] Orc, who represents Lucifer, revolts against Urizen's totalitarianism. In doing so, Orc symbolizes "revolution and the force of liberation from blind tyranny."[12] As Blake does in *Urizen*, the Romantics lauded the idea of the rebellious, independent hero revolting against the constraints of a domineering God and religion, which they exemplified in the doctrine of the Church. They believed Christianity, with its many restrictions, stifled the creative spirit and "suffocate[ed] the soul," and so they sought to rebel against it.[13] They found their inspiration for this anti-religion movement in Lucifer, the heroic rebel who stood against God in order to liberate the human spirit, allowing it to grow and flourish.

While an appealing image for the Romantics and their counterculture movement against established religion and related institutions, this concept of the
devil lost momentum with the resurgence of more conservative values in the
mid–19th century. With those values, often associated with the Victorian period,
came a return to idea of the devil as Satan and a scapegoat for evil.

In satanic horror films, especially those produced in the 1960s and 1970s,
one also finds the image of the devil as Satan, rather than as Lucifer, used as
a scapegoat for the steady erosion of traditional American values. This imagery
coincided with society's growing paranoia over evil, which in the Judeo-Christian tradition stems from Satan, the disfigured prince of hell, as opposed to
Lucifer, the beautiful supreme archangel. The use of Satan also reflected the
conservative mindset of suburban middle America, which embraced many of
the Victorian values and morals espoused in the Church, values and morals
that middle America viewed as under attack by evil forces. As evidence many
pointed to a rise in occult practices, including satanic worship, during the
mid-sixties.

Changing Times and the Devil

According to Jeffrey Burton Russell, "belief in the Devil increased sub-
stantially from 1965 to 1975" and with this belief a revival of satanic worship.[14]
Anton LaVey, the founder and high priest of the Church of Satan in San Francisco, declared "the Satanic Age started in 1966," because "that's when God
was proclaimed dead"— in actuality a re-proclamation of Nietzsche's 1887
statement.[15] Despite LaVey's claims about the satanic age in connection to
God's death, it might be posited that the revival of satanic worship in the sixties better reflected the anti-establishment, counterculture mood of the youth
movement. It was a trend much like the one embraced by the Romantics,
who rejected God, and the restraints of Christianity, in favor of personal freedom and individuality, which they found best conceptualized in the form of
the devil as Lucifer, whom they embraced as a "liberator in rebellion against
the society that blocks the way of progress toward liberty, beauty, and love."[16]
Although the connection to an anti-establishment, counterculture mindset
exists between the Romantics and the Church of Satan, it should be noted
that the latter embraced the concept of the devil as the prince of hell, not as
the supreme archangel, and thus worshipped the demonic and evil elements
associated with Satan. This type of demonic worship and practice led to the
formation of satanic cults like the one created by Charles Manson, the antithesis of what the Romantics originally sought to establish with their anti-establishment, counterculture movement in the 1700s.

The revival of satanic worship in combination with other elements of the counterculture movement (i.e., drugs and "free love") had a profound impact on society, especially in regard to the American family. In conservative Christian religious communities, the prevailing belief was, and is, that a growing moral and ethical decline in the United States stemmed from the dissolution of the American family. The blame for the dissolution rested, primarily, on the so-called sexual revolution of the late fifties and early sixties, which opened the door for pleasure-only relationships. These relationships diametrically opposed the strict sexual mores that mirrored Victorian and Church standards under which sex served as a tool for procreation within marriage only, not for pleasure. Sexual pleasure, especially outside of marriage, was seen as evil and, therefore, associated with the devil; because where there is pleasure, there must be the devil. One finds the association between pleasure and the devil rooted in the story of Eve, who is seen as allowing herself to be seduced into eating forbidden fruit. Had she not given into the temptation of "pleasure," she and Adam would never have been expelled from the Garden of Eden. Likewise, religious conservatives believe, if society had not succumbed to the temptations of the sexual revolution and the lure of sex without consequences — as "the Pill"[17] promised — the American family would have remained intact and the decline in moral values might have been prevented.

Compounding the problem, as conservatives saw it, were groups like the Sexual Freedom League (founded in 1963), whose focus included freedom from sexual discrimination for women and homosexuals.[18] Such a focus was seen as an attack on traditional American morals, for religious conservatives tended to believe that women should be subservient to men, especially in relation to reproductive rights, and that homosexuality was not only a crime, but also a sin against God. Conservative Christians perceived this push for sexual freedom as the beginning of the end of rectitude in the United States.

Another perception in religious communities, especially among traditional, conservative Catholics, is that the beginning of the end of morals and ethics in the United States started with the Second Vatican Council, which began in 1962 and ended in 1965. In convening the council, Pope John's goal was to "modernize the church and to involve it in the concerns of the world."[19] He sought to update the Church "to meet the needs of the time."[20] In addition, he wanted "critical involvement in the new culture" emerging in the sixties, though not "without denying its evils and its needs for transformation."[21] What resulted, however, was what some see as a lapse in Catholic values as the mandates of Vatican II were liberally interpreted, especially in the American Catholic Church. As a result, conservative Catholics saw Pope John's modernization, or updating, of the Church not as a call for man to fall in line with Church doctrine, but rather as a call for the Church to fall in line with secular doctrine, providing, some believed, a perfect opening for the secularization of the Church.

This so-called secularization was also believed to have led to a "decrease in faith, and [a] lessening of respect for [the] authority" of the Church.[22] Considering the counterculture era in which Vatican II took place, in which conservative, traditional points of view, for better or worse, were being shunted aside for more liberal and progressive points of view, it is unsurprising that in faith-based communities these changes were perceived as a weakening of the Church's power to control or even mandate ethical, faith-based behavior. Consequently, traditional morals and values were also perceived as weakening. Because many faithful Catholics could find no other explanation for this sudden mandate for change in the Church or for the social upheaval in America, they turned to the only viable explanation at hand: the devil, the ultimate fall guy. Thus they relieved themselves of any personal responsibility for the world's troubles. By shifting the blame for America's problems to the devil, they performed a transference that occurs "when the true object of [one's] anger is untouchable."[23] The untouchable object proved to be the Catholic Church, possibly the most powerful of all religious and political institutions. Therefore, one finds that the devil, considered "a parasite on the being of humankind [and] ... the being of God,"[24] was "substituted for the real target" and once again made the scapegoat, this time for the secularization of the Church and its inability to stanch the steady erosion of traditional morals.[25]

Marked as society's scapegoat by not only the Catholic faithful, but Americans in general, the devil made an unprecedented step onto the silver screen in the sixties, signaling a cultural shift in the concept of personal morals and ethics, wherein individuals no longer felt compelled to take personal responsibility for their actions, but rather pointed an accusing finger at external forces. In doing so, American society rejected the concept of free will, and instead insisted on blaming its social, political, and personal ills on the ubiquitous Other. In essence this rejection of free will was a rejection of God, who, unlike the devil, insists that individuals take personal responsibility for their decisions and actions. In other words, American society cloaked itself in the mantle of Adam and Eve — the original scapegoats — and declared self-righteously that everything wrong in society was due to evil forces controlled by none other than the devil, "considered simultaneously murderer from the beginning, father of lies, and prince of the world" and consequently, saboteur of free will.[26]

The Three Faces of the Devil

Rosemary's Baby, The Exorcist and *The Omen* are three films that best represent the cultural shift from free will to blaming the devil. In these three films, the devil represents a demonic force of evil, which destroys the lives of the innocent. The personification of the devil as evil incarnate stems from the Bible, wherein one finds three images of the devil: tempter, evil spirit, and demonic torturer or force.

The first and prevailing biblical image of the devil is as tempter. One finds this first illustrated in the Old Testament in the book of Genesis, with Adam and Eve in the Garden of Eden, when the serpent tempts Eve to eat from the tree of the knowledge of good and evil.[27] Another example is in the book of Chronicles, where the devil "tempts David to commit the much-loathed act of holding a census" in direct disobedience to an order given by God.[28] In the New Testament book of Matthew, the devil boldly attempts to lead Jesus astray by tempting to him to do three things: turn stones to bread, test God's ability to save him from death, and turn his back on God by kneeling down to the devil and accepting "all the kingdoms of the world and their splendor."[29] Jesus resisted all three temptations, thus denying the devil the satisfaction of thwarting God's plan to save the human race from damnation.

Undeterred, the devil continues to play the adversary — most often by assuming the role of a demonic entity that can take possession of someone's body, causing a person to scream, convulse, and foam at the mouth.[30] One finds Satan portrayed as a demonic entity throughout the gospels. Probably the most vivid example of demonic possession is from Mark 5:1–20. Here Mark describes a man "with an unclean spirit," so wild that he could not be restrained, "even with a chain," so demented that "night and day ... he was always howling and bruising himself with stones." When asked by Jesus the name of the demon possessing him he replied, "My name is Legion."[31] The episode in many respects mirrors the scene of exorcism in *The Exorcist*. One can even find a similarity between the way Jesus expels the demon into a herd of pigs, which then rush downhill and plunge into the sea, and Father Damien Karras expelling the demon from Regan, taking it into himself, and then jumping out the window. The correlation between the writings found in the Bible and what satanic horror films presented to viewers is what made the movies more frightening and more believable for audiences. Thus the films helped perpetuate the belief that Satan was behind the disruptive changes going on in society.

One finds the third image of the devil in the Old Testament book of Job, where the devil plays the role of a demonic force that can destroy the lives of the innocent without provocation. This image denotes the helplessness of man, for no matter how devout or good one may be, bad things still happen. Life offers no guarantees for either the wealthy or the poor. Man's fate rest in the hands of God, who, on a whim, may decide to turn his back — which the Romantics perceived as a sign of God's darkness — and allow the devil the freedom to destroy one's life. The devil as a demonic force reinforces Nietzsche's "famous [declaration] that 'God is dead,'" which, as noted earlier, many in the sixties believed and re-proclaimed (i.e., LaVey and the Church of Satan).[32] With no God to regulate the behavior of the devil, one loses free will, for how can freedom of choice exist if one's decisions can be negated?

Free Will and the Devil

The image of the devil as a tempter raises the question of free will, the ability of an individual to make a conscious choice between doing right or wrong. Free will posits that without choices "there would be no moral good or evil among creatures, no genuine responsibility or blameworthiness."[33] In other words, without free will, humans lose the ability to make conscious decisions; instead, they become glorified marionettes, subject to the desires of whoever manipulates the strings. However, with the power of free will, one can decide between good and evil, right and wrong, obedience and disobedience. The choice belongs to the individual. What one finds, when the devil plays the tempter, is that more often than not, humans choose to oppose good and right in favor of personal ambition, as illustrated by Adam and Eve whose freedom of choice led to original sin and expulsion from the Garden of Eden.

Christopher Marlowe's *Doctor Faustus* and Stephen Vincent Benét's *Devil and Daniel Webster* represent classic literary portrayals of free will in the face of temptation from the devil. In both cases, the protagonists choose evil over good, and literally sell their souls to the devil in exchange for knowledge and wealth. The satanic horror films produced in the sixties and seventies generally reject this personification of the devil, which represents a manifestation of evil stemming from humanity's deliberate choosing. Instead, it is the image of the devil as a demonic presence that can invade and possess the body of the innocent, and as a demonic force that can destroy the lives of the innocent — neither of which a character has any control over — that frequents the plots of sixties and seventies horror film. This is not to say that the devil as tempter is not present in these films; however, when present, it usually takes second place to the demonic possession or destruction that most plots focus on. One finds this is the case in *Rosemary's Baby*, where the devil's temptation of Guy takes place offscreen, so as not to distract from the main plotline, the demonic destruction of Rosemary's life because of Guy's deal with the devil.

What *Rosemary's Baby, The Exorcist,* and *The Omen* have in common is that they deliberately work against the concept of free will. In each film, an outside entity — the devil — forces an individual to participate in activities against his or her will. In *Rosemary's Baby,* Rosemary is raped by the devil and forced to give birth to his hell spawn. In *The Exorcist,* Regan becomes possessed by the devil and is forced to defile her own body. And in *The Omen,* Damien's ability to choose is denied by virtue of predestination: from the beginning of time he was destined to be the Antichrist and therefore must secure his legacy by any means necessary, even if it means harming his "mother." In each case, free will is an aberration, a thing of myth and fairy tales; and, in its absence, individual freedom of choice is lost and the characters become victims of their circumstances, openly vulnerable to the whims and desires of the devil.

By denying the existence of free will, these films perpetuated the prevalent conceit of the sixties that control over one's fate no longer existed; that choice was an illusion; and that, at anytime, for reasons beyond one's comprehension, the devil could destroy one's life. The portrayal of the devil as a demonic force in these three films also directly corresponds with the concept of the devil as Satan — God's primary adversary — who, after his fall from grace, sought to avenge himself by destroying God's most prized creation, humankind. As portrayed in the satanic horror films of the sixties and seventies, humanity is merely a plaything for the devil, a concept one finds vividly illustrated in the story of Job.

Job, according to the biblical story, was a man of God who lived his life in service of the Lord. As a result, God blessed him with an abundance of money, land, cattle, and children. One day, after wandering the earth, the devil returns to heaven for a council meeting. God asks him if in his wanderings he has had a chance to observe his "good and faithful" servant Job.[34] The devil replies that of course Job is faithful because God has given him no reason not to be. In essence, the devil bets God that if God allows him to take everything away from Job and destroy his life, Job too will turn from God as others have done. Thus begins the devil's reign of terror in Job's life, demonstrating that even the most loyal and faithful of God's servants can be victimized by the devil.

Within this parable of Job, there are two aspects of free will. The first is that at anytime, the devil can take over one's life and literally turn it into a living hell. Under this conceit, free will, as in the ability to choose one's life and circumstances, is lost. The second, grounded in faith, is that no matter one's circumstance, one always has the free will to believe in God, which Job demonstrates. Many see Job's choice to be faithful as the moral of the story.

While a similar moral is often used as a subplot in satanic/horror films —
a call for man to be faithful no matter what evils befall him — what is capitalized on more in these films is the concept of the devil as a force that, no
matter how upright or innocent one may be, can without provocation destroy
one's life. Again the emphasis is on a lack of choice — free will — in one's life,
which in turn reflects a sense of serendipity, as in *The Exorcist*, or predestination, as in *The Omen*.

By making the devil the scapegoat in satanic horror films, the characters
are able to blame their circumstances on someone else, rather than take personal responsibility. This attitude reflects a cultural norm that grew out of
the sexual revolution of the late fifties and early sixties, a norm that freed people from the societal pressures to get married or stay married. Though there
may seem to be a disconnect between marriage and scapegoating, as noted
earlier, conservative Christian religious communities see a direct correlation
between the deterioration of the American family and the decline in morals
and values in the United States. As conservatives see it, this decline in morality
resulted in a universal acceptance of a lack of responsibility in both personal
and professional relationships. Today, one sees examples of this behavior in
the 2009 financial crisis and the 2001 Enron scandal. No one took personal
responsibility for either debacle; instead, those in charge pointed fingers at
external, unnamed Others. In the sixties, however, instead of blaming an
unnamed Other, much of society quickly banded together and declared the
devil the cause for everything wrong in the United States. After all, why blame
one's circumstances on oneself when one can blame the devil? "The devil
made me do it!"

The Devil as the Scapegoat in Satanic Horror Films

Rosemary's Baby exemplifies the blame game. Guy Woodhouse, a failed
actor, blames his wife, instead of his lack of talent, for his failure. Because he
sees her as being at fault, *she* must pay. In light of the counterculture revolution, the fault seems to lie in her inability to "get with the times"— have fun,
live free. Instead, Rosemary, a stay-at-home wife, wants nothing more than
to have a child and start a family — live the American dream. She represents
an outmoded conservative mindset, an impediment to progress. Guy, on the
other hand, represents the liberal, progressive mindset of the sixties, which
fully embraces the new world order. Rather than focusing on the traditions
of hearth and home, he is obsessed with the material offerings of the world —
fame and fortune. In his eyes, Rosemary is holding him back from achieving
his due wealth and recognition because of her conservative values. She is the

sole reason for his lack of his success. Therefore, Rosemary must be held accountable — she must pay, as Eve was forced to pay for instigating the downfall of man.

Guy makes Rosemary pay by "selling" her body to the devil in exchange for a successful acting career, which results in the fame and fortune he craves. Conducted without Rosemary's knowledge, in many ways, the exchange resembles the deal made between Satan and God over Job, in that her life, like Job's, is being bartered and tampered with by forces outside her control. Her free will stolen, she becomes the victim of her husband's underhanded deeds. Guy, however, perceives himself as the only victim — just like Adam, who blamed Eve for his downfall. After all, Guy is merely doing the best he can, given his lack of choice — and talent. As a result, he takes no responsibility for his lackluster career or for the rape of his wife, choosing instead to blame others — the elderly neighbors and, of course, Satan.

The scenario presented in *Rosemary's Baby* clearly connects to the times in which it was released. During the sixties, more often than not, rightly or wrongly, people blamed the country's social and political ills on "the system" rather than on themselves — the public who, over the years, had allowed "the system" to progress without making a stand against it. The reason "the system" had been allowed to progress was because many individuals had, in fact, profited from an imbalance of power in a society that marginalized minorities and women. The result was a backlash against all forms of authority and a rejection of traditional values and morals. This backlash created a new America, one governed by ever-shifting mores that reflected self-centered motivations, such as the ones harbored by Guy. Rather than taking personal responsibility for how "the system" had been allowed to succeed for so long, the religious community pointed their collective finger at the devil for America's perceived fall from grace, and society, along with the movies, took up the mantra. In doing so, society found a scapegoat for its dysfunction, a dysfunction that was having a major impact on the American family, as illustrated in *The Exorcist*, which shows the negative consequences of the sexual revolution on family life: the single parent household.

The end of the traditional concept of marriage and the American family began with the introduction of "the Pill" in 1960, which marked the beginning of the sexual revolution in America. Without the persistent worry of pregnancy, which often resulted in "shotgun weddings," sex became recreational. Moreover, the main function of sex, procreation, became secondary to pleasure. As a consequence, individuals sought pleasure over commitment — the backbone of marriage — and when the sexual pleasure dissipated in their relationships, they moved on to the next partner and the divorce rate soared. Such changes created a new family structure in American culture: the single-parent household. The single-parent household, combined with more women than ever having to enter the workforce in order to support their families and the push towards a "me" self–centered society, helped facilitate the escalation of family dysfunction in America during the late sixties and early seventies. Horror films like *The Exorcist* illustrated this dysfunction, but in the tradition of *Rosemary's Baby*, personal responsibility for the dysfunction was ignored and, instead, the devil became the scapegoat.

In *The Exorcist*, Chris is so involved in her acting career that she neglects her daughter, Regan — although not as badly as Regan's father, who completely ignores the girl. As a result, Regan creates an imaginary friend and father, Captain Howdy, to substitute for her missing parents. She eventually becomes possessed by Captain Howdy, and this demon must be exorcised. What is actually at play in this scenario is the result of the dysfunction in the American family. Chris cannot take ownership of her responsibility for her daughter's neurosis and her possession. Had Chris been a larger presence in Regan's life, Regan would not have fallen victim to the devil — evil — which can be interpreted as all aspects of juvenile delinquency: drugs, alcohol, and premarital sex. Once again, the devil becomes the convenient scapegoat for all that is wrong with the American family.

During the early seventies, the American family was not the only dysfunctional institution in America for which the devil was blamed. On its heels was society's steadily eroding faith in the U.S. government, which began with the assassination of John F. Kennedy in 1963, an assassination swiftly followed by three others: Malcolm X (February 1965), Martin Luther King (April 1968), and Robert "Bobby" Kennedy (June 1968). There was also the war in Vietnam, seen nightly in vivid detail on television screens across America. Seeing the endless parade of the bloodied, mangled bodies of America's youth being lifted from the battlefields of a hostile country also took its toll on society's respect for and belief in the government's ability to do its job. Likewise, the images of fire hoses and attack dogs let loose on African Americans, young and old alike, in the South did little to engender hope in the political system. Reeling from over a decade of turmoil, the United States government took one last blow that seemed would damn it forever: the Watergate scandal and President Nixon's resignation.

There seemed no logical reason for the political or societal chaos of the sixties and seventies, other than what normally might be perceived as an *illogical* reason: that the ill that had befallen the United States was an apocalyptic precursor, a sign of the end-of-days — the work of Satan. Many saw a direct correlation between the instability in society and the predictions they perceived in the New Testament Revelation, wherein God grants the Antichrist dominion over the earth. Everything from the sexual revolution, to the assassinations, to Vietnam, to Watergate, marked a steady march toward the great apocalyptic battle — Armageddon. Paranoia over Satan's Antichrist and the end-of-days fueled the anxieties of an already overstressed, overwhelmed nation.

No film better reflects the growing paranoia in society over the idea of Armageddon than *The Omen*, which, incidentally, was released the same year as the Jonestown massacre, where 913 people committed suicide at the behest of Jim Jones, a charismatic cult leader who many in his following believed was a new messiah. Combined with the political chaos of the day, Jim Jones and the Jonestown massacre served as another indication for some that the end-of-days was fast approaching. *The Omen*, like its predecessors, tapped into this paranoia, "mirror[ing] the social issues and concerns"[35] of the American public, which were grounded in belief in the impending, unavoidable, ascension to power of the church's greatest adversary, Satan's earthly incarnation, the Antichrist.

As originally defined in 2 Thessalonians and 1 John and 2 John of the New Testament, an antichrist means anyone against Christ — an adversary to Christian teachings and doctrines. The image of the Antichrist as "a worker of wonders ... a seducer" of disbelievers and a tempter of believers comes from the Revelation.[36] During the Middle Ages in Europe, as during the sixties and seventies in United States, "the idea of the Antichrist developed into a powerful historical and political factor," often used to explain war and disasters.[37] The Antichrist became the focus of Church tradition, and religious leaders made a concerted effort to interpret, from the myriad "signs" in the Revelation, who the Antichrist might be and when he might arrive. The idea of the Antichrist as Satan in human form stems from these interpretations of John's writings in the Revelation. Today many believe, as did people in the Middle Ages, that the Antichrist is the literal, physical manifestation of the devil on earth and that "the signs of the times" point to his imminent arrival and the "end-of-times."

The Omen, based on a novel by David Seltzer, explores the concept of the Antichrist as "a final human opponent of all goodness"[38] and, as such, the bearer of evil. The evil borne by Antichrist manifests itself in political and social upheaval. For those in the United States during the sixties and seventies, the explanation given in *The Omen* for the chaotic state of affairs resonated. It resonated because Americans were looking for someone other than themselves to blame for the disastrous state of the nation's political and social systems. Moreover, like people in the Middle Ages, Americans focused their attention on external reasons and landed upon the perfect foil, the Antichrist — Satan in human form.

The Omen concentrates on the decay of American political system due to corruption from within. The Antichrist serves as the source of this corruption and thus takes the blame for the disarray of the political system. Once again, Satan plays the scapegoat — because, as noted earlier, it is easier to blame "Others" than to take personal responsibility. One sees this demonstrated perfectly in President Nixon's paranoid belief that his evil enemies were out to get him, which "forced" him to tape his White House meetings and to cover up the Watergate break-in associated with his re-election campaign. What *The Omen* suggests is that by blaming the devil (or, in the case of Nixon, evil political foes) for one's political ills, one can literally get away with anything — including corruption and murder.

The Omen also suggests that man does not control his own destiny. Therefore, not even Damien, the Antichrist, can take personal responsibility for his actions. After all, according to the Revelation, he is predestined to play out the role of world destroyer. Free will, therefore, does not exist; fate has damned Damien to his demonic role.

American society seemed to embrace this concept of predestination in the sixties and seventies, contradicting the belief of self-determination in the United States, which held that Americans possessed the freedom to fashion their own destiny and decide their own fate, be it political or personal. In embracing the idea of predestination, Americans relinquished any responsibility for the chaos around them and, instead, chose to become the victims of their circumstances rather than stand accountable as the instigators.

The Devil Made Me Do It!

Rosemary's Baby, *The Exorcist*, and *The Omen* allude to an insipid lack of personal responsibility in American society, suggesting that during the sixties and seventies, the easiest course of action lay in blaming Others, in particular the devil, for everything wrong in United States. As Geraldine from the *Flip Wilson Show* used to say in jest, "The devil made me do it!"[39] Used by everyone from the 1976 New York serial killer David Berkowitz (aka "The Son of Sam") to Andrea Yates, who claimed in 2006 that the devil told her to drown her five children, Geraldine's statement over the years has lost its comic origins. It has, instead, become the serious mantra for all the evil acts performed both on and off the silver screen since the sixties, an era when the world seemed to turn upside down, when everything good turned bad, when the American dream became the American nightmare and the devil seemed closer to man than God.

NOTES

1. Ellen Burstein, "Fearless," *Guideposts*, 1 April 2007, 65–68.

2. Carrol Lee Fry, *Cinema of the Occult: New Age, Satanism, Wicca, and Spiritualism in Film* (Cranbury, NJ: Rosemont, 2008), 93.

3. Eric Brahm, "Knowledge Base Essay: Scapegoating," in *Beyond Intractability*, available at http://www.beyondintractability.org (retrieved 20 June 2010).

4. "Devil," *Merriam-Webster's Encyclopedia of World Religions* (Springfield, MA: Merriam-Webster, 1999), 270.

5. "Good and Evil," *Merriam-Webster's Encyclopedia of World Religions*, 385.

6. "Satan," *Merriam-Webster's Encyclopedia of World Religions*, 970.

7. Frank S. Kastor, "The Satanic Pattern," in *Satan*, ed. Harold Bloom (Philadelphia: Chelsea House, 2005), 58.

8. Jeffrey Burton Russell, "The Romantic Devil," in *Satan*, ed. Harold Bloom (Philadelphia: Chelsea House, 2005), 167.

9. "Free Will," *Merriam-Webster's Encyclopedia of World Religions*, 359.

10. Russell, "Romantic Devil," 168.

11. William Blake, "Chapter II," *The [First] Book of Urizen*, available at http://www.blake archive.org/exist/blake/archive/work.xq?workid=urizen (retrieved 20 June 2010).

12. Russell, "Romantic Devil," 164.

13. Brian Godawa, *Hollywood World Views: Watching Films with Wisdom and Discernment* (Downers Grove, IL: IVP Books, 2009), 146.

14. Jeffrey Burton Russell, *Mephistopheles: The Devil in the Modern World* (Ithaca: Cornell University Press, 1986), 253.

15. Hal Lindsey and C.C. Carlson, *Satan Is Alive and Well on Planet Earth* (Grand Rapids: Zondervan, 1972), 20.

16. Russell, "Romantic Devil," 160.

17. The Pill celebrated its 50th anniversary May 2010, and as Nancy Gibbs notes in a *Time* magazine article celebrating the anniversary, it is still as controversial today as it was when introduced in 1960. Originally formulated in the 1950s to combat infertility, it has been both maligned for instigating promiscuity and praised for ushering in the women's rights movement. Whether one maligns or praises the Pill, there is no doubt that it influenced, and is still influencing, the social and political landscape in regard to women's rights and issues.

18. "Guide to the Sexual Freedom League Records, 1962–1983," *Online Archive of California*, available at http://oac.cdlib.org (retrieved 20 June 2010).

19. Timothy McCarthy, *The Catholic Tradition: Before and After Vatican II* (Chicago: Loyola University Press, 1994), 62.

20. Ibid., 63.

21. Ibid.

22. Ibid.

23. Rene Girard, *I See Satan Fall Like Lightning*, trans. James G. Williams (Maryknoll, NY: Orbis, 2009), 156.

24. Ibid., xii.

25. Ibid., 156.

26. Rene Girard, *The Scapegoat,* trans. Yvonne Freccero (Baltimore: Johns Hopkins University Press, 1989), 166.

27. See Genesis 3:1–24.

28. Neil Forsyth, *The Satanic Epic* (Princeton, NJ: Princeton University Press, 2003), 37.

29. Matthew 4:8.

30. See, for example, Luke 9:39.

31. See Mark 5:1–20.

32. Eckhart Tolle, *The Power of Now: A Guide to Spiritual Enlightenment* (Vancouver: Namaste, 2004), 13.

33. Robert Kane, *Free Will* (Oxford: Blackwell, 2004), 259.

34. Job 1:1.

35. Fry, 93.
36. "Antichrist," *Merriam-Webster's Encyclopedia of World Religions*, 61.
37. Ibid.
38. Bernard McGinn, *Antichrist: Two Thousand Years of Human Fascination with Evil* (New York: Columbia University Press, 2000), 2.
39. Anthony Calloway, *When the Enemy Attacks* (Bloomington, IN: Author House, 2009), 79.

BIBLIOGRAPHY

Axelrod, Alan, and Charles Phillips. *What Everyone Should Know About the 20th Century: 200 Events That Shaped the World*. Holbrook, MA: Adams Media, 1998.
Benét, Stephen Vincent. *The Devil and Daniel Webster*. (1938.) New York: Dramatists Play Service, 2004.
Blake, William. *The Book of Urizen*. http://www.blakearchive.org/exist/blake/archive/work.xq?workid=urizen. Retrieved 20 June 2010.
Bloom, Harold, ed. *Satan*. Philadelphia: Chelsea House, 2005.
Brahm, Eric. "Knowledge Base Essay: Scapegoating." *Beyond Intractability*. Available at http://www.beyondintractability.org. Retrieved 20 June 2010.
Burstein, Ellen. "Fearless." *Guideposts*, 1 April 2007, 65–68.
Calloway, Anthony. *When the Enemy Attacks*. Bloomington, IN: Author House, 2009.
Carus, Paul. *The History of the Devil and the Idea of Evil*. New York: Gramercy, 1996.
Douglas, Tom. *Scapegoats: Transferring Blame*. London: Routledge, 1995.
The Exorcist. Directed by William Friedkin. Burbank, CA: Warner Home Video, 1997. DVD.
The Flip Wilson Show. Television series. Broadcast 17 September 1970–27 June 1974. NBC.
Forsyth, Neil. *The Satanic Epic*. Princeton, NJ: Princeton University Press, 2003.
Fry, Carrol L. *Cinema of the Occult: New Age, Satanism, Wicca, and Spiritualism in Film*. Cranbury, NJ: Rosemont, 2008.
Gibbs, Nancy. "Love, Sex, Freedom, and the Paradox of the Pill." *Time Magazine*, 3 May 2010, 41–47.
Girard, Rene. *I See Satan Fall Like Lightning*. Trans. James G. Williams. Maryknoll, NY: Orbis, 2009.
_____. *The Scapegoat*. Trans. Yvonne Freccero. Baltimore: Johns Hopkins University Press, 1989.
Godawa, Brian. *Hollywood World Views: Watching Films with Wisdom and Discernment*. Downers Grove, IL: IVP Books, 2009.
"Guide to the Sexual Freedom League Records, 1962–1983." *Online Archive of California*. Available at http://oac.cdlib.org. Retrieved 20 June 2010.
Kane, Robert, ed. *Free Will*. Oxford: Blackwell, 2002.
Lewis, James R. *Satanism Today: An Encyclopedia of Religion, Folklore, and Popular Culture*. Santa Barbara, CA: ABC-CLIO, 2001.
Lindsey, Hal, and C.C. Carlson. *Satan Is Alive and Well on Planet Earth*. Grand Rapids: Zondervan, 1972.
Magistrate, Tony. *Abject Terrors: Surveying the Modern and Postmodern Horror Film*. New York: Peter Lang, 2005.
Marlowe, Christopher. *Dr. Faustus*. Ed. David Scott Kastan. New York: W.W. Norton, 2004.
McCarthy, Timothy. *The Catholic Tradition: Before and After Vatican II*. Chicago: Loyola University Press, 1994.
McGinn, Bernard. *Antichrist: Two Thousand Years of the Human Fascination with Evil*. New York: Columbia University Press, 2000.
Mercatante, Anthony S. *Good and Evil in Myth and Legend*. New York: Barnes & Noble, 1978.
Merriam-Webster's Encyclopedia of World Religions. Springfield, MA: Merriam-Webster, 1999
Muchembled, Robert. *A History of the Devil: From the Middle Ages to the Present*. Oxford: Blackwell, 2003.

The Omen. Directed by Richard Donner and J.M. Kenny. Los Angeles: 20th Century–Fox, 2001. DVD.

Phillips, John A. *Eve: The History of an Idea.* San Francisco: Harper & Row, 1984.

Roberts, Jenny. *Bible Facts.* New York: Barnes & Noble, 1998.

Rosemary's Baby. Directed by Roman Polanski. Hollywood, CA: Paramount, 2000. DVD.

Russell, Jeffrey Burton. *The Devil: Perceptions of Evil from Antiquity to Primitive Christianity.* Ithaca: Cornell University Press, 1987

_____. *Mephistopheles: The Devil in the Modern World.* Ithaca: Cornell University Press, 1986.

_____. *The Prince of Darkness: Radical Evil and the Power of Good in History.* Ithaca: Cornell University Press, 1988.

Szumskyj, Benjamin, ed. *American Exorcist: Critical Essays on William Peter Blatty.* Jefferson, NC: McFarland, 2008.

Tolle, Eckhart. *The Power of Now: A Guide to Spiritual Enlightenment.* Vancouver: Namaste, 2004.

Van Dijkhuizen, Jan Frans. *Devil Theatre: Demonic Possession and Exorcism in English Renaissance Drama, 1558–1642.* Cambridge: D.S. Brewer, 2007.

Waller, Gregory Albert, ed. *American Horrors: Essay on Modern American Horror Films.* Champaign: University of Illinois Press, 1987.

3

Frankenstein's Legacy: The Mad Scientist Remade

Kristine Larsen

The stereotype of the mad scientist overstepping the bounds of what is "natural" and falling into the trap of "playing God" is firmly ingrained in modern culture. As early as 1958, Hirsch noted that the common image of the scientist in the media included the Frankenstein archetype: the scientist as the victim of his own hubris "blasphemously attempting to attack natural or divine law."[1] Four decades later, famed scientist and science writer Carl Sagan noted that many people still picture scientists as "moral cripples driven by a lust for power."[2] Modern marvels such as genetic engineering, nuclear energy, and nanotechnology only further the mistrust of science in the public mind, where science is pictured as a genie released from its bottle with little thought as to the possible outcomes. The general public worries, based on their limited understanding of basic science,[3] whether the Large Hadron Collider will create a black hole that will destroy the earth. As Sagan sagely wrote, "the image of the mad scientist haunts our world — down to the white-coated loonies of Saturday morning children's TV."[4] Over the past half century, media producers and science fiction writers have been all too eager to play on these fears in the name of their craft, extending Mary Shelley's original "Modern Prometheus" through the "Creature Feature" B-movies of the 1950s and 1960s, to *Jurassic Park* and myriad knockoffs populating the Sci-Fi Channel today. Hence we are fed a steady diet of images of megalomaniac protagonists in white lab coats pushing the boundaries of science beyond the limits of ethics in a single-minded attempt to master Mother Nature and wrest from her every secret she, in her modesty, has kept from prying eyes. In the words of Shelley's Victor Frankenstein, scientists have "pursued nature in her hiding-places" in order "to penetrate the secrets of nature."[5]

One might argue that such an unfettered search for knowledge is the job of science. Indeed, science, in the abstract sense, is precisely that: the search for answers to questions posed about the natural world. However, science does not exist in a vacuum; rather, it is the vocation of *scientists*, human beings who are expected to obey the laws of their respective countries and hold to the social mores of their culture, even when doing so might impede their research. In addition, in the process of doing scientific research, technologies are developed and employed that may have applications that may be deleterious to individuals or groups. Some argue that because these future applications cannot always be foreseen, scientists should not be held accountable for them. For example, should Einstein be blamed for the atom bomb, since it was his theoretical equation $E=mc^2$ which made it possible?

Such issues continue to be debated by ethicists and scientists alike. However, when it comes to technologies related to medical and biological research, the ethical lines began to crystallize much more sharply in the 20th century, with ethicists, scientists, politicians, and the general public often reaching a consensus as to what constitutes ethical versus unethical research. An example is human cloning. Many religious groups and much of the American public in general have voiced opposition to human cloning, stating that creating life (especially human life) is the sole province of God, and to "play God" in this way mocks both the creator and his creation. A 2008 poll found that 78 percent of the American public opposed genetically altering or cloning humans.[6] Bioethicist Arlene Judith Klotzko notes that given the complexities of the cloning process and the high incidence of abnormalities seen in animal cloning, "any attempt at human cloning is patently immoral and would result in the ostracism of the scientist by his or her peers."[7] Several countries, including the United States and United Kingdom, have banned reproductive human cloning. Therefore, any scientist who actively engages in cloning humans in order to create a new human being (rather than simply cloning stem cells, which is in itself highly controversial) risks being branded a "mad scientist."[8]

Starting from this concrete example, we can begin to quantify the distinct properties of a so-called mad scientist. His or her research:

1. has an immoral intent (the classic case, often portrayed in the media, is world domination);

2. employs an immoral methodology (such as experimentation on human subjects who have not given their expressed and informed consent to take part in such an experiment, or experimentation which does not treat its human or animal subjects with respect and compassion);

3. has an immoral result (such as the development of a biological weapon);

4. is carried out in secret (out of the sight of peer review or governmental regulations);

5. disregards the ethical considerations and regulations of society in general, professional organizations, and the scientist's nation.

An obvious example from history is the atrocities committed by Nazi scientists in World War II, who experimented on concentration camp victims and other political prisoners with complete disregard for human dignity. Starting from this operational definition, one can recognize that Victor Frankenstein does indeed fit the archetype of a mad scientist. His experiments were done in secret, his creation was certainly not an informed participant in the experiment, and the result — a hideously disfigured creature who had no hope for a normal life — would have certainly been condemned as immoral by the American Medical Association (not to mention the fact that grave robbing is often considered illegal and immoral in its own right).

Creative new twists on Shelley's classic story of science and power have emerged in popular culture over the past decades, inviting the reader or viewer to think more deeply about the complex interplay between science, technology, power, and ethics, and their application to modern marvels. In viewing the mad scientist through the cinematic lens, we come to the uncomfortable conclusion that in many cases we are actually looking into a mirror, as modern medical marvels increasingly force us to examine not only our own mortality, but just how far each of us may be willing to go to control our own bodies and even delay the time of our death. This essay will explore the Frankenstein archetype of the mad scientist in three works which are not often analyzed in this manner: the literary works of J.R.R. Tolkien and the television series *Lost* and *Doctor Who*.

Examples of the single-minded mad scientist at work can be found in the television series *Lost*, which has at its very core an exploration of the dynamic tension between self and Other, with scientists most definitely among the latter. This includes the mysterious DHARMA Initiative and its primary funding source, the Hanso Foundation (THF). While the series has now concluded, significant questions remain concerning both organizations. Much of what has been divulged has been in the form of "orientation videos" which are found both within the text of the series and as stand-alone content available to fans online. An example was *The Lost Experience*, which invited dedicated fans to scour the Internet for clues during the break between seasons 2 and 3. Those clues revealed a nefarious background story for the DHARMA Initiative and the Hanso Foundation.

Viewers of the series first learned about the DHARMA Initiative in Season 2 through the orientation video for the Swan Station (aka the Hatch). The DHARMA Initiative was founded in 1970 by doctoral students from the

University of Michigan, and was intended as a "large-scale communal research compound where scientists and free-thinkers" from around the globe could pursue research. The facility was created on the infamous island through funding provided by the "reclusive Danish industrialist" Alvar Hanso.[9] According to the now-defunct website for the Hanso Foundation,[10] it conducted research in the following six areas:

- Mathematical Forecasting Initiative
- World Wellness and Prevention Development Program
- Mental Health Appeal
- Electromagnetic Research Initiative
- Institute for Genomic Advancement
- Life Extension Project

"Genomic Advancement" sounds suspiciously like a euphemism for "genetic engineering," a term which has largely become synonymous in the public's mind with designer babies and eugenics, while talk of life extension brings to mind the endless search for immortality (the ultimate victory over death and the attainment of the powers of the divine). These last two areas easily raise the specter of Frankenstein. The rest, however, appear to be socially responsible projects. But are they?

The Lost Experience had as its basic plotline the undercover exploits of one Rachel Blake, who hacked into the Hanso Foundation's website and exposed the true activities of the foundation, including "illegal organ harvesting, use of mathematical forecasting to start wars, questionable experiments with genetic engineering and life extension, and the intentional spreading of viruses to limit population growth."[11] For example, THF kept alive comatose patients against their families' wishes in order to provide organs for transplant. This fictional illegal activity speaks to the public outrage over the all-too-real black market in transplant organs in Third World and developing countries. For example, in 2006 the Chinese government was widely criticized for allowing organs from executed prisoners to be harvested without the consent of the next of kin.[12] To make matters worse, lax policing of the organ market has led to a lucrative market in transplant tourism, where desperate Americans and Europeans travel to South America or Asia to receive transplants without going through the normal channels of a donor registry. Not only have executed prisoners donated without their consent, but the desperately poor have been tricked or pressured into donating kidneys.[13]

Another morally questionable project of THF was its Life Extension Project, featuring as its poster child Joop, a supposedly 105-year-old orangutan.[14] For his part, Alvar Hanso proudly supported THF's work in this area, claiming that "given enough time, there is no end to what human beings can accomplish, no frontiers that we cannot cross."[15] Regardless of the intended nobility of the intentions of the individual scientist, the road to controlling nature is indeed a slippery slope. In this way, Hanso is clearly reminiscent of *Jurassic Park's* wealthy and well-intentioned founder, John Hammond, who found he could neither shield the scientists from corruption nor control the natural world. In the end, Hanso himself falls victim to the unscrupulous life extension research being conducted by his foundation, and becomes a prisoner in his own home while undergoing experimental treatments.[16]

While scientific research can cause trepidation in the hearts of some, mathematics can evoke sheer terror in the hearts of those who suffer math anxiety. While the infamous numbers 4,8,15,16,32,42 are well-known to viewers of *Lost*, their true nature is largely unknown to the casual viewer. *The Lost Experience* revealed that they are terms in the Valenzetti Equation, a "mathematical formulation designed to predict nothing less than the exact number of years left before the extinction of the human race."[17] The equation is a series of "core environmental and human factors" which describe various possible means of annihilation such as nuclear war and overpopulation. Each of these core factors is represented by one of the infamous numbers.[18] In his narration in the Sri Lanka Video,"[19] Alvar Hanso explained that the DHARMA Initiative was actually formed to try and find a means of changing one of the numerical values of the core factors.

The Sri Lanka Video then turned to a present-day lecture by chief scientist Dr. Thomas Werner Mittelwerk, addressing an audience of fellow scientists. Blake surreptitiously taped this event, because she discovered that Mittelwerk, "a mad scientist with a Messiah complex," was actually running THF in Hanso's absence.[20] Careful viewers of the series had already come across Mittelwerk in *Bad Twin*, a *Lost* tie-in novel supposedly written by Oceanic 815 crash victim Gary Troup. Here Mittelwerk was described as having "everything but morals ... everything except a conscience."[21] Among Mittelwerk's unethical plots was THF's Mental Health Appeal's incarceration of mathematicians against their will, in order to work on the Valenzetti Equation. Among their discoveries was the suggestion that a virus with a 30 percent mortality rate was "optimum" for Valenzetti research.[22]

The messianic symbolism is interesting, given that the tension between science and religion is central to the *Lost* mythos. In another *Lost* spinoff, the "Mysteries of the Universe" promotion for Season 6, the DHARMA Initiative is described by an unnamed former member as "a cult. Not religious, but it certainly had the same feeling, and actions of cult." The former member had left the organization precisely because its actions had "crossed the line" according to his personal ethics.[23]

The end of the Sri Lanka Video captured Mittelwerk explaining his plans to purposefully infect two unsuspecting villages with a virus disguised as a vaccine. When one horrified scientist argued that the intended experimental subjects were "innocent human beings," Mittelwerk launched into a speech worthy of Victor Frankenstein or John Hammond: "If you knew, with mathematical certainty, that you could end all famine, war, and poverty, what would you do? Exactly, you'd find the best way to get it done — precisely, surgically, without allowing for any more suffering that is absolutely necessary."[24] Mittelwerk's plan was exposed; however, in a secret message he vowed to continue his work, claiming, "Humanity needs me, now more than ever. I have the virus, I have the will, and I will not fail."[25] Mittelwerk is therefore a classic example of the public's worst scientific fears, namely a rogue, truly "mad" scientist. Can Mittelwerk be stopped? Can his real-life counterparts? Only the future will tell.

If death is the subject of unethical scientific practices in *Lost*, it is not surprising that perversions of science are also being committed relative to the beginning of life. The "Others" (the inhabitants of the island who have taken over the DHARMA Initiative's village and scientific equipment) recruited fertility specialist Juliet Burke to join their ranks in order to find out why pregnant women on the island (and their unborn fetuses) die in the second trimester. Juliet is a researcher (originally in her ex-husband Edmund's lab) specializing in making impossible pregnancies possible. For example, she managed to impregnate a male field mouse, but the pregnancy did not go to full term. She stole an experimental drug from the lab in order to help her sister, Rachel (who had undergone chemotherapy), become pregnant. Rachel gloats to her sister, "Tell that bastard ex-husband of yours what he can do with his ethics," as both clearly believe the end justifies the questionable means.[26] When Edmund discovers that the unauthorized experiment has succeeded, he proclaims Juliet's research on her sister, the "guinea pig," to be "potentially genius" but with some obvious ethical and legal concerns. But rather than report her to the appropriate ethical oversight group or the police, he demands to be in on the research, to "win prizes and drink champagne and do good for people." One seriously suspects that the first two reasons are truly driving his intentions.[27]

Representatives from the Mittelos Bioscience Corporation, apparently a front for the Hanso Foundation, succeed in convincing Juliet to join their company for a short stint, falsely assuring her she will return in time for the birth of her niece or nephew. As Richard Alpert points out to Juliet, she has accepted the position despite the fact that she knows that no one in the scientific community has ever heard of their laboratory. When she briefly hesitates, Alpert appeals to her Promethean spirit: "You took a woman, your own sister, whose reproductive system was ravaged by chemotherapy, who was sterile. And you made her pregnant. You created life where life wasn't supposed to be. That's a gift, Juliet. You have a gift. And don't you think you're meant to do something significant with it?"[28] It is easy to compare Juliet's accomplishment to that of Frankenstein, who "succeeded in discovering the cause of generation and life."[29] Just as Victor fell victim to his hubris, so too did Juliet Burke.

On the island, Juliet finds herself impotent to stop the dying, and when she protests that she cannot fix the problem, Benjamin Linus (a complex character worthy of his own essay on the line between good and evil) coldly tells her that they will just find more mothers for her to experiment on.[30] Thus begins Juliet's role in a convoluted plotline to kidnap a pregnant survivor of the Oceanic 815 crash and test other women for possible pregnancies, involving fake vaccines and in one case the implantation of some kind of device which will create false symptoms in a woman who has recently given birth. In typical *Lost* fashion, Juliet finds herself a veritable prisoner on the island several years after the birth of her sister's child, and moves between the island's various factions as she tries to escape at any cost. She has become a pawn in the greater story of good versus evil on the island, and only regains a portion of her free will at the end of the fifth season, when she willingly gives her own life to try and reset the timeline and prevent the crash of Oceanic 815 from occurring in the first place.

The final example of a Frankenstein character in the *Lost*-verse is Stuart Radzinzky, the head of research for the DHARMA Initiative on the island, who was obsessed with harnessing the unique electromagnetic energy "for the betterment of mankind and advancement of world peace."[31] Unfazed by the gruesome deaths of several members of his drill team, Radzinsky continues despite the protestations of fellow scientist Pierre Chang (who himself originally wished to use the energy in order to achieve time travel). The Swan Station is Radzinsky's brainchild, his ill-conceived "baby," which he will protect at any cost. As the drill team approaches its ultimate goal (and destruction), Radzinsky's behavior becomes more obsessive and erratic, and when Chang tries to get him to consider more carefully what he is doing, Radzinsky launches into a Frankenstein-like soliloquy: "If Edison worried about the consequences we'd all still be sitting in the dark. I came to this island to change the world, Pierre. That's exactly what I intend to do."[32] In true Frankenstein fashion, the monster cannot be controlled; there is a tremendous explosion, and the Swan Station instead becomes a massive degaussing station, where Radzinsky and later other DHARMA workers spend years pressing a computer button every 108 minutes in order to discharge the buildup of electromagnetic energy. The genie has been let out of the bottle, and is only sent back to hell when Desmond Hume later engages the failsafe and implodes the station.[33] As for Radzinsky, he is driven utterly insane, and after years of trying to control the monster he has unleashed upon the world, he commits suicide within the womb-like station which gave birth to his bastard child. From fertility to life extension, organ transplantation to possible effects of electromagnetic fields, *Lost* therefore forces its viewers to confront some of the timeliest intersections between science and ethics.

The characters of *Lost* seamlessly travel between past, present, and parallel realities. Fans of the fantasy works of J.R.R. Tolkien keep their feet planted in a hypothetical distant past of our own world, where elves, dwarves, ents, and wizards fight side by side with humans in a classic battle of good versus evil. But to read Tolkien with too tight a focus on philosophy and morality is to miss the complexity of the tapestry which this philologist wove together over six decades. His grand mythology of Middle-earth contains an impressive litany of astronomical knowledge (including constellations, phases of the moon, and meteors) as well as attention to biological detail, such as the observation that "Elves and Men are evidently in biological terms one race, or they could not breed and produce fertile offspring."[34] Even his choice of a career — "I am primarily a scientific philologist" — reflected his keen love for the natural world and its scientific study.[35] Perhaps the clearest statement of his personal view on the preferred relationship between the scientific and the artistic cultures is found in a letter to Milton Waldman, where he writes, "The Light of Valinor (derived from light before any fall) is the light of art undivorced from reason, that sees things both scientifically (or philosophically) and imaginatively (or sub-creatively) and says that they are good...."[36] However, in this same passage Tolkien draws our attention to one of the main themes of his — and, he argues, all — stories, namely the Fall. As Birzier explains, pride is the cause of nearly every fall, the "desire to be something more than God, or what God intended."[37] This pride can be intimately intertwined with science (and its application as technology), as in the classic cases of Prometheus, Icarus, Faustus, and Frankenstein. Pandora's tale warns us that curiosity can sometimes do much more than kill the cat, and in the book of Genesis Adam and Eve's taste of the fruit of the forbidden tree of knowledge ultimately led to humanity's fall and expulsion from the Garden of Eden. While some scientists have vociferously argued against placing what they see as artificial boundaries on what questions they can ask, and which paths they might take in answering these questions, in the aftermath of abuses of the scientific method such as those perpetrated by Nazi scientists, such limitations have become a reality in our modern world. It is therefore useful to explore Tolkien's works as a cautionary tale of the potential of science (and scientists) to suffer a fall, despite the idealistic purity to which science aspires, and the presumed good intentions of those who practice it.

The first instance of sin in Middle-earth is unequivocally a sin of desiring forbidden knowledge. Melkor, the mightiest of the angelic powers, or Ainur, was given by the supreme deity Ilúvatar "the greatest gifts of power and knowledge."[38] He was not satisfied with these gifts, and like Frankenstein, he became so consumed with the desire for more of both that he fell from being the chief among the Powers to the Great Enemy. Melkor sought to gain ultimate knowledge and power over the very spark of life, the so-called Flame Imperishable. Here we see an interesting twist on the tale of Prometheus. Rather than stealing the divine fire in order to help humanity, Melkor's motivations are strictly self-aggrandizing. Through his desires he fell into evil and sin, and through his introduction of discord into the Ainur's song of creation, evil became intertwined into the very fabric of reality. Among his blasphemous thoughts was the desire to "bring into Being things of his own," kindled by his impatience in what he perceived as Ilúvatar's slowness in filling the Void.[39] Here we find two of the most important recurring themes in the fall of science in Middle-earth: the desire to be a creator (a role assumed to belong solely to God), and the desire to change the pace of the natural world through artificial means. Melkor continued to battle the Valar (those among the Ainur who came down into the world to be its protectors), his ultimate desire nothing less than complete dominion over the world. Failing in this, he resorted to twisting both the physical environment and various life forms to suit his nefarious needs. Further failing to subjugate the natural world to his desires, he fell into what Tolkien called "nihilistic madness" and would have destroyed the world if it had been within his power.[40]

Geneticist J.B.S. Haldane wrote in his famed 1923 essay "Daedalus" that "if every physical and chemical invention is a blasphemy, every biological invention is a perversion."[41] Tolkien illustrates this point most dramatically through his writings on the roles of Melkor, Sauron, and Saruman in the unholy origin of orcs, Uruk-hai, and trolls.[42] Although he sought internal consistency within the entirety of his secondary universe, like Frankenstein Tolkien could only achieve an ugly, patchwork parody of life in his attempt to write an origin for the orcs and related creatures. For he firmly believed that evil had no power to create, and thus orcs could only be a blasphemous corruption of creatures which already existed.[43] Tolkien wavered between a number of unsatisfactory explanations, alternately calling orcs corrupted elves, humans or even animals.[44] The orcs are depicted as "short crook-legged creature(s), very broad and with long arms that hung almost to the ground," having claws, jowls, and hairy ears.[45] The modern reader cannot help drawing a direct connection between such twisted and unnatural creatures and their most famous archetype, Frankenstein's monster. For as Tolkien realized, "we cannot really conceive of *beautiful evil*."[46]

Like Shelley's classic tale, Tolkien's *The Simarillion,* the prequel to *The*

Hobbit and *The Lord of the Rings* that focuses on the elves and Valar, contains a cautionary message against trying to create life. Aulë, the craftsman — or engineer — of the Valar, was given by Ilúvatar "skill and knowledge scarce less than to Melkor."[47] But like Victor Frankenstein, Aulë tried to master the secret of creating life and thereby make living beings of his own. Frankenstein and Aulë initially believe their motivations justify their actions, but are eventually forced to face the folly of their experiments. Aulë wished to have living beings whom he could teach, and had grown impatient waiting for the arrival of the elves. Like Frankenstein, Aulë knew that his peers would not understand his motivations, and labored in secret, but was unable to keep his actions hidden from the true creator. Upon crafting the seven dwarf fathers, Aulë was visited by the Voice of Ilúvatar, who chided: "Why dost thou attempt a thing which thou knowest is beyond thy power and thy authority?"[48] Demonstrating his infinite love and pity, Ilúvatar adopts the dwarfs and gives them the autonomous spirits (souls), which Aulë does not have the power to bestow.

A similar example of the downward spiral into sin can be found in Saruman. His transformation from the chief of the wizards, emissary of the Valar, and student of Aulë into a mad scientist consumed by a "mind of metal and wheels"[49] is one of the more obvious cautionary lessons of *The Lord of the Rings*. As Saruman succumbs to his lust for knowledge and power, he falls into sin and abuse of the natural world. So too does his laboratory, Isengard, transforming from a beautiful tower where "wise men" had once engaged in observing the heavens (an example of pure science) into a "child's model or a slave's flattery of that vast fortress, armory, prison, furnace of great power, Barad-dûr, the Dark Tower."[50] Saruman's desire for knowledge and power led him into a Faustian deal with the devil — Sauron in this case — and despite Saruman's prideful belief that he could somehow manipulate the deal to his benefit, the reader understands Tolkien's message that this is utter folly.

Humans are also not free from Frankensteinian desires in Middle-earth. The noblest of the human bloodlines, the kings of the island of Númenor, became discontent with their several-centuries-long life spans, and seek to prolong their lives unnaturally; they even seek the secret of immortality. Tolkien recounts how "their wise men labored unceasingly to discover if they might the secret of recalling life, or at the least of prolonging of Men's days. Yet they achieved only the art of preserving incorrupt the dead flesh of Men, and they filled all the land with silent tombs in which the thought of death was enshrined in the darkness."[51] The Númenóreans were therefore easily swayed by the counsel of Sauron, who promised them life eternal if they would worship Melkor and attack the Blessed Lands of the Valar. Knowledge led to a fall from grace, and the rebellious Númenóreans find themselves not only cast out of Eden, but the victims of a Noachian disaster which destroys their beautiful island. Unfortunately, when the survivors of Ilúvatar's wrath arrived on the eastern shores of Middle-earth and founded the kingdom of Gondor, the lesson of their previous homeland was too soon forgotten, and they still "hungered after endless life unchanging."[52] But immortality is not to be sought after, nor actually achievable, in Tolkien's world, as even the elves and the Valar themselves may ultimately pass away in the End of Days. An important recurring theme in tales of the fall (not only in Tolkien but also in other classic works of science fiction and fantasy) was articulated by Tolkien in a 1951 letter, when he explained that a love of the supreme creator's world and frustration with their own mortality will lead individuals to become sub-creators, mimicking the actions of the true creator in an "obsessive, clinging" attempt of each individual to be the "Lord and God of his private creation." This is what leads to rebellion against the creator and the desire for power.[53]

In a draft of his famous essay "On Fairy-stories" Tolkien mused that "science (so noble in origin and original purpose) has produced in alliance with sin nightmare horrors and perils of the night before which the giants and demons grow pale."[54] If Tolkien were alive today, he would most certainly make connections between the creations attempted by Aulë, Sauron, Saruman, and Melkor and the current medical marvels of cloning, genetic engineering, and extreme fertility treatments. Victor Frankenstein realized too late the horror which he had unleashed upon the world. While Sauron and Melkor never regretted their actions, they showed no more mercy towards their creations than Frankenstein did towards his, and Tolkien notes not only that the Great Evil Powers would sacrifice their own minions without a second thought, but also that they in turn hated their creator and tormentor.[55] How similar this is to the tension between Victor Frankenstein and his creation, who laments, "Yet you, my creator, detest and spurn me, thy creature, to whom thou art bound by ties only dissoluble by the annihilation of one of us. You purpose to kill me. How dare you sport with this life?"[56] But Frankenstein will not be swayed, and after his creature causes the deaths of those closest to him, he pursues the unnamed abomination into the Arctic with the sole thought of exterminating that which he has given life.

"Exterminate, exterminate!" We hear the madness of Melkor and Frankenstein both echoed in the mantra of Davros and his Daleks, among the most enduring enemies in the long-running BBC series *Doctor Who*. A brilliant scientist, Davros observed the increasing incidence of genetic mutation among his own people—the Kaleds—due to the chemical weapons used in a millennium-long racial war on his home planet of Skaro against the rival Thals. He discovered the ultimate form his people would be destined to assume, a squid-like creature that would require an artificial housing for transportation. Davros himself is a mutant, confined to a motorized wheelchair and life support system which encompasses his body beneath the waist. His bald head is covered with grey, wrinkled skin reminiscent of the radiation-burned mutants in the *Planet of the Apes* films, and because his eyes are useless he relies on a blue artificial eye on his forehead in order to see. One hand is paralyzed, while the other is withered. His voice is mechanical and alternates between icy coldness and maniacal hysteria.

Sliding down the long slope toward madness, Davros began eugenics experiments on his own people, accelerating the rate of mutation in an effort to create a super-race which could not only win the planetary war, but ultimately conquer the universe. It is no coincidence that the Kaled officers dress in black uniforms eerily reminiscent of the SS, and that the Kaleds (and the Daleks they become) are obsessed with "racial purity."[57] A helpless, invertebrate mass of biological mush housed within a nearly impenetrable mechanical shell, the Daleks (as Davros christens his creations) personified the most excessive case of artificial parts possible, a far more extreme case than the more famous cyborg Darth Vader. Too late does the Kaled government realize Davros's true plan, working "without conscience, without soul," propelled by his "fanatical desire to perpetuate himself in his machines."[58] Like their creator, the Daleks are devoid of compassion or pity and obsessed with a single-minded mission to destroy all those who are not of their (superior) race, and as such the Daleks embody pure evil.

Case in point is a discussion between Davros and the Doctor concerning the ethical responsibilities of scientists. Despite the time-traveling Doctor's foreknowledge of the destructive power of the Daleks, he cannot bring himself to destroy the nascent race out of hand. Instead he asks their creator if he could hypothetically allow the use of a killer virus which he had created himself. Davros's response epitomizes the stereotype of the mad scientist: "To hold in my hand a capsule that contained such power. To know that life and death on such a scale was my choice. To know that the tiny pressure of my thumb, enough to break the glass, would end everything. Yes, I would do it. That power would set me up above the gods. And through the Daleks I shall have that power!"[59] The Doctor's presence at the creation of the Daleks (in this past timeline) was facilitated by the Time Lords' high council, in the hopes of preventing the species' creation or at the very least altering it to prevent their ultimate conquest of numerous planets. The Doctor manages to effect some change, because Davros does not die in the final battle (but is instead buried in suspended animation), and his presence in the new timeline is a chaotic one, as the continued tension between the creator and his creations is a sufficient distraction to prevent the Daleks from achieving their true destructive potential. Like Victor Frankenstein, Davros assumes that his "new species would bless me as its creator and source.... No father could claim the

gratitude of his child so completely as I."[60] Like Frankenstein, Davros is sorely
mistaken. He is also unable to control the monster he has unleashed upon the
world, and at the end of the episode the new-born Daleks refuse to obey their
creator. Tolkien's Melkor rebelled against Ilúvatar in the very beginning, and
the humans of Númenor later fell in their disobedience; likewise the Daleks
failed to live up to their creator's original intent.

Just as Frankenstein's monster, though loath to admit it, needs his creator
(to make him a mate), the Daleks also return to their creator time and time
again. For example, in "Destiny of the Daleks," the Daleks free Davros from
his entombment in the ruins of Skaro because they have come to an impasse
in their ongoing war against the Movellans, a race of robots. Davros openly
bristles at the idea that his children are ruled by a "Supreme Dalek" because
he believes his creations should obey only him without question. In "Resurrection of the Daleks" the ruthless creatures free their creator from a prison
space station because they need his scientific expertise to find a cure for a
virus unleashed upon them by the Movellans. The Daleks openly discuss
among themselves the fact that they are using Davros, but concede that without him they are doomed. Again, this reluctant symbiosis between creation
and creator mirrors that of Victor Frankenstein's creation and his maker. Like
Victor Frankenstein, Davros finally understands that in their disobedience
his creations are hopelessly flawed (and therefore evil, according to his personal
definition) and desires to destroy them (by allowing them to fall prey to the
virus). Unlike Shelley's protagonist, however, Davros does not wish to rid the
universe of his creations, but merely to start again from a clean state with a
new and improved, re-engineered version of his monsters.

Davros's next round of genetic engineering is displayed in "Revelation
of the Daleks," in which he has taken up residence on the planet Necros,
where the rich and powerful from across the galaxy repose in suspended animation, awaiting cures for their fatal diseases. Hiding behind the ironic name
of the "Great Healer," Davros succeeds in finding cures for the myriad diseases
which plagued the residents of the necropolis, but for his own nefarious purposes. Those who were deemed unworthy to become Daleks were converted
into a high-protein foodstuff (analogous to the foodstuff Soylent Green in the
1973 film of that title), while the unlucky chosen were engineered into a new
type of Daleks.

Davros's revised plan for universal domination is momentarily interrupted
by the arrival of "regular" Daleks, who arrest their creator and return him to
Skaro to stand trial. However, Davros is able to regain power and engineers
the "Imperial Daleks," with Davros as their emperor. In "Remembrance of
the Daleks" the new Imperial Daleks are revealed, with "functional append-
ages" and a prosthetic limb grafted onto their squid-like form. However,

Davros is revealed to have lost many of his humanoid characteristics and looks increasingly like a Dalek (i.e., more machine than organic).

Although Davros himself is absent from the Daleks' next appearance, his Frankenstein-like experiments continue to be carried out, now by the Daleks themselves. In "Daleks in Manhattan"/"Evolution of the Daleks" the four Daleks of Davros's Cult of Skaro use horrific human-animal and Dalek-human hybridization in order to evolve into a more deadly form. The experiment is deemed a failure by the Daleks themselves (who are wedded to their own concept of racial purity), and a single survivor, Dalek Caan, escapes. The intertwined fate of Caan and Davros is revealed in "Stolen Earth"/"Journey's End" when Davros returns with a new army of Daleks. Having failed to destroy the inferior species of the universe, Davros has now fallen into complete nihilism (akin to that of Morgoth) and uses the combined gravity of kidnapped planets (including Earth) to create a weapon that will disrupt the electromagnetic field which binds matter together. As Davros maniacally explains to the Doctor, "Behold the apotheosis of my genius.... This is my ultimate victory, Doctor! The destruction of reality itself!"[61] Davros plans to keep his Daleks safe within their spacecraft, to become the rulers of a new universe. More horrifying still, it is revealed that the new army of Daleks was created from Davros's own cells, as he proudly displays that much of his remaining flesh had been removed from his body. Thus in the case of Davros, not only does he fall into the madness of power lust, but he himself finally becomes that which he has created, a Dalek, after suffering numerous mutations and physical injuries. The experimenter has become the experiment, to the undeniable detriment of both.

Davros's plan includes causing his nemesis, the Doctor, to face the blood accumulated on his own hands, not only in the destruction of the original Dalek army (and the Time Lords' home planet of Gallifrey) in the Time War, but in the Doctor's unconscious engineering of many of his formerly innocent companions into soldiers and "monsters." "I made the Daleks, Doctor," Davros boasts. "You made this."[62] It is revealed that Dalek Caan actually helped to bring together the Doctor and his companions, most notably Donna Noble, for the expressed purpose of destroying Davros and the Daleks once and for all. "I saw the Daleks, what we have done, throughout time and space," the prophetic yet insane Caan explains. "I saw the truth of us, Creator, and I decreed no more!"[63] In a plot twist far too complex to explain in this brief synopsis, the Doctor is saved from having to commit genocide because a hybrid-clone of himself (a combination of his and Donna's genetics called the "meta-crisis") does the deed for him. As he and Caan die in flames, Davros curses the Doctor, naming him "Destroyer of Worlds," and the Doctor is forced to face that he has indeed followed the path of Frankenstein. The

episode ends with the meta-crisis clone — his monster — and Rose Tyler, arguably the companion dearest to him, being banished to an alternative parallel
universe where the monster can wreak no further havoc. Just as Frankenstein's
monster ends his days in the icy wasteland of the Arctic Circle, the Doctor's
monstrous doppelgänger is banished to Bad Wolf Bay, Norway, on a desolate
beach in a parallel reality.

Turney[64] argues that if we are going to have an earnest dialogue on debates
of science and society, "fictional representations [of science] matter.... We
need to attend, not just to the internal development of science, but to the
history of science in popular culture." In today's society, the first-time reader
of Shelley's *Frankenstein* too often comes to the work with the mistaken
impression that Frankenstein is the name of the creation instead of the creator.
However, they soon learn that Frankenstein truly is the name of the monster,
namely the scientist who has perversely over-stepped the boundaries of morality. In the case of the island of *Lost*, Middle-earth, and the planet Skaro, the
potential abuses of science — and their consequences — are clear, but delivered
with a fresh face which is sometimes lacking in derivative works. They are all
worthy descendants of Shelley's masterpiece, and carry on Victor Frankenstein's plaintive caution: "Learn from me, if not by my precepts, at least by
my example, how dangerous is the acquirement of knowledge and how much
happier that man who believes his native town to be the world, than he who
aspires to become greater than his nature will allow."[65] In the early years of
the 21st century, this lesson is now more imperative than ever.

NOTES

1. Walter Hirsch, "The Image of the Scientist in Science Fiction: A Content Analysis," in *American Journal of Sociology* 63, no. 5 (1958), 510.
2. Carl Sagan, *The Demon-haunted World* (New York: Ballantine, 1997), 373.
3. The National Science Board has been tracking the public's attitudes towards and knowledge of science for several decades. The latest results, *Science and Engineering Indicators: 2010*, can be found at http://www.nsf.gov/statistics/seind10/ (retrieved 5 June 2010).
4. Sagan, 11.
5. Mary Shelley, *Frankenstein or, The Modern Prometheus* (New York: Signet Classics, 2000), 39.
6. *Science and Engineering Indicators: 2010*, Chapter 7, page 41, http://www.nsf.gov/statistics/seind10/pdf/c07.pdf.
7. Arlene Judith Klotzko, *A Clone of Your Own? The Science and Ethics of Cloning* (Cambridge: Cambridge University Press, 2006), xxi.
8. Arlene Judith Klotzko, ed., *The Cloning Sourcebook* (Oxford: Oxford University Press, 2001), 22.
9. "Orientation," *Lost*, 2005.
10. For example, *Lostpedia*, available at http://lostpedia.wikia.com/ (retrieved 5 June 2010).
11. Pandora, "The Lost Experience," *SledgeWeb's Lost ... Stuff Forum*, available at http://lost.cubit.net/forum/index.php?topic=2204.0 (retrieved 5 June 2010).
12. "China Officially Admits Executed Prisoners Are the Basis of Organ Trafficking," *Asia*

News (16 November 2006), available at http://www.asianews.it/index.php?l=en&art=7771 (retrieved 5 June 2010).

13. Brian Handwerk, "Organ Shortage Fuels Illicit Trade in Human Parts," *National Geographic* (16 January 2004), available at http://news.nationalgeographic.com/news/2004/01/0116 _040116_EXPLorgantraffic.html (retrieved 5 June 2010).

14. Pandora, "The Lost Experience."

15. Truffula, "Truffula Surfs the *Lost* Webmaze," *Lost Online Studies 1.1*, available at http://loststudies.com/1.1/truffula/maze.html (retrieved 5 June 2010).

16. Pandora, "The Lost Experience."

17. "Valenzetti Equation," *Lostpedia*, available at http://lostpedia.wikia.com/wiki/Valenzetti_Equation (retrieved 5 June 2010).

18. Pandora, "DHARMA and the Sri Lanka Video," *Sledge Web's Lost ... Stuff*, available at http://lost.cubit.net/essentialsView.php?id=97026 (retrieved 5 June 2010).

19. This video is posted on various websites, including http://lostpedia.wikia.com/wiki/Sri_lanka_video (retrieved 5 June 2010).

20. Cecilia, "The Lost Experience: The Summary," available at http://www.lostblog.net/lost/tv/show/the-lost-experience-the-relatively-short-summary-for-nonplayers (retrieved 21 June 2010).

21. Gary Troup, *Bad Twin* (New York: Hyperion, 2006), 150.

22. Pandora, "The Lost Experience."

23. "Mysteries of the Universe." *Lostpedia*, available at http://lostpedia.wikia.com/wiki/Mysteries_of_the_Universe (retrieved 5 June 2010).

24. http://lostpedia.wikia.com/wiki/Sri_lanka_video.

25. Pandora, "The Lost Experience."

26. "Not in Portland," *Lost*, 2007.

27. Ibid.

28. "One of Us," *Lost*, 2007.

29. Shelley, 37.

30. "One of Us," *Lost*, 2007.

31. "The Man Behind the Curtain," *Lost*, 2007.

32. "The Incident," *Lost*, 2009.

33. "Live Together Die Alone," *Lost*, 2006.

34. Humphrey Carpenter, ed., *The Letters of J.R.R. Tolkien* (Boston: Houghton Mifflin, 2000), 189.

35. Carpenter, 345.

36. Ibid., 148.

37. Bradley Birzier, *J.R.R. Tolkien's Sanctifying Myth* (Wilmington, DE: ISI Books, 2002), 95.

38. J.R.R. Tolkien, *The Silmarillion* (Boston: Houghton Mifflin, 2001), 16.

39. Ibid.

40. J.R.R. Tolkien, *Morgoth's Ring* (Boston: Houghton Mifflin, 1993), 396.

41. Jon Turney, *Frankenstein's Footsteps: Science, Genetics and Popular Culture* (New Haven, CT: Yale University Press, 1998), x.

42. See Tolkien, *Morgoth's Ring*, 405–23.

43. See ibid., 417.

44. Ibid., 410.

45. J.R.R. Tolkien, *The Two Towers* (Boston: Houghton Mifflin, 1993), 50, 55.

46. Verlyn Flieger and Douglas A. Anderson, eds., *Tolkien on Fairy-stories* (London: HarperCollins, 2008), 256.

47. Tolkien, *The Silmarillion*, 19.

48. Ibid., 43.

49. Tolkien, *The Two Towers*, 76.

50. Ibid., 160–1.

51. Tolkien, *The Silmarillion*, 265–6.

52. Tolkien, *The Two Towers*, 286.

53. Carpenter, 145.
54. Flieger and Anderson, 269.
55. Tolkien, *Morgoth's Ring*, 406.
56. Shelley, 81.
57. For example, see "Genesis of the Daleks," "Remembrance of the Daleks," "Daleks in Manhattan," *Doctor Who*, 1975.
58. "Genesis of the Daleks," *Doctor Who*, 1975.
59. Ibid.
60. Shelley, 38–9.
61. "Journey's End," *Doctor Who*, 2008.
62. Ibid.
63. Ibid.
64. Turney, 13.
65. Shelley, 38.

BIBLIOGRAPHY

Birzier, Bradley. *J.R.R. Tolkien's Sanctifying Myth*. Wilmington, DE: ISI Books, 2002.
Carpenter, Humphrey, ed. *The Letters of J.R.R. Tolkien*. Boston: Houghton Mifflin, 2000.
Cecilia. "The Lost Experience: The Summary." Available at http://www.lostblog.net/lost/tv/show/the-lost-experience-the-relatively-short-summary-for-nonplayers. Retrieved 5 June 2010.
"China Officially Admits Executed Prisoners are the Basis of Organ Trafficking." *Asia News*, 16 November 2006. Available at http://www.asianews.it/index.php?l=en&art=7771. Retrieved 5 June 2010.
Doctor Who. Television series. Broadcast 23 November 1963–6 December 1989, 26 March 2005–present. BBC.
Flieger, Verlyn, and Douglas A. Anderson, eds. *Tolkien on Fairy-stories*. London: HarperCollins, 2008.
Handwerk, Brian. "Organ Shortage Fuels Illicit Trade in Human Parts." *National Geographic*, 16 January 2004. Available at http://news.nationalgeographic.com/news/2004/01/0116_040116_EXPLorgantraffic.html. Retrieved 5 June 2010.
Hirsch, Walter. "The Image of the Scientist in Science Fiction: A Content Analysis." *American Journal of Sociology* 63, no. 5 (1958): 506–12.
Lost. Television series. Broadcast 22 September 2004–23 May 2010. ABC.
Lostpedia. Available at http://lostpedia.wikia.com/. Retrieved 5 June 2010.
Klotzko, Arlene Judith. *A Clone of Your Own? The Science and Ethics of Cloning*. Cambridge: Cambridge University Press, 2006.
_____, ed. *The Cloning Sourcebook*. Oxford: Oxford University Press, 2001.
Pandora. "The Lost Experience." *SledgeWeb's Lost... Stuff Forum*. Available at http://lost.cubit.net/forum/index.php?topic=2204.0. Retrieved 5 June 2010.
_____. DHARMA and the Sri Lanka Video," *SledgeWeb's Lost... Stuff*. Available at http://lost.cubit.net/essentialsView.php?id=97026. Retrieved 5 June 2010.
Sagan, Carl. *The Demon-haunted World*. New York: Ballantine, 1997.
Science and Engineering Indicators: 2010. Available athttp://www.nsf.gov/statistics/seind10/. Retrieved 5 June 2010.
Shelley, Mary. *Frankenstein or, The Modern Prometheus*. New York: Signet Classics, 2000.
"Sri Lanka Video." Available at http://lostpedia.wikia.com/wiki/Sri_lanka_video. Retrieved 5 June 2010.
Truffula. "Truffula Surfs the *Lost* Webmaze." *Lost Online Studies 1.1*. Available at http://lost-studies.com/1.1/truffula/maze.html. Retrieved 5 June 2010.
Tolkien, J.R.R. *Morgoth's Ring*. Boston: Houghton Mifflin, 1993.
_____. *The Silmarillion*. 2nd ed. Boston: Houghton Mifflin, 2001.
_____. *The Two Towers*. 2nd ed. Boston: Houghton Mifflin, 1993.

Troup, Gary. *Bad Twin.* New York: Hyperion, 2006.
Turney, Jon. *Frankenstein's Footsteps: Science, Genetics and Popular Culture.* New Haven: Yale University Press, 1998.
"Valenzetti Equation." *Lostpedia.* Available at http://lostpedia.wikia.com/wiki/Valenzetti_Equation. Retrieved 5 June 2010.

4

Focus on the Family:
Good and Evil Vampires
in the *Twilight* Saga

A.J. Grant

The Problem of Evil in Twilight

The problem of evil in the *Twilight* saga is that there is not much of a problem. And this *is* a problem — at least for vampires, who, traditionally, *are* evil and commit one evil deed after another. Bram Stoker's *Dracula* wreaks havoc on small towns and villages in Transylvania and later sets up forty-eight coffins throughout London, obviously planning mayhem for England. Dracula sells his soul to the devil and is thereby damned for all eternity, because he trades mortality for immortality, at the expense of countless human lives. What is terrifying about 19th century vampires is that they are *essentially* evil — evil to the core — and in every way imaginable. They are theologically evil, having made an eternal pact with the devil. They are morally evil, in the sense that they *intend* evil: the classic components of *intentional* evil, malice and forethought, are present in Lord Ruthven, Carmilla and Dracula. In addition, 19th century vampires resemble natural forms of evil — earthquakes, floods, fire and lightning — because they strike randomly: "who lives and who does not depends on contingencies that cannot be deserved or prevented."[1] This combination of evils is what makes 19th century vampires so terrifying.

The traditional Western categories of evil — metaphysical, natural and moral — are readily identifiable within the Christian theological frame of Bram Stoker's *Dracula*. If metaphysical evil refers to "the degeneration inherent in the limits of the substance of which the physical world is made,"[2] then vampires like Dracula have been freed from this evil since they are immortal. In order to remain "undead," however, Dracula, and other traditional vampires, must inflict "natural evil" or pain, suffering, and death on humans. In traditional Christian theodicies (like Leibniz's), moral evil "refers to the crime for which natural evil is the just punishment."[3] In other words, bad things happen to bad people. A causal connection exists between sin and suffering. Here we begin to see clearly the terror of the vampire: in *Dracula*, the causal connection between natural and moral evil is sundered. Lucy and Mina are both innocents before their encounters with the Count, but Lucy in her changed state is evil to the core, an evil signified by her sexual wantonness. When the vampire hunters encounter her at her grave, we see a profound change in her from virgin to whore: "The sweetness was turned to adamantine, heartless cruelty, and the purity to voluptuous wantonness." Her eyes were now "unclean and full of hell-fire, instead of the pure gentle orbs...."[4] When Lucy first encounters Holmwood in her changed state, she approaches him seductively "with a languorous, voluptuous grace" and moans, "Come to me, Arthur.... My arms are hungry for you. Come and we can rest together."[5] It is a transmogrified Lucy, a nightmare for a decent Victorian woman, but it could just as easily have been Mina.

For the more recent vampire stories of Anne Rice, Chelsea Quinn Yarbro and Charlaine Harris, the traditional 19th century theological framework is abandoned altogether, significantly altering the traditional categories of evil associated with vampires, and, perhaps, the idea of evil itself as an appropriate descriptor for vampires. Gone is the theological dualism of God and the devil and with this the power of crosses, rosary beads and holy water. The new vampires are freed of metaphysical evil in these contemporary series since they are far more powerful than Dracula or Carmilla and impossible to kill — Lestat fails to end his life by a flight into the hot desert sun. The new vampires, like Louis, St. Germaine and eventually Lestat, refuse to drain humans, and, longing for their lost humanity, attempt to reclaim it through the cultivation of the arts and good deeds. In other words, they are not morally evil, nor do they strike arbitrarily like earthquakes or floods. If they do attack humans, they attack only evildoers — murderers, rapists and other thugs — which both justifies the attacks and humanizes the attackers. These "chic" vampires, according to Sandra Tomc, are "not subhuman so much as ultra-human," but, in addition, they have also gone through a "process of domestication" which removes them far from Dracula and other 19th century monsters.[6]

The *Twilight* saga, on the face of it, is a modern, secular vampire story in the tradition of Rice, Yarbro and Harris, but deceptively so. Meyer's saga reflects categories of good and evil that from afar look like those presumed common among Americans, but up close turn out to be peculiarly Mormon.

These less evil and more human vampires account, in part, for the current popularity of vampires across all literary genres and communication media. What Meyer shares with Rice, Yarbro and Harris' secular vampires is the fact that vampires are not quite as evil as *Dracula*; rather they are ultra-humans who mourn the loss of their humanity and refuse to prey on humans. But for Meyer, vampires are ultra-humans not because God is absent and sin doesn't matter (as in Rice's, Yarbro's and Harris' worlds), but because all humans were once spirit children of God, the Father, and are in varying stages of progress toward godhood. God the Father and Jesus, according to traditional Mormon theology, were once human, but have, through obedience, progressed to the point of godhood — the *telos* for all humans. Meyer's vampires, as ultra-humans, are simply one step closer to becoming gods, because they are already immortal.

The cosmic struggle between God and the devil is present in Mormon theology, but is less important than the struggle of humans toward godhood. All humans and angels, including Satan and his minions, are moving toward godhood or turning from it. No being is evil *by nature*. Similarly, the vampires and werewolves of *Twilight* are not *essentially* evil like Dracula or Carmilla. They *can* change and are therefore judged on whether or not they have chosen membership in a good family, rather than going solo or joining a coven that feeds on humans.

In addition to an emphasis on free agency and a focus on the family, *Twilight* features humans and vampires who embrace traditional values. Bella, Edward and Jacob are all obedient American teenagers: they honor their parents and refrain from lying, stealing, committing adultery, murdering, and coveting others' possessions. Perhaps it is more accurate to say that the heroes and heroine of *Twilight* are good *Mormon* kids, because in addition to keeping the six commandments just listed they also don't swear, drink alcohol (or caffeine), smoke, or do drugs. And they refrain from premarital sex. This is the cultural and moral frame of the series and those who live within this frame prosper, while those who live outside the frame falter and perish. This is not to say that our heroes and heroine do not suffer — they suffer a great deal, but they eventually triumph over their struggles and predicaments, because they make moral choices. This is neither comedy nor tragedy (in spite of multiple references to Romeo and Juliet in *New Moon*) and this is certainly not satire; rather, this is classical romance,[7] since our romantic hero and heroine transcend their own limitations by coming together (in a chaste fashion) and triumphing over the evil that is almost sure to overwhelm them. And this transcendence and triumph are made possible because of Bella and Edward's commitments to traditional values, free agency, family, and sacrificial love.

The Solution to Evil: Free Agency and the Family

In a 2005 interview with William Morris, Stephenie Meyer noted, "Unconsciously I put a lot of my beliefs into the story. Free agency is a big theme, as is sacrifice."[8] Mormon theology presents free agency (or moral agency) as an eternal gift of God the Father given to all his spirit children before the creation of the world. In this sense, evil does not exist eternally but comes into being with the *choice* of Lucifer to rebel against God's plan of salvation involving Christ. Lucifer suggests to God an alternative plan, which would have involved the removal of free agency and the eternal enslavement of humans. God rejects Lucifer's plan and the angel of light is transformed into Satan, God's adversary. From Adam and Eve on, according to Mormon theology, every human being knows the difference between good and evil and possesses the ability to choose between the two:

> [B]ecause that they are redeemed from the fall they have become free forever, knowing good from evil; to act for themselves and not to be acted upon, save it be by the punishment of the law at the great and last day, according to the commandments which God hath given. *Wherefore, men are free according to the flesh*; and all things are given them which are expedient unto man. *And they are free to choose liberty and eternal life*, through the great Mediator of all men, or to choose captivity and death, according to the captivity and power of the devil [emphasis added].[9]

This doctrine of free agency differs from traditional (Augustinian) Christian doctrine that argues that because of original sin, all humans are by nature evil, which means that all actions are always and only sinful. Apart from redemption, it is not possible for humans not to sin (*non posse non peccare*).[10] It is only as humans are infused with grace that they are able to overcome their "sin nature" and begin to choose good over evil. In other words, humans cannot choose God; God must choose them. For Mormons, the fall was both necessary and felicitous, because it creates the possibility for the exercising of free agency for all humans.

Mormons have a sunnier view of human nature. All humans once lived as spirit children in God's presence for eons before the earth was created. During this time each and every human grew in their knowledge of God. At some point, however, these spirit children needed to be born into human bodies in order to continue their spiritual growth toward godhood. Thus, all humans are born with the potential to be divine as is clearly stated in the *Doctrine and Covenants 132.20*: "Then shall they be gods, because they have no end; therefore shall they be from everlasting to everlasting, because they continue; then shall they be above all, because all things are subject unto them. Then shall they be gods, because they have all power, and the angels are subject unto them."[11]

This sounds a lot like the Cullens in *Twilight*. Though vampires are, by "nature," destined (or determined) to survive on human blood, and their free agency is thus replaced by an iron-clad determinism, nevertheless, in Meyer's vampire world, as in Rice's and Harris,' blood substitutions are possible, so choice is reinstated. Throughout the *Twilight* saga, but especially in *New Moon*, the notion of choice is paramount, and as the good vampires consistently choose good over evil, they move ineluctably toward godhood — Edward and Bella choose not to have sex; Carlisle chooses to heal humans as a medical doctor; and the whole Cullen family chooses not to feed on humans, instead drinking the blood of animals. The result is that the family grows physically and mentally stronger as it prepares for the final showdown with the Volturi.

Vampires actually turn out to be excellent popular culture figures to illustrate the struggles that free agency imposes. In fact, Meyer says that free agency is the underlying "metaphor" of her vampires: "It doesn't matter where you're stuck in life or what you think you have to do; you can always choose something else. There's always a different path."[12]

In addition to the importance of free agency, Stephenie Meyer also mentions "sacrifice," which involves individuals' giving up opportunities or privileges for the good of the group — and the primary group, for Mormons, is the family. "The family is the center of life on earth. Through eternal covenants made in Holy Temples, husbands and wives and their families can be sealed together throughout eternity."[13] This focus on the family, taken together with free agency, marks, metaphysically, the division between a good life and an evil life in the *Twilight* saga. To be alone is to be subject to temptation and evil; to be part of a family is to be shielded from temptation and evil. Bella is thus in a tenuous position at the beginning of *Twilight*, because in addition to being the only child of divorced parents, she chooses to leave her mother, Renee (who has recently remarried), and live with her father, Charlie, in Forks, Washington. In short, she has a broken family, and her divorced parents act more like children than adults. "It was to Forks that I now exiled myself— an action that I took with great horror. I detested Forks," says Bella. Renee tells her that she doesn't have to live with her father, and Bella feels a twinge of guilt: "How could I leave my loving, erratic, harebrained mother to fend for herself. Of course she had Phil now, so the bills would probably get paid...."[14]

Bella is more parent than child, and immediately after moving in with Charlie, she takes on the cleaning and cooking responsibilities for the household. Charlie, like Renee, is a child — hardly the wise, protective father valued by Mormons. Here we have the twin notions of free agency and sacrifice at play—Bella sacrifices her own desires and preferences for the greater good of her dysfunctional parents. But this places her in a highly vulnerable position, from a Mormon standpoint. She is all alone. She needs a family and eventually finds in the Cullens the potential for a new family, in fact, an eternal family of vampires.

Good, Bad and Ugly Vampires

In the *Twilight* saga, vampires are not evil by nature. As Edward explains the origin of his "family," Bella wants to know how it all started, so Edward turns to speculations about evolution and creation and suggests a very Mormon doctrine of the creation by God, the Father (Elohim):

> Couldn't we have evolved in the same way as other species, predator and prey? Or, if you don't believe that all this world could have just happened on its own, which is hard for me to accept myself, is it so hard to believe that the same force that created the delicate angelfish with the shark, the baby seal and the killer whale, could create both our kinds together?[15]

Traditional Christian theology argues that the world was created "very good" (read "perfect") and that the fall is responsible for the entrance of metaphysical, natural and moral evil. In other words, there are no predators or prey before the fall in Mormon theology. Edward's speculations are very much in line with the Mormon belief that Elohim used preexistent matter to shape the universe into its current form, a creation that includes natural evil. Moral evil enters the world through the fall, but the fall is absolutely necessary for humans to experience the "oppositions" in life, for without sorrow one cannot know joy—"Adam fell that men might be; and men are, that they might have joy."[16] Thus, vampires and humans, according to Edward, could be another example of opposition, another instance of God pairing predator with prey.

Since no creature is evil by nature, including the vampire, it only follows that there are good vampires in the *Twilight* saga, vampires like the Cullens, a "family" of "vegetarian" vampires who refuse to live on human blood. And there are *bad* vampires, like the Volturi, an ancient (and mostly corrupt) vampire council that polices vampire activity throughout the world and enforces vampire laws (e.g., turning a child, speaking or acting in a manner that draws attention to vampires, etc.). The Volturi are bad because they feed regularly and arbitrarily on humans, like normal vampires. And they are potentially trouble for the Cullens, because they are jealous of their preternatural gifts, cannot understand their abstinence from human blood, and would prefer to have the more gifted of them, Edward and Alice, swear allegiance to Aro, Caius and Marcus. But there are also *ugly* vampires, rogue vampires, like James and Victoria, predators who disregard both human and vampire laws.

In terms of vampires, then, none are evil by nature, rather it is a matter of free agency or choice. Those who, through sacrifice and self-denial, refuse human blood and choose to form "families" based on love (the Cullens and Tanya's "family") are good. Those, like the Volturi, who choose power over love and continue to drain humans, are bad. Those who choose to disregard vampire and human laws, rogue vampires like James and Victoria, are evil. In short, vampires in the *Twilight* saga are more or less evil based on their commitment to the traditional Mormon values of sacrificial love, free agency, and the family.

The Good

What then does evil look like for a vampire in *Twilight*? As previously noted, vampires are evil only if they choose to follow their natural desire for human blood (unless it's in a drip bag). The good vampires are those who refuse human blood and choose a life of self-restraint and sacrifice by forming an eternal family. Free agency and family values — the Cullens. There are seven of them. To outsiders they appear a mother, a father, and five adopted children, though in reality they are three vampire couples — Carlisle and Seem, Emmett and Rosalie, Jasper and Alice — and Edward. Seven is the number of perfection in biblical numerology and the Cullens are the perfect family, but there is room for one more, since Edward is single, and Bella Swan seems the best candidate, except that she is not a vampire and Edward refuses to even contemplate turning her. In fact, one of the central conflicts in the saga is Bella's desire to become a vampire and Edward's refusal to allow it. In the end, the question of joining the Cullen's eternal family is put to a vote — each member has a voice and a choice in the matter.

And what does a good vampire family look like? Pretty traditional. The father, Carlisle, is a renowned medical doctor; Seem, the mother, stays home and keeps house; and the five children dutifully respect their "parents" and attend the local high school. From Charlie's perspective the town is lucky to have Dr. Cullen, who "is a brilliant surgeon" and could have chosen any hospital in the world and made "ten times the salary he gets" in Forks.[17] And the kids are "well-behaved and polite" according to Charlie, Bella's father, in spite of early reservations about them. They're all "very mature."[18] And pretty rich: Edward drives a new Volvo, Rosalie a red BMW M3 series, and the other kids a new Jeep. Their home is actually a secluded country estate nestled in the woods.

And they are pretty pretty. They are all, of course, vampires and *ipso facto* "chalky pale," but they are also "devastatingly, inhumanly beautiful. They were faces you never expected to see except on the airbrushed pages of a fashion magazine. Or painted by an old master as the face of an angel."[19] When she first encounters the Cullen children, Bella has difficulty determining who is more beautiful — "the perfect blond girl, or the bronze-haired boy."[20] Throughout *Twilight*, Bella catches herself staring at her "Adonis" and constantly commenting on his beauty and strength. The transfiguration of Edward that occurs in the meadow on a Saturday hike reveals Edward in all his statuesque glory: "His skin ... literally sparkled, like thousands of tiny diamonds were embedded in the surface. He lay perfectly still in the grass, his shirt over his sculpted, incandescent chest, his scintillating arms bare.... A perfect statue, carved in some unknown stone, smooth like marble, glistening like crystal."[21] Bella gazes in wonder and hesitantly touches first his hand, then his arm. When he sits up suddenly, his "angel's face" is only a few inches from hers. But as he leans in, presumably to kiss her, he's suddenly gone, twenty feet from her in an instant.

And pretty godlike. Edward is well on his way to godhood. In *Twilight*, while Bella waits outside of Spanish class, she describes Edward as "looking more like a Greek god"[22] than a high school senior. Later, on their hike to the clearing, Bella notes, "He was too perfect, I realized with a piercing stab of despair. There was no way this godlike creature could be meant for me."[23] Shortly after Edward meets Charlie, Bella describes Edward again as a "godlike creature" and when she finally visits the Cullen estate, Edward notes that Carlisle often painted the master vampires — Aro, Marcus and Caius — as "gods."[24] Finally, when Edward tells his story of being turned, Bella pictures him in her mind as "terrible and glorious as a young god, unstoppable"[25] in his hunting down of criminals to satisfy his blood lust.

And pretty white. According to Bella, "Every one of them was chalky pale, the palest of all the students living in this sunless town. Paler than me, the albino."[26] They own a huge three story *white* house in the country located miles down an unmarked country road next to a river. The inside of the house is "very bright, very open and very large."[27] The whole back of the house is glass, which has a view of the perfect lawn stretching away to the river. There is a "massive, curving staircase" in the foyer and "[t]he walls, the high-beamed ceiling, the wooden floors, and the thick carpets were all varying shades of *white*" (emphasis added).[28]

And pretty strong and heroic. Edward saves Bella from being crushed by Tyler's van sliding across a sheet of ice in the school parking lot, and he saves her again from four men intent on harming her in Port Angeles. Edward runs miles through the woods with her the night of the Cullen "baseball game," where the outfielders stand a quarter of a mile from home plate. They only play during thunder storms because the crack of the ball and bat and the sound of collision is "like the crash of two massive falling boulders."[29] Edward whisks Bella away from the field when the three rogue vampires — Laurent, Victoria, and James — break up the family baseball game. To Bella, Edward has it all: "Interesting ... and brilliant ... and mysterious ... and perfect ... and beautiful ... and able to lift full-sized vans with one hand."[30]

And these are vampires? Well, yes, but they are far more human than vampire, and far more godlike than the vampires conceived by Bram Stoker, Stephen King and Elizabeth Kostova or even Rice or Yarbro. Bella comes across an entry for the *Sturgeon benefice* when she googles "vampire" and finds this definition: "An Italian vampire, said to be on the side of goodness, and a mortal enemy of all evil vampires."[31] The Cullens are clearly, in Nina Auerbach's words, "children of the light" (not "children of the night") who have chosen self-sacrifice, denial of lust, and a life dedicated to serving humans from the shadows.[32] From the perspective of the Volturi, the overly zealous vampire "hall monitors" (according to Alice), the Cullens are "abnormal" and "unorthodox."[33] Alice explains the difference to Bella on their trip to Valera, Italy, to rescue Edward:

> We Cullens are unique in more ways than you know. It's ... abnormal for so many of us to live together in peace.... Carlisle speculates that abstaining makes it easier for us to be civilized, to forms bonds based on love rather than survival or convenience. Even James' little coven of three was unusually large — and you saw how easily Laurent left them. Our kind travel alone, or in pairs, as a general rule. Carlisle's family is the biggest in existence, as far as I know, with the one exception, the Volturi.[34]

Sacrifice, self-denial and the love of a family make the Cullens unique as vampires and empowers them to overcome both the evil within and the evil brought on by other non-familial vampires. This is big love indeed.

The Bad

The Volturi is the "bad" group of vampires in the saga — at least from the perspective of the Cullens and naïve humans. There are five of them: the three "masters," Aro, Caius and Marcus, and two gifted female vampires who serve them, Jane and Alec. In addition, there are nine guardians, which brings their numbers to fourteen (or twice the Cullens without Bella). The three masters are over 3,000 years old and possess great powers as well as a keen "love of power,"[35] the opposite of the power of love that fuels the Cullen family. Alice and Edward refer to them as vampire "Royalty" and the "Ruling

Class." The Volturi are responsible for policing other vampires and ensuring that all obey the main law of vampirism, as noted by Alice to Bella: "We just have to keep our existence a secret."[36] Edward, out of despair over the "death" of Bella, has decided to break this law in Volterra so that the Volturi will kill him.

The Volturi are bad, because though they have indeed formed a family, it is a family based on power and not love. They have a long history, but it is a history of slaughtering and enslaving others. They are not willing to deny themselves human blood like the Cullens, and they live together not for love, but in order to consolidate power. The Volturi are presented, in the final showdown, as an unnatural, snake-like collective, gliding over the snow: "They came in a rigid, formal formation. They moved together, but it was not a march; they flowed in perfect synchronicity from the trees — a dark, unbroken shape that seemed to hover a few inches above the white snow, so smooth was the advance."[37] In addition, the Volturi are evil because free agency has been surrendered to the lordship of the three masters. So, in addition to being pictured as serpent-like, they are all clad in black. Meyer continues her description of their approach for the final showdown: "The outer perimeter was gray; the color darkened with each line of bodies until the heart of the formation was deepest black. Every face was cowled, shadowed. The faint brushing sound of their feet was so regular it was like music, a complicated beat that never faltered."[38] The Volturi are a collective with a black heart comprised of the three masters. And their faces? Pale with blood red eyes rather than the liquid bronze, brown or black eyes of the abstaining vampires. The three masters are very old with "paper thin" skin and "milky" eyes, images of aging repulsive to our adolescent culture (which is Meyer's primary audience). The individual Volturi are clad in capes with hoods, both of which are indexically associated with evil.

The Ugly

The ugly vampires in the *Twilight Saga* obey neither human nor vampire laws. Laurent, James and Victoria emerge from the woods into the clearing where the Cullens are playing baseball, "one by one" and "ranging a dozen meters apart." They are loners, banded together only for the hunt, and as they approach the Cullens, they "close ranks" and appear as "a troop of predators as it encounters a larger, unfamiliar group of its own kind."[39] Bella notices immediately "how different they were from the Cullens" — "Their walk was catlike, a gait that seemed constantly on the edge of shifting into a crouch."[40] They are animal-like in appearance, their clothes are "frayed," and they are barefoot. Victoria's hair is a "startling shade of red" and chaotic. Their eyes are not the brown or black typical of the Cullens, but "a deep burgundy color that was disturbing and sinister."[41]

Laurent introduces himself first and then Victoria and James. Carlisle introduces himself and says, significantly, "This is my *family* [emphasis added], Emmet and Jasper, Rosalie, Esme and Alice, Edward and Bella." Bella notes, "He pointed us out in groups, deliberately not calling attention to individuals."[42] Later, while discussing hunting ranges, Carlisle describes their house as a "permanent residence nearby" and then he invites them to come back to their "home." "James and Victoria exchanged a surprised look at the mention of the word 'home'...."[43] Throughout the conversation, the Cullens are pictured as refined and civilized over and against the wild and uncivilized appearance and manners of the three rogue vampires. Ideas of family and home are contrasted sharply with the nomadic life of the rogues.

Laurent, Victoria and James have been hunting humans in the Seattle area, unlike the Cullens, who hunt only animals. As far as groups go, these vampires are bottom feeders, mere animals of instinct moving from place to place and feeding on humans when hungry. And they are not a family. We learn later that James and Victoria are lovers while Laurent had only joined them recently. In terms of free agency, these creatures have lost control over their appetites and when they finally catch a scent of Bella, they want to kill and feed. They are slaves to their dark passions, and, we learn later, violating at least two vampire laws: bringing public notoriety to vampires and infringing on other vampires' territories.

Conclusion: A Family Romance

The *Twilight* saga is a romance in the classical sense of the word. There is a hero and a heroine and they both overcome small personal flaws and insurmountable difficulties in order to triumph over circumstance and adversity. The saga is a *modern* romance as well, since the first four volumes are really about Edward and Bella's move from being a teenaged, high school couple to a married couple with a child. One Internet critic dubs *Twilight* "an incredibly silly novel, a dime-store passion play along the lines of *Romancing the Stone*."[44] And it *is* silly, but the romance appeals not only to teenage girls (divided into Teams Edward and Jacob), but to older women as well. Both *Twilight* and *New Moon* have both been described as good "date movies."

But *Twilight* is a modern romance without the sex. Stephenie Meyer reports that her editor wanted premarital sex in the story, but she refused.

The effect of this strict morality amounts to what *Time* critic Lev Grossman calls an "erotics of abstinence":

> What makes Meyer's books so distinctive is that they're about the erotics of abstinence. Their tension comes from prolonged, superhuman acts of self-restraint. There's a scene midway through Twilight in which, for the first time, Edward leans in close and sniffs the aroma of Bella's exposed neck. "Just because I'm resisting the wine doesn't mean I can't appreciate the bouquet," he says. "You have a very floral smell, like lavender ... or freesia." He barely touches her, but there's more sex in that one paragraph than in all the snogging in Harry Potter.[45]

This erotics of abstinence is right in step with what Katie Roiphe calls the "new narcissism" of contemporary novelists Dave Egger, David Foster Wallace, Michael Chabon, and Jonathan Franzen, whose characters prefer hugging to sex: "The current sexual style is more childlike; innocence is more fashionable than virility, the cuddle preferable to sex."[46] Bella and Edward clearly prefer the cuddle and manage to abstain from sexual activity (and from turning Bella) through four long novels — until they are married and form a family.

Jana Reiss, who has written on vampires (*What Would Buffy Do: The Vampire Slayer as Spiritual Guide*) and Mormonism (*Mormonism for Dummies*), sees significant Mormon influence in the saga: "The most obvious Mormon influences can be seen in the ways Meyer has her teenage heroine stand up for marriage and, ultimately, motherhood."[47] But Mormon readers are split on what to do with a vampire saga that has been variously called "Mormon Gothic," "Big Mormon Love," and "the Great Mormon Novel" by Mormon readers. It has been banned at a Mormon middle school and not stocked in a Mormon bookstore, in spite of its popularity.[48]

Tyler Chadwick, a literary critic, explores the appeal of *Twilight* through Freud's notion of the "uncanny" and suggests that Mormons ought to read these and other gothic works "to fulfill the obligation and opportunity to progress" (toward godhood) by being "willing to explore alternate, rhetorical lives."[49] In addition, Chadwick argues, "If we deny ourselves the vitality of such experience in our venture toward godhood by refusing an invitation into the uncanny ... it just may take us ... 'four billion earth lives' (give or take a million) to experience what we need to experience to become like God."[50]

How account for the popularity of a romance based on Mormon theological principles? Because, as Tolstoy once observed, "the Mormon people teach the American religion."[51] *Twilight* is popular because the principles of love, self-sacrifice, individual choice and family are all *so very* American. In addition, the girl gets the boy, and the boy and girl get married, and the boy and girl (literally) live happily (for)ever after. To most readers, Edward and

Bella are simply good, non-churchgoing, moral kids raised by nominally Christian parents. By the end of the fourth book in the saga, however, it is clear that both have progressed significantly toward godhood, because of their moral choices and their focus on the family.

Combine an "erotics of abstinence" with a focus on the family and what we have is a vampire saga that reads more like a Jane Austen novel than a Charlotte or Emily Bronte novel. It is Elizabeth and Mr. Darcy vamped University Press, not Catherine and Heathcliffe or even Jane Eyre and Rochester. In fact, Bella possesses a well-worn compilation of Austen's novels, which she reads regularly.[52] Elizabeth (*Pride and Prejudice*) and Emma, like Bella, could have made significant contributions in a profession, but they can't have careers without upsetting the social order. Austen's vision of the world is actually quite similar to Stephenie Meyer's: a world free of sex, vulgarity and brutality, filled with polite people who abide by the dominant cultural code. Premarital sex is unthinkable and evil in Austen's and Meyer's world, so even though Edward and his male vampire counterparts are able to have sex (unlike St. Germaine and Lestat), Edward chooses marriage and family before sex with Bella.

The problem of evil in the *Twilight* saga is that there isn't very much of a problem, at least for a vampire story, and the evil isn't terribly powerful, and it's either eradicated or held at bay by the good vampires. Curiously, living on animal blood rather than human blood supposedly makes for weaker vampires, but not when these vampires have embraced the eternal bonds of a good family. Good clearly triumphs over evil. The Cullens defeat James and Victoria and are able to halt the aggression of the much more formidable Volturi. The white vampires defeat the black-clad vampires as a family based on love and free agency (as opposed to power and convenience) always will. And Edward, Bella and Rename (half-human/half-vampire) form a unique eternal family of their own based on free agency, love and sacrifice. The last chapter in the fourth book is entitled "The Happily Ever After." Edward attempts to make love to Bella, as he has so often throughout the saga, but he is blocked by Bella's "shield," a unique force field she has learned to generate. Edward is upset, because he's been waiting for four volumes to have uninterrupted sex, but Bella reminds him, "We have plenty of time to work on it," to which he responds, "Forever and forever and forever."[53]

NOTES

1. Susan Neiman, *Evil in Modern Thought: An Alternative History of Philosophy* (Princeton, NJ: Princeton University Press, 2002), 282.

2. John Hick, "The Problem of Evil," in *The Encyclopedia of Philosophy* (New York: Collier, 1967), 136.

3. Ibid.
4. Bram Stoker, *Dracula,* ed. Nina Auerbach and David J. Skal (New York: Norton, 1997), 217.
5. Ibid., 218.
6. Sandra Tomc, "Dieting and Damnation: Anne Rice's *Interview with the Vampire,*" in *Blood Read: The Vampire as Metaphor in Contemporary Culture,* ed. Joan Gordon and Veronica Hillinger (Philadelphia: University of Pennsylvania Press, 1997), 95–113.
7. Romance, according to Hayden White, "is fundamentally a drama of self-identification symbolized by the hero's transcendence of the world of experience, his victory over it, and his final liberation from it — the sort of drama associated with the Grail legend or the story of the resurrection of Christ in the Christian mythology. It is a drama of the triumph of good over evil, of virtue over vice, of light over darkness, and of the ultimate transcendence of man over the world in which he was imprisoned by the Fall" (8–9). White continues, "The archetypal theme of satire is the precise opposite of the Romantic drama of redemption; it is, in fact, a drama of diremption, a drama dominated by the apprehension that man is ultimately a captive of the world rather than its master, and by the recognition that, in the final analysis, human consciousness and will are always inadequate to the task of overcoming definitively the dark force of death, which is man's unremitting enemy" (9). Unlike romance and satire, "Comedy and Tragedy ... suggest the possibility of at least partial liberation from the condition of the Fall and provisional release from the divided state in which men find themselves in this world.... In Comedy, hope is held out for the temporary triumph of man over his world by the prospect of occasional *reconciliations* of the forces at play in the social and natural worlds. Such reconciliations are symbolized in the festive occasions which the comic writer traditionally uses to terminate his dramatic accounts of change and transformation" (9). The *Twilight* saga is clearly romance, though it is peculiarly American and Mormon in its social and theological underpinnings.
8. William Morris, "Interview: Twilight Author Stephenie Meyer" (26 October 2005), available at www.motleyvision.org (retrieved 7 December 2009).
9. *Book of Mormon,* 2 Nephi 2:26–27.
10. This distinction is drawn from Augustine's fourfold state of human nature: (1) Before the Fall, for Adam and Eve, it was possible to sin or not to sin (*posse peccare posse non peccare*). (2) After the Fall, the possibility of not sinning was removed and human nature became sinful (*non posse non peccare*). (3) When grace is infused into the soul, the ability not to sin is restored (*posse peccare posse non peccare*). (4) In heaven, the saint is fully redeemed and not capable of sinning (*non posse non peccare*). Augustine's view of human nature as essentially evil deeply influenced Roman Catholic theology as well as Protestant theology through the writings of Martin Luther and John Calvin.
11. Joseph Smith, *The Doctrine and Covenants of the Church of Jesus Christ of Latter-Day Saints* (1843), available at www.scriptures.lds.org (retrieved 12 January 2010).
12. Quoted in William Morris, "Stephenie Meyer's Mormonism and the 'Erotics of Abstinence,'" 2 May 2008, available at www.motleyvision.org (retrieved 7 December 2009).
13. *Mormon Doctrine of Salvation.* 2010. Available at www.mormonbeliefs.org (retrieved 5 January 2010).
14. Stephenie Meyer, *Twilight* (New York: Little, Brown, 2005), 4.
15. Ibid., 308.
16. 2 Nephi 2.25.
17. Meyer, *Twilight,* 36.
18. Ibid.
19. Ibid., 19.
20. Ibid.
21. Ibid., 260.
22. Ibid., 206.
23. Ibid., 256.
24. Ibid., 340.
25. Ibid., 343.
26. Ibid., 18.

27. Ibid., 322.
28. Ibid.
29. Ibid., 370.
30. Ibid., 79.
31. Ibid., 135.
32. Nina Auerbach, *Our Vampires, Ourselves* (Chicago: University of Chicago Press, 1995), 120.
33. Stephenie Meyer, *New Moon* (New York: Little, Brown, 2006), 427–428.
34. Ibid., 428.
35. Ibid., 429.
36. Ibid., 430.
37. Stephenie Meyer, *Breaking Dawn* (New York: Little, Brown, 2008), 679.
38. Ibid.
39. Meyer, *Twilight*, 375.
40. Ibid., 376–377.
41. Ibid., 376.
42. Ibid., 377.
43. Ibid., 378.
44. Geoff B., "*Twilight*: Vampires and Mormons." *The Millennial Star*, 28 October 2008, available at http://www.millennialstar.org (retrieved 21 June 2010).
45. Quoted in Morris, "Stephenie Meyer's Mormonism."
46. Katie Roiphe, "The Naked and the Conflicted," *New York Times Book Review* (3 January 2010), 8.
47. Steve Rabey, "*Twilight* Author's Mormon Faith a Big Influence in Books & Film," *Religious News Service* (23 November 2008), available at http://www.sj-r.com/beliefs (retrieved 15 January 2009).
48. "Censorship Dateline," *Newsletter on Intellectual Freedom*, available at www.members.ala.org (retrieved 15 January 2009).
49. Tyler Chadwick, "Reading the Mormon Gothic," *Dialogue: A Journal of Mormon Thought*, 42.2: 137–140, available at https://dialoguejournal.com (retrieved 21 June 2010).
50. Ibid., 140.
51. Quoted in Harold Bloom, *The American Religion* (New York: Simon & Schuster, 1992), 116.
52. See Meyer, *Twilight*, 147–148.
53. Meyer, *Breaking Dawn*, 754.

BIBLIOGRAPHY

Auerbach, Nina. *Our Vampires, Ourselves.* Chicago: University of Chicago Press, 1995.
B., Geoff. "*Twilight*: Vampires and Mormons." *The Millennial Star*, 28 October 2008. Available at http://www.millennialstar.org/. Retrieved 21 June 2010.
Bloom, Harold. *The American Religion.* New York: Simon & Schuster, 1992.
The Book of Mormon. Trans. Joseph Smith. Salt Lake City: Church of Jesus Christ of Latter-day Saints, 1961.
"Censorship Dateline." *Newsletter on Intellectual Freedom.* Available at www.members.ala.org. Retrieved January 2009.
Chadwick, Tyler. "Reading the Mormon Gothic." *Dialogue: A Journal of Mormon Thought,* 42.2, 137–140. Available at https://dialoguejournal.com. Retrieved 21 June 2010.
Hick, John. "The Problem of Evil." *The Encyclopedia of Philosophy.* New York: Collier, 1967. 136–140.
Meyer, Stephenie. *Breaking Dawn.* New York: Little, Brown, 2008.
_____. *Eclipse.* New York: Little, Brown, 2007.
_____. *New Moon.* New York: Little, Brown, 2006.
_____. *Twilight.* New York: Little, Brown, 2005.

Mormon Doctrine of Salvation. 2010. Available at www.mormonbeliefs.org. Retrieved 5 January 2010.

Morris, William. "Interview: *Twilight* Author Stephenie Meyer." 26 October 2005. Available at www.motleyvision.org. Retrieved 7 December 2009.

_____. "Stephenie Meyer's Mormonism and the 'Erotics of Abstinence.'" 2 May 2008. Available at www.motleyvision.org. Retrieved 7 December 2009.

Neiman, Susan. *Evil in Modern Thought: An Alternative History of Philosophy.* Princeton, NJ: Princeton University Press, 2002.

Rabey, Steve. "*Twilight* Author's Mormon Faith a Big Influence in Books & Film." *Religious News Service,* 23 November 2008. Available at http://www.sj-r.com/beliefs. Retrieved 15 January 2009.

Roiphe, Katie. "The Naked and the Conflicted." *New York Times Book Review* 3 January 2010: 8–9.

Smith, Joseph. *The Doctrine and Covenants of the Church of Jesus Christ of Latter-Day Saints.* 1843. Available at www.scriptures.lds.org. Retrieved 12 January 2010.

Stoker, Bram. *Dracula.* (1896.) Ed. Nina Auerbach and David J. Skal. New York: Norton, 1997.

Tomc, Sandra. "Dieting and Damnation: Anne Rice's *Interview with the Vampire.*" In *Blood Read: The Vampire as Metaphor in Contemporary Culture.* Ed. Joan Gordon and Veronica Hillinger. Philadelphia: University of Pennsylvania Press, 1997. 95–113.

White, Hayden. *Metahistory: The Historical Imagination in Nineteenth Century Europe.* Baltimore: Johns Hopkins University Press, 1973.

5

The Dichotomy of the Great Mother Archetype in Disney Heroines and Villainesses

Sarah Lynne Bowman

The Wonderful World of Disney has provided Western culture with models for "proper" gender identification and moral behavior for nearly a century. Since Disney's inception in 1923, the world-famous company has offered "safe," wholesome entertainment for children and adults alike. Meanwhile, from a strictly ideological point of view, the phrase "Disney film" promises characters and plots that feminists can easily read as overly simplistic, naïve, sexist, or even culturally offensive.

Why, psychologically speaking, are people still drawn to these images? One can dismiss this question as irrelevant, claiming that we are culturally conditioned to enjoy these sorts of stories. While such a critique certainly holds merit, the symbology inherent in Disney films draws from a much deeper well than any particular socio-cultural moment: the well of the collective unconscious. Regardless of one's intellectual orientation toward psychoanalysis, comparative religion theorists such as Carl Jung, Erich Neumann, and Joseph Campbell have offered impressive proof that certain symbols replicate cross-culturally across time and space. These symbols often hold similar or even identical meanings in disparate societies, suggesting a certain universality of archetypes, which arise ultimately from our basic human language structures. As humans evolved over time, so too did our consciousness, our comprehension, and our symbolic and verbal representations of the world. This process imprinted upon us a genetic predisposition toward understanding reality in terms of a handful of basic symbols that remained important for the survival of early humankind.

Embedded within these symbols are two universal elements of existence: survival and reproduction. As Darwin famously put forth in his natural and sexual selection theories, any creature alive on the planet is a success story — a product of both reproduction and survival — in its birth and its continued existence. Some organisms live to reproduce, which is the story of how each one of us came to exist on this planet. If survival and reproduction are the two most basic elements of existence, then even in the vast complexities of human culture, these themes will remain constant. We will, necessarily, harbor deep concern for these elements, replicating them in our cultural manifestations in various narratives and symbols. How do we best survive in the world around us? How should we behave in order to increase our chances? What qualities should we exhibit in order to get along best in the social order? What aspects should we seek in a mate? How do we avoid death, isolation, and despair? These questions form the basis of much of our psychic and cultural life. Indeed, we have literally been programmed to exhibit concern for our own well-being and our reproductive potential.

With these concepts in mind, the content of many Disney films — and of the far older fairy tales upon which they are built — is far more comprehensible. These narratives function as a form of secular mythology, providing explanatory models for young and older minds alike. These "cautionary tales" detail the actions an individual should take in order to ensure happiness, survival, and reproductive viability.

Thus the representation of "proper" feminine and masculine behavior in these films is no trivial or childish matter. The mind recognizes key archetypes from the depths of its own evolutionary consciousness, and then memorizes the narrative "lessons" presented by the tales. Ultimately, the preoccupation in Disney films with sexual presentation, gendered behavior, and the relative value of certain parenting tactics resonates deep within us as we pose another basic question of social existence: What sort of man or woman do I need to become in order to achieve my "dream" — the dream of continued existence, wealth, and reproductive success?

Within this framework, Disney films become far deeper and more intriguing. I could detail the archetypal symbolism behind nearly every image within my films of study, citing several uses of those same symbols cross-culturally to produce a similar psychological and cultural effect. However, the primary focus of this essay will remain rooted within the Archetypal Feminine. How are positive and negative representations of femininity symbolically coded by Disney films?

More specifically, I wish to examine the relationship between heroine and villainess. I have chosen four Disney films that feature females as both the primary protagonist and the antagonist: *Snow White, Cinderella, Sleeping Beauty,* and *The Little Mermaid*. Each of these films also derives from fairy tales, implying a cultural symbology far older and richer than the relatively new development of Disney. I will focus primarily on the Archetypal Feminine as defined by Erich Neumann in his fascinating book *The Great Mother*.

Neumann's theory encompasses all aspects of femininity, working to heal the "good girl/bad girl" dichotomy. For Neumann, the Great Mother archetype embodies both the "Good" and "Terrible" aspects of femininity. Through what he terms "the principle of opposites,"[1] this dichotomy is often emphasized in mythological structures worldwide, but Neumann convincingly proves this distinction false. Both the Good and Terrible aspects of the Archetypal Feminine are contained within what he calls the Great Round.[2] Furthermore, the dichotomy between masculinity and femininity can also become a false opposition, for both male and female are present in the uroboric whole that is the primordial pre-consciousness.[3]

From an ideological perspective, the myths within Disney films provide a clean and easy cultural explanation for why people should view certain personality aspects as favorable over other qualities. Disney movies code socially preferable characteristics — such as humility, obedience, nurturing, and innocence — as "good," offering the reward of "happily ever after" at the conclusion for girls who exhibit these qualities. Alternately, the characteristics of selfishness, vanity, seduction, cruelty, and ambition are coded as "evil," promising rejection, expulsion from society, and even death for those who choose this path. From a survival perspective, the qualities on the first list offer greater chances for reproductive success and low-conflict mating, whereas the qualities on the second list may lead to cuckolding, abuse, and neglect from the mother figure. Therefore, the "proper femininity" emphasized by Disney films provides not only an instruction manual for the docile characteristics patriarchy prefers in women; the "evil" aspects of the Feminine may also prove dangerous to both mates and offspring in terms of reproductive success.

However, with Neumann's theory as a model, I suggest that this distinction between the Disney princess and her Terrible Mother nemesis is, ultimately, a false dichotomy. Though the films clearly code these two figures as distinct, each character offers personality features present in the Great Mother as a whole: creation and destruction, nurturance and negligence, protection and confinement. Thus, despite the eventual "happy endings" of these films, the princess and villainess figures remain inextricably linked; they are, indeed, defined by one another and thus both create and destroy each other symbolically.

The Great Mother in Her Various Manifestations

Erich Neumann, a depth psychologist who studied under Carl Jung, was instrumental in providing clear explanations for how the Great Goddess in mythology originally contained all aspects of femininity. Unlike later patriarchal myths, ancestral cosmology gave the Divine Feminine precedence over the Masculine. According to Neumann, in early historic times, goddess figures presided over heaven, earth, and sea. Ancient peoples organized their ritual life around the conception of the Great Goddess as giver of both life and death, offering sacrifices in order to win her favor.[4] With the rise of patriarchy and, subsequently, more advanced forms of civilization, the Great Mother was divided, her life-bearing elements isolated from her more dangerous aspects.

In *The Great Mother,* Neumann attempts to articulate and reemphasize the essential power of the goddess archetype in her many forms. Offering hundreds of examples from ancient mythology, ritual, and art, Neumann presents a staggering amount of evidence to support his claim, spanning the entire globe and thousands of millennia. Attempting to replicate his research in any sort of satisfying form here remains far beyond the scope of this particular study. However, I will focus upon several of the primary symbols associated with the Great Goddess in both her "Good" and "Terrible" forms in order to explicate the coded symbology associated with the female protagonists and antagonists in Disney films.

These particular images trigger age-old archetypes deep in the reaches of the human mind, encoded with a constellation of meanings that reflect early humankind's essential desires and anxieties. Neumann writes:

> The function of the image symbol in the psyche is always to produce a compelling effect on consciousness. Thus, for example, a psychic image whose purpose it is to attract the attention of consciousness, in order, let us say, to provoke flight, must be so striking that it cannot possibly fail to make an impression. The archetypal image symbol corresponds, then, in its impressiveness, significance, energetic charge, and numinosity, to the original importance of instinct for man's existence. The term 'numinous' applies to the action of beings and forces that the consciousness of primitive man experienced as fascinating, terrible, overpowering, and that it therefore attributed to an indefinite transpersonal and divine source.[5]

In terms of the Great Mother archetype, in ancestral populations, goddess figures worldwide were associated with their life-bearing elements, but also with their potentially dangerous, ensnaring, death-dealing aspects. Within the Great Mother archetype dwells the anxiety of survival, for in early stages of life, the human child is completely dependent on the Mother figure for nourishment and protection. Neumann refers to the child's early interconnectedness with the Mother in the womb as the *uroboros*, the initial state of unity.[6] Cast out from the womb and fostered by the Mother, the child then must learn to extricate himself or herself from this dependence in order to become a functional, individuated adult in the world. The child must learn to seek his or her own inner comprehension or enlightenment as the primary guide to survival.

Therefore, the Mother Goddess archetype is imbued with dual elements in order to articulate this tension. She is the container, or *vessel*, indicating her essential nature as bearer and nurturer of life. She represents the return to the uroboric state — to sleep and to the womb. This relationship also connects her to the tomb, to death, and to the intoxicating lure of the unconscious. This splitting of the Great Mother into two elements, dubbed "the principle of opposites" by Neumann, helps the psyche come to terms with her power and articulate it.

In addition to the split of the Great Mother into the elementary aspects of Good and Terrible, Neumann also emphasizes another dichotomy: the Virgin versus the Intoxicating Enchantress. For Neumann, the word "virgin" does not represent the female's lack of sexual experience, but rather her spiritual transcendence beyond the realm of the physical. The Virgin possesses a certain inherent quality that allows her to bear children as a result of supernatural insemination. The Virgin also encourages the ego-consciousness to seek spiritual enlightenment, which Neumann refers to as the Sophia element of her nature. Her ability to inspire the transformation of a normal mortal to higher states of light and awareness contrasts sharply with the Enchantress' lures of sexual ecstasy and intoxication. These latter temptations threaten to overwhelm the ego-consciousness, ensnaring the individual into a darker, more asleep state.

The development of human consciousness, according to Neumann, mirrors the maturation of the individual — the initial worship of the Mother and desire to return to the womb which must then be disavowed in order for the person to reach an individuated state of consciousness. The Mother shifts from a figure of abundance to a figure of great terror, threatening to quell the nascent, developing ego.

The ultimate archetypal expression of the Terrible Mother is embodied in the dragon, the beast that the hero must slay in order to ascend to the next stage of life: marriage and the creation of progeny. The Terrible Mother also manifests in many other symbols in mythology including mermaids, witches, enchantresses, sirens, succubae, wights, and nymphs. As Neumann explains:

> In the early phase of consciousness, the numinosity of the archetype consequently exceeds man's power of representation, so much that at first no

form can be given to it. And when later the primordial archetype takes form in the imagination of man, its representations are often monstrous and inhuman. This is the phase of the chimerical; creatures composed of different animals or of an animal and a [female]—the griffins, sphinxes, harpies, for example—and also of such monstrosities as phallic and bearded mothers.[7]

Regardless of her manifestation, the hero must overcome the powerful lure of the Mother, which represents the return to sleep, sexual ecstasy, and death. Once the Mother in her Terrible guise is slain, the hero may obtain what Campbell refers to as the "life-transmuting trophy," which generally means the hero's princess bride.[8] Having overcome the lure of the Mother, the hero can safely mate with the princess, asserting himself as masculinized—in other words, a full adult.

However, despite the patriarchal "triumph" over the power of the Archetypal Feminine in the monomyth, Neumann asserts that the essential life and death giving aspects of the Mother continue to exist, embedded deep within our symbolic language from its time of inception. He refers to the goddess's ability to give and take life as her *elementary* character.[9] The Great Mother also possesses a *transformative* character.[10] The elementary character represents the passive, eternal, and primordial element of woman-as-vessel. This aspect emphasizes her nature as the womb—the place of gestation, nourishment, and comfort—but also as the tomb—the lure of the unconscious towards sleep, regression, and death.

The transformative aspect of femininity also possesses both a positive and negative aspect. The Divine Feminine can represent the impetus toward spiritual seeking and the attainment of enlightenment; the desire for Disney princes to attain their princesses forces them to confront the dark aspects of the Divine Feminine and ascend toward greater states of bravery and consciousness. This impetus arises from the Virgin's nature as physical and spiritual inspiration. However, the alternate side of the Virgin is embodied in the Enchantress. Instead of inspiring the hero to rise to greater potential, the Enchantress provides challenges that the hero must face in order to break free of her intoxicating nature. These challenges take the form of a trial or test, such as solving a riddle or resisting seduction. If the hero fails, he devolves into a state of lesser consciousness, such as belligerence, sloth, or sexual captivity. Thus the presence of the Feminine can take the shape of both negative and positive transformative elements.

Regardless of what form she takes, the Great Mother is instrumental to the hero's development. The young child could not come into existence and live to maturity without the influence of the Good Mother; the hero could not reach his potential without his struggle with the Terrible Mother. Either

way, the Mother's very presence insists upon psychic and spiritual transformation; whether as a helper or an impediment, she encourages the child to
grow. Though the hero in the monomyth may ultimately demonstrate his
independence, his growth is wholly dependent on the Mother. Thus the hero's
journey is inextricably linked with the power of the Great Mother.

The Great Mother Archetype in Disney Films

The Disney animated features *Snow White, Cinderella, Sleeping Beauty,*
and *The Little Mermaid* present a fascinating study with regard to the Great
Mother archetype in that the hero's journey remains more implicit than
explicit. Though in each story the hero must ultimately conquer the Terrible
Mother figure of the villainess in order to attain a "happily ever after" ending
with the princess, all three of these narratives emphasize the subjectivity of
the princess herself as the primary protagonist. Based upon Western fairy
tales, these stories serve as an instruction manual for proper and improper
femininity on a surface level. However, when examined from a depth psychology perspective, they articulate the inherent power of the Archetypal Feminine
over the psyche, a power which women must learn to navigate within themselves.

The splitting of the Great Mother into the princess and the witch exemplifies the dual nature of the goddess. While clearly preferring the safe, elementary, passive maternal element of the Good Mother, the archetype also
offers an explication of the transformative powers of both the Good and Terrible Mother. The narratives ultimately feature the triumph of the nurturing,
life-bearing elements of the woman-as-vessel, but they also emphasize the
alchemical power of the deathly, ensnaring elements of the woman-as-
temptress, which lures people to a less evolved state of consciousness. It is
important to note, however, that *both* the princess and the witch transform
the prince; the princess serves as life-transmuting trophy that fuels his quest,
and the witch represents the test or obstacle that he must overcome to fulfill
his goal.

The following analysis will examine the Archetypal Feminine as embodied in Disney films. First, I will describe the roles of each of the female characters within the framework of Neumann's theory — Virgin, Good Mother,
Enchantress, and Terrible Mother. Then, I will identify key symbols within
these texts that have historically represented the Mother on a cross-cultural
level, including imagery pertaining to animals, plants, earth, water, weaving,
pottery, and other vessels of containment. Analysis of these symbols should
help future viewers decode the heavily embedded archetypes within the text

and enhance their appreciation of the surprising depth contained within these seemingly simplistic images. The films code these symbols as either "good" or "evil" depending on whether they are associated with the princess or villainess; for example, a cauldron in *Snow White* provides sustenance and even a bed when Snow White utilizes it, but it produces poisonous potions of transformation in the hands of the queen.

The Virgin and Good Mother in Disney Films

In each of the movies listed, the princess represents the Virgin, both in her sexual inexperience and in her essential ability to encourage the male figures to attain their next state of social responsibility — and perhaps even spiritual consciousness. In *Snow White and the Seven Dwarfs*, the prince plays the most passive role of all the Disney heroes, though he does offer the ultimately transformative kiss of true love. The true heroes of *Snow White* are actually the dwarves, who experience a profound transformation when Snow White enters their cottage and lives. Assisted by her woodland friends, she cleans their cottage, with particular emphasis on the dirty dishes. She encourages them to wash before supper, similar to a ritual baptism.[11] When they learn she might be in danger, they rush to her aid like the heroes of old. When the dwarves realize that Snow White remains beautiful even in (apparent) death, they create the glass coffin as a testament to her importance in their life, a ritual altar at which they continuously pay homage until the prince arrives. Though Snow White does not actually give birth to the dwarves, her presence in their lives and her maternal nature act as spiritually transformative elements characteristic of the power of the Virgin Mother.

In *Sleeping Beauty*, Aurora/Briar Rose represents the Virgin in providing the impetus for Prince Philip to break free from the shackles of the Terrible Mother's prison and fight her in both thorny bush and dragon form. When he confers upon Aurora the transformative kiss, they marry and ascend into a castle in the clouds, emphasizing her nature as spiritually transformative and light-bringing. Even her name — Aurora — means "the dawn," the moment of the breaking of light onto a new day.

Similarly, in *Cinderella*, we first see our heroine awakening from sleep and opening the shutters to her room in the tower of the chateau, awake before everyone else in the house. This sequence emphasizes her relationship with the breaking dawn and essential essence of light-giving properties. She represents a ray of hope for both the king and the prince. While the prince desires true love, the king desperately wishes for grandchildren to carry on his legacy. This desire is revealed in the king's Freudian slip when the prince shows no interest in any of the marriageable women arrayed before him. The king exclaims, "I can't understand it! There must be one who'd make a suitable *mother*! Errr ... a suitable *wife*." Cinderella's appearance offers hope that her virginal quality will transform prince into viable king, as well as providing the promise of her own evolution into a future Good Mother role for the children of the kingdom.

Finally, in *The Little Mermaid*, Ariel also represents the virginal, light-bringing quality. She desperately desires to "ascend" from her watery home — representing the unconscious — to join those on the land as "part of [their] world." Her very name can alternately be spelled Aerial, defined by Merriam-Webster as "existing or growing in the air rather than in the ground or in water."[12] Her positive transformative character is emphasized when she rescues the prince from an assuredly watery grave, a symbol of the negative elementary character of the Terrible Mother. Bringing him to land, she literally carries him from darkness to light. The mermaid often represents the siren in mythology, the powerful Enchantress who is half-human, half-sea creature, whose charms lure men to their deaths. However, we see the mermaid represented here as the Virgin in her positive, elementary element.[13]

Though the princesses in *Snow White* and *The Little Mermaid* do not receive the aid of a benevolent Mother figure, this archetype is manifest in the other films. The Good Mother element is evident in the names of the characters, literally coded in *Cinderella* as "fairy godmother" and as the "good fairies" in *Sleeping Beauty*. In *Cinderella*, once the wicked stepmother and ugly stepsisters have destroyed her ball gown, Cinderella retreats to the back of the chateau, crying under a weeping willow and next to a fountain. Both trees and bodies of water are symbols of the Great Mother.[14] As if summoned by these elements, the fairy godmother materializes to comfort Cinderella. She provides Cinderella with the means to attend the ball by transmuting a pumpkin into a carriage (vessel); lower forms of animals into higher consciousness beings (horse into human, mice into horses); and rags into a new gown and glass slippers (garments). As I shall explain in the next section, vessels of all forms represent the womb and the Mother's ability to give nourishment as food and water containers. Garments and the act of weaving are also the traditional domains of the Feminine and remain important elements throughout these films.[15]

Similarly, the good fairies in *Sleeping Beauty* represent the Good Mother. They are aptly named Flora, Fauna, and Merryweather, indicating the goddess's connection with the plants, animals, and seasons. They take on the role of Good Mother when they raise Aurora, excited at the prospect of being able to "take care of the baby," getting to "feed it and wash it and dress it and rock it to sleep," all symbols of the Divine Feminine. They also are able to transmute items in the service of aiding Aurora and Prince Philip. They bestow upon Aurora three gifts at birth with their magic wands: beauty, song, and eternal sleep instead of the death ordained by Maleficent's curse. In addition, they are able to use their powers to do the following: create a dress and birthday cake for Aurora; clean the messy house; unshackle Prince Philip and his horse, releasing him from the Terrible Mother's bondage; transform rocks to bubbles; change arrows into flowers; create rainbow shields to protect Philip from the scalding oil of the Terrible Mother's caldron; summon bridges of energy to help Philip avoid failing into a chasm; and cast a sleep spell over the entire kingdom to protect the inhabitants until Aurora awakens. In addition to protecting Philip, they also give him the implements of war necessary to defeat the Terrible Mother: the Sword of Truth and the Shield of Virtue, adorned with the Christian cross. In this regard, the fairies become both protectors and goddesses of war.[16] They cast the final spell that allows Philip to slay Maleficent, who has transformed herself into the archetypal symbol of the *anima*, the dragon.[17] The good fairies use both their maternal and transformative qualities in the service of the Virgin goddess, allowing the hero to triumph over the Terrible Mother.

The Enchantress and Terrible Mother

Disney villainesses represent the other half of the life-giving, light-bringing principle of the Great Mother. Instead of providing nurturance, abundance, and encouragement to the princesses, Disney villainesses deprive, confine, and derogate their counterparts. They represent the dark Feminine in her Terrible Mother and Enchantress aspects. While the essential element of femininity represents containment, providing the vessel for the child to be nurtured and fostered, that vessel can also be viewed as corrupt or dangerous. In Disney, the Terrible Mother figure is unfair, vain, and petty. Some villainesses, such as the queen and Maleficent, seek to kill the princess, whereas Ursula and the wicked stepmother simply wish to make the heroines their slaves. Regardless of the manifestation, this form of the archetype represents deprivation and destruction. Where the Good Mother protects, the Terrible Mother endangers. Where the Good Mother releases the child into the next phase of adulthood, the Terrible Mother confines. Where the Good Mother encourages the child's beauty to shine, the Terrible Mother instead emphasizes her own, forcing the princess to dress in rags. Where the Good Mother provides emotional and physical nourishment, the Terrible Mother neglects. The Terrible Mother represents the negation of the positive Feminine essential principle.[18]

The other aspect of the dark goddess is her transformative nature as witch or enchantress.[19] Each of the Disney villainesses exhibits these powers; indeed, their transformations of themselves and other characters provide the needed fuel for the protagonists to grow into the next phase of life. In *Snow White*, the queen wishes to remain the "fairest one of all," confining and enslaving the princess her whole life. The queen also commands the spirit of the mirror with the words: "Slave in the magic mirror, come from the farthest space. Through wind and darkness, I summon thee. Speak; let me see thy face." These first words of the movie emphasize the queen's control not only of the kingdom, but also of extra-dimensional spirits, as well as her emphasis on physical beauty and vanity. This vanity takes an ironic turn when, in order to tempt Snow White with the apple, the queen creates a magic potion that transmogrifies her visage into that of an old crone. Falling to her death in a chasm while the dwarves chase her away, the queen dies in this less attractive state. Unsatisfied with the beauty she possesses, she dies alone and old; her ambition is the cause of her demise.

The queen also transforms fruit into poison. This action transmutes a usually nourishing food into something deadly; the queen intends for Snow White to fall into deep sleep and to get buried alive. There is a loophole — the spell can be released by love's first kiss — but the queen does not anticipate that kiss's coming to pass. As in the Eden story of Genesis or the Demeter and Persephone myth from ancient Greece, the lure of the of the red fruit of fertile womanhood, representing the womb, sexuality, and menstruation,[20] enchants the young woman, and Snow White is drawn into the confinement of sleep and the vessel of the coffin.[21] However, the powers of the Earth Mother help save her and bring her back up to the surface, embodied here by the vigilant dwarves and woodland creatures waiting at her side. Unlike Persephone, Snow White forsakes the underground realm for the rest of her life, able to marry her princely love, rather than remaining chained to the side of the lord of the Underworld in Hades. Here, a kiss from her prince awakens her, a life-giving, "good" symbol, as opposed to the deathly kiss of a dark Mother creature such as a succubus.

Sleeping Beauty also features a powerful witch figure in a long, black cloak: Maleficent. Her name means "doing evil or harm; harmfully malicious."[22] Unlike the queen in *Snow White* or the wicked stepmother in *Cinderella*, Maleficent has no familial relation to Aurora. Her intention seems solely to cause problems for Aurora's parents, King Stefan and his queen. Coded as a witch from the pagan tradition, Maleficent was a magic staff to curse Aurora, teleport, and transform herself into a dragon. Her minions are pig-snouted; the pig is an ancient animal associated with the Great Mother.[23] They dance around the fire as one would at a pagan ritual. Paganism is connected with the Christian concept of evil in this film, exemplified both by these hell-fires and by Maleficent's complaint about her minions: "They're hopeless. A disgrace to the forces of evil." Furthermore, the good fairies bestow two gifts upon Prince Philip to fight Maleficent — the Sword of Truth and the Shield of Valor — the latter of which is adorned with the Christian cross like a protective ward. Maleficent wears a hat with long, horn-like protrusions, coding her as demonic. She commands the Earth, calling forth thorns to ensnare the king's castle, much as she captures Philip with her web of ropes and traps him in her dungeon. He must escape from her dark underworld, overcome the vines of the Earth, and eventually slay Maleficent in her dragon form before peace can be restored to the land. This progression is a clear representation of the hero slaying the Great Mother in Neumann's theoretical formulation.

In *Cinderella*, we find the least obvious example of the transformative element of the Great Mother. The wicked stepmother and ugly stepsisters possess no magical powers. The wicked stepmother married Cinderella's father under the auspices of loving him; the film explains that "it was upon the untimely death of this good man, however, that the stepmother's true nature was revealed. Cold, cruel, and bitterly jealous of Cinderella's charm and beauty, she was grimly determined to forward the interests of her own two awkward daughters." While the cause of death of Cinderella's father remains uncertain, the film offers the potential for the audience to interpret the wicked stepmother as a black widow, a spider-like Great Mother figure that ensnares and kills her mates in order to gain their fortunes.[24] The wicked stepmother claims to behave fairly toward Cinderella, while hypocritically forcing her into servitude. This ensnaring quality is emphasized by the spider webs in the staircase leading up to Cinderella's room in the tower, the site where the wicked stepmother eventually imprisons Cinderella. The hero's journey in this case takes place with the mice Gus and Jacques, who must avoid death at the hands of the stepmother's familiar, the cat Lucifer. At several points in the movie, these mice are captured in a teacup — a symbol of the elemental nature of the woman-as-vessel — and almost discovered or burned by scalding liquid. The male mice must rescue the phallic object of the key from the wicked stepmother's grasp and ascend the steps to Cinderella's tower. In addition, the old, tired dog, Bruno, eventually scares away Lucifer, indicating that the Virgin's power over the animals is superior to the dark Mother's.

The Little Mermaid offers a fascinating example of the Terrible Mother in the sea-witch Ursula. Like Maleficent, Ursula wishes to undermine the patriarchy-dominated underworld of King Triton, coded as a Poseidon figure. She uses Ariel's desire to explore land and her love for the prince to her advantage, luring Ariel into her underwater realm and ensnaring her into a bargain that could potentially take hold of the mermaid's soul. Ursula has the body of an octopus — another symbol of the Great Mother[25] — and her eight tentacles are similar to the eight legs of a spider in their ensnaring imagery. She is able to transmogrify Ariel from mermaid to human, as well as to capture the souls of those who lose in her bargains. She captures Ariel's singing voice — the princess's defining feature, as with all the other Disney princesses. Ursula further transforms her own otherwise old and bulbous form into a seductive Enchantress figure, using the Virgin's voice to try to ensnare the prince into marriage. This maneuver attempts to force Ariel to lose her end of the bargain, giving Ursula dominion over the princess's soul and leverage in her battle against Triton for dominion of the underwater realm. In this respect, the Terrible Mother represents the guardian of the dead in the Underworld; she also represents a potentially castrating force to a patriarchal kingdom, just as Maleficent does.[26]

These films explicate the theme of the ingénue as bringer of original sin. The Eve and Pandora myths are extremely important to our notions of femininity in Western culture. By eating the forbidden apple or opening the box, these Virgins expose the world to the negative aspects of existence, including death. The apple represents temptation for Snow White; similarly, giving in to temptation results in Sleeping Beauty's "trance" when she is lured by Maleficent to touch the spindle. Sleeping Beauty collects berries when she first meets the prince, another red fruit representing the womb, menstruation, sexuality; the spindle draws a drop of her blood, a symbol of menses and sexual initiation and transgression. In both stories the villainesses are the source of temptation, utilizing deceptively benign feminine symbols of nurturance to lure the Virgins, quite literally, to the "dark side." From the perspective of Neumann's theory, this dark side represents the Terrible aspect of the Great Mother inherent within each of these protagonists.

Imagery Related to the Great Mother

Each of these four Disney films replicates imagery specifically coded as related to the Great Mother when aligned with Neumann's book. The Divine Feminine is associated with the following: any sort of vessel; cooking and the making of pottery[27]; various plants and animals; the act of weaving and making other forms of clothing; sleep and death; water and earth. While patriarchal gods tend to represent an ethereal being in the high cosmos, the Mother's dominion is everywhere in the practicalities of daily life. As Neumann states:

> Just as the unconscious reacts and responds, just as the body "reacts" to healthful food or poison, so [the Great Mother] is living and present and

near, a godhead that can always be summoned and is always ready to intervene, and not a deity living inaccessible to man in numinous remoteness and alienated seclusion.[28]

These films consistently reinforce the imagery pertaining to the Great Mother in both her Good and Terrible guises. The daily activities of the protagonists and antagonists center upon these recurring images of the Archetypal Feminine.

Vessels of all kinds appear throughout these films. Most of them are connected to the kitchen, including pots, pans, cups, and pitchers. Snow White and Cinderella both spend a good deal of time cooking and cleaning dishes. They provide sustenance for others, reaffirming their role as the fecund, virginal womb. Alternately, the good fairies have difficulties cooking, cleaning, and sewing without magic, comically marking them as post-menopausal and past their prime fertility-wise. The vessel can also brew poison in these films, illustrated most clearly by the queen in *Snow White*, who uses her cauldron and beakers to create potions to age herself and put Snow White into a deep sleep.

However, vessels need not always relate to food. In *The Little Mermaid*, the prince's ship bears a woman carved on the hull, indicating the vessel's connection with the Feminine.[29] The ship is initially a place of safety, but when the storm breaks this vessel, Ariel must carry the prince to land, protecting him against the wrath of the dark Mother and a "watery grave." This watery grave is associated with Ursula, the representative of the dark goddess in the film, who also uses a magical cauldron for her nefarious plots. In addition, coffins are considered vessels as well, such as the glass coffin within which Snow White sleeps. Thus the vessel can be a womb-like container providing nourishment or a place associated with death and the tomb.

The woman-as-nourishment concept also connects to the imagery of the breast. According to Neumann, all milk-giving animals are often associated with the Great Mother. Maleficent's pig-snouted minions also represent another suckling animal — the sow. *Cinderella* features an extended scene of the cat Lucifer drinking milk. The wicked stepmother demands that the cat be fed before everyone else in the house. Lucifer quite literally takes sustenance away from Cinderella and the mice, emphasizing the dark Mother's influence in the lower realm of the house. Lucifer terrorizes the rats and acts superior to Cinderella. Cinderella mentions that he "must have *some* good qualities," implicitly connecting him with the Terrible. The very name Lucifer indicates evil; he represents an extension of the Mother's arm throughout the home, repeatedly trying to thwart the good characters.

Many other animals are featured in these films. Neumann refers to the Great Mother as Lady of the Beasts, indicating her connection and dominion over the lower forms of consciousness on the planet.[30] Both the protagonists and antagonists in each of these films have animal companions. An exhaustive explanation of these familiars is beyond the scope of the present inquiry, but *Snow White*, *Cinderella*, and *Sleeping Beauty* all feature birds and other wild creatures. The bird-friends of the Virgin figures tend to be colorful with beautiful voices, just like their feminine counterparts. Alternately, the bird-friends of the Terrible Mother are black-colored ravens, crows,[31] and vultures,[32] symbols of ill portent and potential death. The black of their feathers matches the black of their mistresses' clothing. Similarly, the cat Lucifer in *Cinderella*, the snake-like eels in *The Little Mermaid*, and the dragon in *Sleeping Beauty* are all black, symbolically tied to the dark Mother's dominion over death, prophecy, and the underworld.

The Divine Feminine is also connected to the Earth, fruit, and plant-life.[33] The forest remains a place of refuge for the virginal princesses in *Snow White*, *Cinderella*, and *Sleeping Beauty*. The cottage-in-the-woods motif represents the vessel's relationship to the wilderness, a place of potential safety or of potential danger. The apple in Snow White offers the intoxicating lure of nourishment, while actually causing deep sleep. The red fruit as a lure to the underworld is also featured in the Greek Persephone myth, representing the mysteries and dangers of menstruation and sexuality.

Finally, one of the most potent symbols of femininity in these films is the act of weaving and sewing, which Neumann attributes to the Great Mother as well. Both *Cinderella* and *Sleeping Beauty* emphasize the importance of perfecting the Virgin's dress to aid in her transformation. Consequently, the Terrible Mother figures in Disney often attempt to sabotage this transformation. The wicked stepmother forces Cinderella to constantly clean the laundry and mend her clothes, then allows the ugly stepsisters to rend asunder Cinderella's dress for the ball. Similarly, the queen forces Snow White to dress in rags. The most potent image, though, of the Great Mother's connection to weaving is the spindle in *Sleeping Beauty*; Maleficent transforms this object of creation into an object of potential sleep and death. Each of these symbols emphasizes the Great Mother's power as both creator and destroyer, epitomized in the creation and destruction of garments.

Conclusion

With Neumann's formulation of the Great Mother as the necessary component to psychological evolution, the Archetype — whether in the form of the repressed feminine (the *anima*), the bestial form, or actually embodied as a female character — becomes more difficult to label as strictly evil in the classical sense. The female villainesses in Disney films certainly behave in self-interested, disrespectful, and often abominable ways, but their actions provide the needed impetus for the protagonists to ascend to the next level of consciousness. Furthermore, despite the preferred reading of these texts, some viewers may find valid points of identification within these antagonist characters. Ultimately, the archetype of the great goddess in *each* of her aspects is necessary for — and therefore integral to — the psychic development of the individual.

NOTES

1. Erich Neumann, *The Great Mother*, trans. Ralph Manheim (Princeton, NJ: Princeton University Press, 1991), 8.
2. Ibid., 211–239.
3. Ibid., 18.
4. Ibid., 147–149.
5. Ibid., 5.
6. Ibid., 18.
7. Ibid., 12–13.
8. Joseph Campbell, *The Hero with a Thousand Faces* (Princeton, NJ: Princeton University Press, 1973), 193.
9. Neumann, 120–210.
10. Ibid., 211–338.
11. Ibid., 326–327.
12. "Aerial," *Merriam-Webster Online Dictionary*, Merriam-Webster Online, available at http://www.merriam webster.com/dictionary/aerial (retrieved 2 April 2010).
13. Neumann, 276.
14. Ibid., 48–49.
15. Ibid., 227–233.
16. Ibid., 172.
17. Ibid., 33.
18. Ibid., 147–210.
19. Ibid., 74.
20. Ibid., 262.
21. Ibid., 45.
22. "Maleficent," Dictionary.com. *Dictionary.com Unabridged*, Random House, Inc., available at http://dictionary.reference.com/browse/Maleficent (retrieved 2 April 2010).
23. Neumann, 45.
24. Ibid., 177.
25. Ibid., 66.
26. Ibid., 151.
27. Ibid., 133–137.
28. Ibid., 330–331.
29. Ibid., 256ff.
30. Ibid., 268–280.
31. Ibid., 164, 165.
32. Ibid., 149.
33. Ibid., 240–267.

BIBLIOGRAPHY

"Aerial." *Merriam-Webster Online Dictionary*. 2010. Merriam-Webster Online. Available at http://www.merriam-webster.com/dictionary/aerial. Retrieved 2 April 2010.

Campbell, Joseph. *The Hero with a Thousand Faces*. Princeton, NJ: Princeton University Press, 1973.

Cinderella. Directed by Clyde Geronimi, Wilfred Jackson, and Hamilton Luske. Los Angeles: Walt Disney Home Entertainment, 2005. DVD (Two-Disc Special Edition).

The Little Mermaid. Directed by Ron Clements and John Musker. Los Angeles: Walt Disney Home Entertainment, 2006. DVD (Two-Disc Platinum Edition).

"Maleficent." Dictionary.com. *Dictionary.com Unabridged*. Random House, Inc. Available at http://dictionary.reference.com/browse/Maleficent. Retrieved 2 April 2010.

Neumann, Erich. *The Great Mother*. Trans. Ralph Manheim. Princeton, NJ: Princeton University Press, 1991.

Sleeping Beauty. Directed by Clyde Geronimi. Los Angeles: Walt Disney Home Entertainment, 2008. DVD (Two-Disc Platinum Edition).

Snow White and the Seven Dwarfs. Directed by David Hand. Los Angeles: Walt Disney Home Entertainment, 2009. DVD.

6

Exploring the Relay Gaze in Hollywood Cinema: Serial Killers and the Women Who Hunt Them

Sarah Lafferty

"Everything you saw, I wanted you to see."
— Illeana Scott, *Taking Lives*

Crime is a significant part of American culture, both in reality and in the fictional media. In response to this concern, a new character type, the female FBI agent, is, I believe, directly tied to America's evolving national identity. As a figure of power within a male institution, the female agent displays pseudo-feminist tendencies in her struggle for acceptance and relevance in a traditionally masculine profession. She is a seemingly powerful figure who, when analyzed, proves to be overwhelmingly devoid of individual power. Instead, it is her relationship to distinctly male forces of power, particularly evil figures, that allows her to enter into a position of control in regard to the camera gaze. This new form of gaze — what I define as the "relay gaze" — investigates the agent's overall social and sexual roles. In popular culture, the female FBI agent, explicitly coded, consistently falls into the same struggle, both with her male counterparts and the male serial killers who are obsessed with her.

This chapter analyzes the provocative relationship between the female FBI agent and the male serial killer in *Silence of the Lambs, Hannibal, Taking Lives,* and *Untraceable.* Media depictions of these figures are important because they, like all media texts, shape the conceptions of the agents and Bureau as a whole to both American and global audiences. It is within this context that I analyze how the female agent develops into a hero. This development occurs through challenging and stretching the boundaries of the good/evil dichotomy and heteronormative sexual paradigms.

The representations of the female FBI agents are socially significant because of the effects they can have on film audiences. The roles — the attributes they are encoded with and are therefore held by — can reflect the time period and cultural climate. The gendering of character types is also relevant. Positioning these women, and referring to them as heroines instead of heroes, is not an argument that can be cast aside as simply semantics. Thomas Gramstad in his article "The Female Hero: A Randian-Feminist Synthesis" strengthens my argument by stating, "What we need is not 'heroines' (who are usually reduced to passive prize objects/rewards for male heroes), but *female heroes* (active heroes who happen to be female)."[1] I question, therefore, why we still automatically gender the hero figure as male. When one analyzes the positioning of these women, one can recognize they have evolved to a point where they are just as much a hero as any other typical heroic character. The term hero itself is polysemic. For example, Batman of the *Batman* series, John McClane of the *Die Hard* series, and Luke Skywalker of *Star Wars* are all accepted as hero figures, yet they are also widely different in both their actions and personalities. So why are gendered actions, related to the hero, any different?

The definitions of hero and villain are expansive; I do not believe that a universal descriptor of the hero figure is the level of morality or admiration felt by characters within the film and by extension, the film audience. I also argue that they are not merely the protagonists of the text. The main trait of the hero lies in the concept of the rescue. What sets the hero apart, especially from the heroine figure, is the ability to self-rescue. This attribute highlights that Illeana Scott and Jennifer Marsh are the heroes of their respective films. The importance of proving hero roles is twofold: One, it shows that even characters who are coded as evil villains, such as Hannibal Lecter, can still be deemed heroes. Two, it proves that the female FBI agent figure evolved to a point in film narrative function that she is not the heroine or damsel in distress, but the personification of the hero.

Serial killers are common evil figures in Hollywood cinema, especially in the horror and psychological thriller genres. They are insidious and grotesquely harming figures with which we, as a culture, have an abject fascination.[2] These figures, both fictional and real, fascinate in part due to their gender. They are as trapped in their heteronormative gender roles as the female agents. It is significant that these grotesque, powerful serial killer figures occupy the masculine role in the heteronormative paradigm, because our culture demands it. While it may be socially okay for female agents to have an amount of agency and power through the relay gaze, it is not okay for the male figures to be emasculated. The serial killers in these films play a crucial role in how the female agents develop as characters. This is significant, particularly with respect to the gender relationship. This inherent binary between male and female affects the way their development unfolds. This is the crux of the role that "evil" plays. The role of evil is always present, as the male figures are serial killers; however, it is how evil is treated within the narratives that allows the audience to accept and support evil's role. The killers in these films are stereotypes of the more sensationalized aspects of profiled serial killings: cannibalism, sexual violence, and proxy murder. Hannibal Lecter is a fictional representation of the cannibal serial killer, the most famous in American crime being Jeffrey Dahmer. Martin Asher represents the charming and sexual predator, akin to America's Ted Bundy. Finally, Owen Reilly represents the proxy killer, a killer who manipulates people into committing the act of murder in his or her place; his most famous counterpart in American crime is Charles Manson.

The camera gaze is important to consider when analyzing the relationship between the male serial killer and the female agent. Traditionally, the camera's gaze has been gendered as male,[3] privileging the male viewpoint. Since the traditional camera gaze privileges the masculine viewpoint, there is also an underlying sexual framework with implicit power roles (male over female). The female agent is complex because she challenges this tradition, established through the relay gaze, but in a limited capacity, i.e., she does not transcend the implied framework in which we encounter her, as she is still within a masculine agency. She does establish herself, through time, as a powerful figure within said institution, which suggests subversion, but the initial dynamic between herself and the villain reasserts the masculine/feminine power dynamic. Therefore, with the advent of the female FBI agent, the traditional gaze is no longer male, but instead one that is based in the relationship between the two characters, oscillating between them. I have termed this new concept the relay gaze. This concept is one of the major patterns found in media texts with lead female FBI agents.[4] This new gaze is significant because it does not inherently privilege one gender or the other, but instead shifts power between the two figures.

This specific relationship, between the male serial killer (a figure understood as evil) and the female FBI agent (a figure understood as good), is narratively rebellious because it highlights the fact that the two figures need each other in order to complete their functions — neither is relevant without the other half. This subversive relationship is treated differently within each of the texts, from a teacher figure (Lecter in *Silence* and *Hannibal*), to lover

(*Taking Lives*), and finally to child (*Untraceable*). The various relationships correspond directly to the female character's position within the film, therefore positioning the serial killer as the male counterpart to the female agent. The positioning of the women requires a particular sexual and cultural framework that is deeply embedded in our culture. There is an interesting development between the three movies: from non-consummated relationship, to consummated, to Oedipal. Implications of the sexual issue in the three relationships directly tie in to the tipped power balance and to the issue of the relay gaze, as again, power equals control of the gaze. The typical male/female power dichotomy is subverted as the roles change. Starling demonstrates the typical assumption that women lack power — therefore she is positioned as the student to Lecter's teacher. Her relationship to Lecter is also stripped of sexuality and they remain in a platonic relationship. Scott grows from that role and moves the female FBI figure into a more equal role in terms of power, as the lover. Her relationship with Asher is consummated and it is ultimately this consummation that gives her control. Finally, Marsh moves the figure to a higher position of power, as the mother to Reilly's child. This relationship is acceptable in terms of power because it is a socially comfortable role in which the audience can view Marsh. Her relationship to Reilly is a clear Oedipal one, and because of this positioning, she takes on the power characteristics, camera gaze, and hero status typically allotted to a male figure.

The killers in these films are considered from the start to be evil villains, not accounting for the spectrum of character types the male killers actually represent. The evil role thus places both the male and female characters in these films into slightly disjunctive hetero-normative gender roles, as the powerful, good female figure is not normative. When one looks at the male and female characters within the narratives together, and not apart as most feminist film scholars do, you see a direct balanced relationship between them. Since the male figure is the "evil" half, then this has important implications for the development of the female as the "good" figure. This is subversive, insofar as the hero is traditionally defined as a masculine role in our cultural narratives.

Relationships

Hannibal Lecter and Clarice Starling:
The Mentor and the Protégée

The symbiotic tie between Starling and Lecter is a strong and disconcerting one through both films. Starling begins *Silence of the Lambs* as a rookie. Her concern and focus on her career is, therefore, different from Scott's and

Marsh's because she is not an established agent, but a child figure at the start of her life in the FBI. Her first meeting with Lecter cements this role. Bruce Robbins, in his article "Murder and Mentorship: Advancement in *Silence of the Lambs*," discusses the implications of Starling's position. He points out that it is Lecter who knows Starling's goals. She is not interested in the traditional gender role of mother and he intuitively sees this within her before she fully understands her own motivations. Instead, "what this working class woman really wants is professional achievement or advancement."[5] Robbins positions her career desires as replacement for her sexual ones, which falls in line with her position as a rookie childlike figure. She is new, naïve, and malleable. She develops, both in her profession and sexually, through the course of *Silence* and *Hannibal* with direct influences from both Lecter and the FBI.

There is a divide in academic material focusing on these characters, between those who link Lecter and Starling's connection sexually and those who argue that their relationship is professionally platonic. Robbins takes the side of professionalism: "He [Lecter] enthusiastically embraces this asexual, ethically generous interpretation of his interrogator's [Starling] deepest motives and indeed derives from his knowledge a pleasure equivalent to erotic pleasure, which clearly marks him as the good mentor."[6] While I agree with Robbins that their relationship is one of teacher and student, both in age and professional status (rookie and seasoned professional), in *Silence of the Lambs*, by the time *Hannibal* comes around ten years later they have equaled out; both are established professionally and therefore are on equal footing, which allows for a possible development into a deeper, more sexual relationship. The fact that Lecter's attempt at a sexual relationship ultimately is rebuffed points to their character types' inability to fall into such a change in relationship status.

Starling's relationship to Hannibal, while it fulfills the traditional heroine-to-hero function, is still difficult for the viewer to accept because of her role as a female agent. The two require a continued relationship in order for either character to exist, but her role as agent and his role as villain frustrate the heteronormative framework that defines their gender. Mizejewski, looking at investigative films, states that "the attraction between investigator and criminal is a traditional fold in this genre.... [T]here's nothing straightforward or conventional about what Lecter and Clarice need in each other, as the sequel makes clear."[7] This ties back to Propp's idea that the hero's function, one of them, is to save the princess — Lecter needs Clarice in order to be considered a hero figure. Clarice needs Lecter from the first moment she meets him, not only to navigate the FBI but to survive personally. *Hannibal* pushes the boundaries of their relationship further than *Silence*, as they have both grown as characters, Clarice more than Lecter. "The film pushes this coupling [Hannibal and Starling] slightly.... [T]he isolated close-up of his finger running down hers is the first time a man touches her."[8] This points to evidence that Clarice does fulfill the princess/virginal heroine role. The blur between his role as her protector and his role as a sexual mate for her, traditionally the conclusion of the hero/heroine role, is thus activated.

Once these traditional gender roles have been established, the significance of the relay gaze becomes apparent. As Halberstam states, the film allows us different identities: "the woman detective alters traditional power relations and changes completely the usual trajectory of the horror narrative."[9] Halberstam's remarks on the relationship between Hannibal and Clarice give ending points wrapping up the conclusion that they are indeed hero and heroine, as well as the mentor/protégée: "his story requires her story, and hers depends on him."[10] What is interesting, however, is the reason that Halberstam sees in how the relationship plays out: "*Silence* is a horror film that is not designed to scare women, it scares men instead with the image of a fragmented and fragile masculinity."[11] This is not just applied to Bill's character; the FBI is also slowly becoming an "image of a fragmented and fragile masculinity" with the hiring of female agents.

Having departed from the standard male-oriented gaze, we find in *Silence* and *Hannibal* that the masculine viewpoint is no longer privileged as normative. The presence of the female agent challenges the power structure of the culture in which she operates and, in doing so, reveals through her relationship with Lecter that the FBI is not a wholly "good" institution. What the villain permits, then, is a different gaze, the relay gaze, that undermines the sexual paradigm that relegates the female agent to the childlike role, as well as the assumption that the masculine FBI, the supposed province of good, is problematic in its own right. The audience, in order to accept the film, needs a fall guy so that the real villain, a much scarier one (the FBI), isn't easily detected.

Illeana Scott and Martin Asher: The Lovers

Illeana Scott and Martin Asher are the next step from Clarice Starling and Hannibal Lecter because they are in fact lovers. Their ages are relatively equal, as are their abilities in their respective fields. They are distinct from Starling and Lecter, who were decades apart in age and therefore had a different relationship. The relative equality of Scott and Asher allows for a tighter, more intimate relationship. The film emphasizes this point when it allows the audience to see that Scott and Asher (who is posing under the name James Costa) are on an equal footing before they meet each other. Scott is an established, talented FBI special agent and Asher is an equally experienced killer by this point. They are stable and come into their relationship with established identities.

The shared intensity in their professional ability, as well as their commitment to their job, anticipates the sexual relationship between the two. When they are in physical proximity, their professional similarities play off of their gender roles. When she is fully performing the role of the investigator, also as the fullest example of the female heroine investigator figure, and when he is fulfilling the *homme fatale* role by being James Costa, they are at their strongest. This occurs twice in the film: the first time they meet in person and then in the final showdown. It is interesting to mention that both times this occurs, the location privileges Scott. The first meeting takes place in an interrogation room at the police station. Scott sees "James Costa"—currently known to her and the audience only as a witness and victim of Martin Asher— from the other side of the interrogation room's double mirror. This control Scott has of the look, of the camera gaze, also reappears in the final scene. She is given the chance to see "Costa," analyze him, before he even knows of her existence. When she enters the room they are also visually separated and linked at the same moment. When she enters she is wearing a black suit, while he is wearing a white shirt, the exact opposite of her suit. Once she sits and they begin to talk, their relationship begins and the characters are inextricably linked from this point forward. When she sits, they are on an even level, especially when she takes off her suit jacket to reveal a white shirt as well. They are now visually equal, and also continue to enact their abilities, feeding off of each other. This is an explicit example of the relay gaze, as neither figure is objectified within this scene. The change in camera angles equals their visual positioning, as well as their narrative positioning.

While they are seen as equals here, they do not remain equals by the end of the film, when Scott gains control and power over Asher. This is complicated when she sees him in the elevator, the moment at which Scott finds out that Costa (her lover) and Asher (the monstrous serial killer) are one and the same. Desire in horror also, according to Williams, lies between the woman and the monster, and although the female has some control of the gaze, at the same time the monster eclipses her power, stripping away agency because "the woman's look of horror paralyses her in such a way that distance is overcome; the monster's own spectacular appearance holds her originally active, curious look in a trance like passivity that allows him to master her through her look."[12] While this describes Scott's paralytic reaction to seeing Costa as Asher, as a monstrous figure, she is not ultimately controlled by him, as many other horror heroines are. This subverts both the power dynamics of the female agent as powerless and the implied power dynamics between lovers.

In the final showdown, the audience learns that she constructed and orchestrated the entire scene following her breakdown over finding out that Costa was Asher, the entire seven months he spent watching her living alone on a farm in rural Pennsylvania. After she stabs him she says, "Everything you saw I wanted you to see," pointing directly to the fact that she is now fully in control of what is gazed at. The control of the camera gaze, and also of the narrative, is Scott's, as this undercover operation was also hidden from the audience as a plot twist. Her control of what is gazed at, what is seen, fools both Asher and the audience, proving to be a successful plot twist. The faked pregnancy as an undercover operation is successful because it was a plausible for a typical female heroine. Scott's non-gender conforming actions not only saved her life, but also saved the character type. The fact that this was a seven-month-long deep cover assignment proves her dedication to her profession, as well as the possibility and hope for strength as a hero figure.

Scott and Asher, as profiler and killer, complement each other, understanding their need for each other. Their relationship is also one, as I have discussed before, that leads to a consummation of their sexual desire, which is closely tied to their personal actions. Their attraction to each other is somewhat constructed by Asher as, under the identity of James Costa, he is able to be what he believes she needs. The first time he moves towards this is after she first interrogates him. He sees Paquette corner her in the office and he goes up to them, asking to speak with Scott. Costa/Asher then lies, telling her that he could see Paquette had trapped her (having previously seen her expression with his three sisters). He attempts to establish trust with Scott, reading her as she is attempting to read him. He again interrupts her at the bar as she is working on the case file. He sits by her, commenting on the fact that she is analyzing the Band-Aids on his fingers. As they size each other University Press, she decides to give him her personal cell phone number, falling slightly for his nice guy/innocent victim guise. This scene, her slip in judgment, reinforces the more traditional male gaze/gender paradigm; however, it is momentary. The narrative as a whole tells the audience that she was acting out of character. This mistake, however, leads to monumental consequences — necessary because the consequences highlight the fact that Scott does not fit in the heroine stereotype.

He uses his status as victim two more times to get closer to Scott. After an alleged break-in at his art gallery he requests that Scott drive him home. While in the car he asks her why she does what she does. She lets her guard down and tells him the origins of her decision to enter law enforcement. She says that the job is the only one she could ever picture herself doing, that it is "a compulsion, not a punishment." She explains that when she was twelve someone had broken into her house and she grabbed a knife and killed him.

This could easily have been constructed as a possible negative in her life, something that she sought punishment or forgiveness for, like Starling trying to escape the lambs. Instead, for Scott, it was a career maker in a more positive way. Her career, she explains, is important. He inquires about the wedding ring on her finger. She tells him that she has never been married, that the ring is to keep people at bay. This also symbolizes her marriage to her job, something that she has completely devoted herself to. For Scott, her role as a female agent is not ultimately prohibited from her sexuality, unlike with Starling. This foreshadows that she will eventually mix up her professional and her sexuality, which emphasizes, in the end, how her role as female agent advances the alternative gaze suggested in the relationship between Starling and Lecter.

After the Costa/Asher reveal, Scott is punished and shunned by the other detectives, and to this point, the audience as well. She is the one who broke protocol by sleeping with a witness and entering into a physical relationship with him, placing her career, her livelihood, in jeopardy. There is the professional boundary that she crosses, which can only be crossed (within a heteronormative paradigm, of course) by a woman. In sleeping with the witness, then, she is transgressive both as an agent and as a woman. This also represents a stereotypical female response to defer to the male in the relationship — to give up her individual life goals for him. This is short lived, however, because with Scott this cannot ultimately work. She is unable to be codependent; she can function only on an interdependent level. As she breaks, and is blamed and tossed off of the case, she becomes someone she is not. She cries in her hotel bathroom, scrubbing him off of her body, acting like a victim. At the same time Asher, on the other hand, immediately becomes someone else on the train. The audience then assumes the opposite of what is about to occur. As the scene flashes back and forth between a naked, crying Scott and an active Asher capturing his next victim, the audience is lured into expecting what typically happens at this point to heroines in these situations: they break and are unable to regroup, needing instead to be saved by the male hero. This does not work or last because ultimately Scott is more active and advanced than Starling was, and she regains her position.

Owen Reilly and Jennifer Marsh: The Son and Mother

Jennifer Marsh and Owen Reilly represent the next step in the agent/serial killer relationship. As I mentioned earlier, it is this Oedipal relationship that empowers Marsh, at the expense of her sexuality.[13] She is the maternal figure to the killer and also has the most independence and agency. This hero positioning must be balanced, however, as the other relationships were. This balance is equaled in its mirror image to Starling and Lecter. Marsh takes the level of strength and power that Lecter had, but as an experienced agent in her field. Reilly therefore takes Starling's place as a rookie — a fledgling killer. This balance causes the killer to be somewhat of a weakened figure; as one is strong, the other must complete the balance with a calculated level of weakness. The introductions of the characters also display their various stages of life, as mother and son.

The film opens on a young male using a handheld camera. As he sets the camera down the screen shows him setting a kitten up on a glued sheet in what looks to be a basement. While his identity is not revealed at this point, he is Owen Reilly. Similarly, our introduction to Marsh is almost as hidden. We first see her walking into a building, with her jacket hood University Press, so until she decides to remove it, the audience cannot guess her gender. She removes her hood in the elevator, showing that she is a middle aged, attractive woman. She walks to the security stand and flashes her badge, showing her name and also confirming that she is an FBI agent. As she sits at her desk it is revealed that she is working in the cyber crimes division, and it is quickly shown that she is good at what she does. The moment she gets in, she immediately closes a fraud case, orchestrating the field team to take the suspects down. The complete balance in camera gaze for the introductions highlights the concept of the relay gaze. Both characters are given POV control over their introductions — introductions that showcase their power. Reilly is setting up his first torture/murder scene — he is skilled, but clearly new at what he is doing.[14] Marsh, on the other hand, is in complete control as she effortlessly coordinates the successful completion of a case.

Marsh and Reilly, like the others, have matched skill sets, which in their case is computer technology. Reilly's abilities are tied directly to his murder set-ups and the way in which he uses them (streaming through the website). Marsh's talents are equally matched and are the focus of her professional life and also bleed into her personal life. When Marsh is in the car driving home from the office she depends on the OnStar system to see the traffic route, highlighting her constant use of updated technology. Her abilities also exceed those of her boss. When she explains the site to him he asks her to speak without using the technical jargon. Frequent close-ups of Marsh's hands, her tool in her field, underline her strength in technology. There are also multiple close-ups of Reilly's hands as he types in information about the victims for the perusal of various site members and guests. While Marsh and Reilly are matched in skill level they also go back and forth in having the upper hand, like Scott and Asher. Later in the film when Marsh is driving away from the hotel, her car stops in the middle of Broadway Bridge. The news she hears over the radio right before it cuts out is the story about Reilly, calling him the Internet Killer and the perpetrator of the most serious Internet crime to date.

Unlike Starling and Scott, Marsh has a flourishing, positive family life and is able to juggle work and home successfully. What is also important is the struggle Marsh makes for her family. We learn that she does not even want to continue on the case at first because she does not want to take away from her scheduled time with her daughter, Annie. Her dedication is towards her family first. Reilly is similarly motivated, but in a more visceral, deviant manner, fulfilling the role of the noir psychopath. The impact of his father's suicide was so severe that he had to be institutionalized. Once he was released, he was driven purely to avenge the death of his father. Towards the end of the film it is revealed that all of the deaths, including the kitten, on kill-withme.com are related. Reilly not only avenges the death of his father, but also makes a point of using the skills his father taught him to do it. The death most closely linked to the connection between Reilly and his father is Griffin's. Griffin is killed with sulfuric acid, which was taken from the same university where Dr. Reilly taught. It is important that Griffin specifically died via this method because of what Griffin represents to Reilly.

Griffin, a younger agent who works with Marsh, is seen as the good son to Reilly's bad son. Griffin sits by Marsh in the office, their desks connected, and they work together on cases. As he is much younger than she is, she acts as a mother figure throughout the film for him. Griffin represents everything that Reilly is not. He not only assists Marsh on a professional level, but also interacts with her and Annie away from the office, as an added family member. When he kills Griffin, Reilly makes a point of pinning Griffin's FBI badge into his naked chest, to again point out Griffin's overachieving status of the "good son." True to that status, before Griffin dies, he also solves the case. Harking back to his discussion with Marsh earlier in the film about learning Morse code in Boy Scouts, Griffin blinks his eyes in Morse code to give Marsh the information she needs to capture the killer.

Marsh is in control of the gaze from the beginning of the film, which is natural because her job — sitting at a computer looking through other people's computers — makes her a legal voyeur whose job depends on her ability to watch others. While Marsh also has power in the ability to not be seen, being able to be behind a computer screen in an office, Reilly has control over what is seen. Because he controls his website — and, in effect, the camera angles — the audience does not see or know who he is until Griffin is sacrificed. It is when Marsh steps out of her normal job at the desk and into the field that Reilly sees her. Up until the point that she visits one of the crime scenes, the house where Reilly kidnapped one of his victims, she monitors the killer's actions through her computer in the office as well as her home computer.

Bringing her job home, however, is a punishable action. When she brings her job into the house, blending her two roles, Reilly is given a chance to spy on her through a video game hack Annie is given.

As the camera gaze oscillates slightly between them, it is the connection, their relationship, that is important. Marsh and Reilly are connected from the beginning when she is tipped onto his website. While they are not physically proximal to each other, or aware of their identities at first, they are still connected through the means of their skill base: computer technology. Reilly can be seen as a new killer, a rookie, even before the audience is given his actual age. Marsh takes note of the fact, when she views his work with the kitten, that he, like most killers, is escalating. The kitten, while relevant in his killing pattern,[15] is a test before he moves upwards to human victims. Marsh and her team also notice that Reilly is not actually performing the murders himself; he is setting them up. He is somewhat disconnected by setting up the murders. Instead he is forcing the members and guests of his website to control the force of the death via the number of people logging onto the site. This attempt to circumvent directed responsibility is inherently juvenile in nature, again highlighting his position as the son figure. This affects the "motherly" response from Marsh because she moves into the role of the disciplinarian.

When Reilly captures Marsh, he treats her differently from the men. He does videotape her capture, however, transferring the power of the camera gaze control into his favor, albeit for a limited time. All of the site visitors, including her fellow agents at the office, are watching the events take place in real time. He takes her to her own basement and hangs her upside down, also binding her hands and feet. When he sets her up it is completely non-sexualized visually. Whereas the male victims were shown with exposed chests or legs, Marsh is kept in her jeans and a tucked-in long sleeved shirt. This indicates that Reilly does not see her in an overtly sexual way, as she represents more of a maternal figure to him. He does, however, comment on the faceless website visitors: "I wonder if they'll kill you faster or slower. Awful things men do to women that other men pay to watch, it will probably be faster ... much faster." Reilly is correct; Marsh's capture brings the site the most visitors to date, a fast eighteen million. The most visitors, however, log in after their struggle. She begins to swing her body, eventually catching the pipe, opening it up to push the steam into Reilly's face. She gets herself down and fights him. She gets her gun back and is forced to shoot him. It is here that he loses all of his control again; he fails at being a serial killer because he has gone beyond his boundaries in trying to kill her, beyond his goals of only killing the people related to his father's death. She regains all of her power in defeating the villain, and also regains control over the camera gaze — literally. She crawls up to the camera, which has been knocked onto the floor, and makes a point of looking directly at the camera into the eyes of all of the Internet viewers and flashes her badge, her symbol of authority and power. Marsh's control over the camera, and therefore the camera gaze for the audience, finally establishes her as the hero of the text. Not only does she defeat the villain alone, but she also claims power over the gaze of the camera.

Conclusion

Analyzing the characters in relation to each other throughout these texts does show there is hope in resistance of the traditional, heteronormative roles of girl, young woman, and mother. By the end of each film's narrative, not only has the woman rebelled against her assigned gender role (as student, lover, or mother) in relation to the killer, but she ultimately succeeds as a professional — therefore coming full circle and making the case for the female hero figure. As the character-type develops, from Clarice Starling to Illeana Scott and Jennifer Marsh, it has also gained the all important final element of solidifying the character as a hero, and not a heroine: self-rescue. This skill is crucial because of the agents' similar relationships to the killers within the films, both in plot and in physical location. The location itself gains more power for these women because of the history of struggle with which it is laced. By reappropriating control in these settings, the female FBI agent also makes positive strides throughout the film toward the label of hero.

All of the final showdowns occur in domestic settings. Starling and Lecter confront one another in Paul Krendler's kitchen; Scott and Asher, in the farmhouse kitchen and living room; Marsh and Reilly, in Marsh's basement. The home is the ultimate representation of the domestic setting, and historically, the roles of women in the home come with burdens of gender oppression and inequality. The concept of the stay-at-home mother, the dutiful wife, stuck within the confines of a suburban home is a stereotype understood and used within American culture. It is this cultural understanding of the history of women in the home that infuses the provocative placements of the films' final showdowns with power. The movements through the home also display evidence of the evolution of the female FBI agent character type. In *Hannibal*, again, the final showdown takes place in the kitchen. The kitchen has long been associated with the stereotype of the American housewife, commonly connected with this room as opposed to any other within a typical house structure. Since Starling is still a heroine, not yet a full hero, as she does not save herself, the kitchen is an appropriate setting. This does not, however, strip agency from her character. She does fight and rebel against Lecter, refusing his sexual advances, choosing her career instead. This choice is extremely important because it leaves room for advancement in gender representation for subsequent films.

Taking Lives has a final showdown, as previously noted, that begins in the kitchen and ends in the living room. The movement out of the kitchen and into a more gender-neutral space serves as a *mise-en-scène*[16] highlight to Scott's actions. When capturing Scott, Asher believed her to be pregnant and helpless. Scott's ruse, a faked pregnancy, worked because it manipulated common conceptions of gender roles. The success of Scott's plan, then, reveals the extent to which Asher (and by implication the audience) assumed that because Scott is a woman she was helpless in this situation. Instead she saves herself and defeats the villain, Asher, because she orchestrated the undercover operation and controlled the entire situation.

Jennifer Marsh, in *Untraceable*, gains her hero status through self-rescue because the final showdown begins in her basement with her bound by Reilly. The basement is distant from the kitchen and away from gendered territory. Notably Marsh saves herself (from being bound upside down, hanging above a lawn mower) because of her knowledge of the space and utilization of various elements (pipes, tools, etc.) in order to surprise and defeat Reilly. The expectations that come from the heteronormative paradigm (and its assumptions about how women should function within it) are disrupted by these female agents. They show a competence that surprises because of how deeply the masculine Other assumes the female agent will behave in a particular capacity (because the villain, like the audience, accepts the paradigm in question).

I have defined a hero based in narrative structure with a focus on the importance of the ultimate self-rescue. It is stripped of the character's moral standings and decisions, as I am looking at the function of the character type and not the overall personality and psychological makeup of the figure. Due to this definition, as I have discussed, while there is a female hero figure, most prominently in Jennifer Marsh, there are also heroes found in places typically not associated with common conceptions of the term "hero." Labeling the female FBI agent as the hero figure is significant because it is acceptable that women in our time period and political climate realistically hold these positions and hold them well. Women are active in the FBI, as well as many other federal and state agencies and the military, unlike in decades before. Therefore it should only be natural, as genre and film are social mirrors, that these women are represented within fictional narratives as powerful, independent heroes. Ultimately it is through the relay gaze that the women reach the role of hero. The oscillation of power between two figures that the relay gaze allows, gives both figures equal chance at control.

The irony of this development is that the good institution, the FBI, ultimately requires evil villains to enable the woman to succeed. While finally having evidence of a female hero is socially significant, so, by extension, is the labeling of Hannibal Lecter. The fact that he fulfills the hero role further supports the idea that previous hero/villain roles are no longer relevant or viable. The lines have been blurred; the idealistic concepts of easily categorized villains and heroes have reached the point where they are utopian ideas. They are not a reflection of reality; they are not even satisfying as fiction. With the breakdown of the simple definition of hero and villain, these films expose and challenge the masculine stereotypes and power structures that traditionally require such simplified notions of good and evil. While this idea creates anxiety and paranoia, an overall sense of unease, it is nonetheless relevant and systemic.

NOTES

1. Thomas Gramstad, "The Female Hero," in *Feminist Interpretations of Ayn Rand*, ed. Mimi Reisel Gladstein and Chris Matthew Sciabarra (University Park: Pennsylvania State University Press, 1999), 351.

2. John Douglas, former FBI profiler, also finds this to be true, opening his *Crime Classification Manual* with "Crime and the criminal have always fascinated society" (1).

3. The scene in which Buffalo Bill hunts down Starling through night vision goggles is an explicit example of the camera gaze in *Silence of the Lambs*. In the scene, the gaze of the camera places the audience in the POV of the male figure, giving him visual and narrative power.

4. Breaking out of the thriller genre, both *Miss Congeniality* films center around Gracie Hart and the more comical serial killer in each story. Television shows with FBI characters, such as *The X-Files* and *Profiler*, have major story arcs surrounding the agent's relationship with a serial killer.

5. Bruce Robbins, "Murder and Mentorship: Advancement in *The Silence of the Lambs*," *Boundary* (1st ser. 23, 1996), 72.

6. Ibid., 83.

7. Linda Mizejewski, *Hard Boiled and High Heeled* (New York: Routledge, 2004), 186.

8. Ibid., 185.

9. Judith Halberstam, *Skin Shows* (Durham, NC: Duke University Press, 1995), 166.

10. Ibid.

11. Ibid., 168.

12. Linda Williams, "When the Woman Looks," in *Re-Vision: Essays in Feminist Film Criticism*, ed. Mary Anne Doane, Patricia Mellencamp, and Linda Williams (Los Angeles: University Publications of America, 1983), 86.

13. The audience learns that Marsh lost her husband, another law enforcement agent, in the field, and has since devoted her time to her family and her job — not to actively searching for another sexual partner.

14. Killers, as John Douglas highlights in *Crime Classification Manual*, escalate in their crimes. Typically they start with animals and progress to humans.

15. The kitten is owned by one of the men Reilly blames for the sensationalism of his father's death.

16. *Mise-en-scène* is a film term that refers to everything that in the composition of a shot: set design, lighting, camera movement, and the general visual environment. The direct French translation is "put in the scene."

BIBLIOGRAPHY

Altman, Rick. *Film/Genre*. London: British Film Institute, 1999.
Berger, Arthur Asa. "Propp, DeSaussure and the Narrative." *Popular Culture Genres*. London: Sage, 1992.
Cawelti, John. *Adventure, Mystery and Romance*. Chicago: University of Chicago Press, 1976.
Clover, Carol J. "Her Body, Himself: Gender in the Slasher Film." In *Horror, the Film Reader*. Ed. Mark Jancovich. New York: Routledge, 2002. 77–90.
Cowie, Elizabeth. "The Popular Film as a Progressive Text — a Discussion of *Coma*." In *Feminism and Film Theory*. Ed. Constance Penley. New York: Routledge, 1988. 104–140.
Degh, Linda. *American Folklore and the Mass Media*. Bloomington: Indiana University Press, 1994.
Douglas, John E., Ann Burgess, and Robert K. Ressler. *Crime Classification Manual*. San Francisco: Jossey Bass, 1992.
Douglas, John E., and Mark Olshaker. *The Anatomy of Motive*. New York: Scribner, 1999.
Freeland, Cynthia A. "Feminist Frameworks for Horror Films." In *Film Theory and Criticism*. Ed. Leo Braudy and Marshall Cohen. Oxford: Oxford University Press, 2004. 742–763.
Garrett, Greg. "Objecting to Objectification: Re-Viewing the Feminine in *The Silence of the Lambs*." *Journal of Popular Culture* 27 (1994): 1–12.
Gilet, Peter. *Vladimir Propp and the Universal Folktale*. New York: Peter Lang, 1998.
Gramstad, Thomas. "The Female Hero." In *Feminist Interpretations of Ayn Rand*. Ed. Mimi Reisel Gladstein and Chris Matthew Sciabarra. University Park: Pennsylvania State University Press, 1999.
Halberstam, Judith. *Skin Shows*. Durham, NC: Duke University Press, 1995. 161–177.
Hannibal. Directed by Ridley Scott. Los Angeles: MGM, 2004. DVD.
Inness, Sherrie A., ed. *Action Chicks: New Images of Tough Women in Popular Culture*. New York: Palgrave Macmillan, 2004.
_____. *Tough Girls*. Philadelphia: University of Pennsylvania Press, 1999.
Kaplan, E. Ann. "Is the Gaze Male?" In *Feminism and Film*. Ed. E. Ann Kaplan. New York: Oxford University Press, 2000. 119–135.
Miss Congeniality. Directed by Donald Petrie. Burbank, CA: Warner Home Video, 2004. DVD.
Mizejewski, Linda. *Hard Boiled and High Heeled*. New York: Routledge, 2004.
Mulvey, Laura. "Afterthoughts on 'Visual Pleasure and Narrative Cinema' Inspired by King Vidor's *Duel in the Sun* (1946)." *Visual and Other Pleasures*. Bloomington: Indiana University Press, 1989.
_____. "Visual Pleasure and Narrative Cinema." *Visual and Other Pleasures*. Bloomington: Indiana University Press, 1989.
Profiler. Television series. Broadcast 29 September 1996–1 July 2000. NBC.
Propp, Vladimir. *Morphology of the Folktale*. Austin: University of Texas Press, 1968.
Reynolds, Quentin. *The FBI*. New York: Random House, 1954.
Robbins, Bruce. "Murder and Mentorship: Advancement in *The Silence of the Lambs*." *Boundary* 1st ser. 23 (1996): 71–90.
Schopp, Andrew. "The Practice and Politics of 'Freeing the Look': Jonathan Demme's *The Silence of the Lambs*." *Camera Obscura* 2nd ser. 18 (2003): 125–151.
Sharrett, Christopher. "The Horror Film in Neoconservative Culture." In *The Dread of Difference*. Ed. Barry Keith Grant. Austin: University of Texas Press, 1996. 253–276.
The Silence of the Lambs. Directed by Jonathan Demme. Los Angeles: MGM, 2004. DVD.
Spicer, Andrew. "Gender in Film Noir." *Film Noir*. Harlow, Essex, UK: Pearson Educational, 2002. 90–93.
Taking Lives. Directed by D.J. Caruso. Burbank, CA: Warner Home Video, 2004. DVD.
Untraceable. Directed by Gregory Hoblit. Culver City, CA: Sony Pictures, 2008. DVD.
Williams, Linda. "When the Woman Looks." In *Re-Vision: Essays in Feminist Film Criticism*. Ed. Mary Anne Doane, Patricia Mellencamp, and Linda Williams. Los Angeles: University Publications of America, 1983. 83–99.
The X Files. Television series. Broadcast 10 September 1993–19 May 2002. 20th Century–Fox Television.

7

Wanting the White Witch

Bryan Dove

As much as I fought with my sister as a boy, I would have never sold her
out to a witch for a box of candy. Whether it was this, or the fact that my
parents had taught me from a very young age not to trust adults trying to
give me candy, I never quite understood why Edmund was tempted by that
box of bewitched Turkish Delight that the White Witch offers in the opening
chapters of *The Lion, the Witch and the Wardrobe*. To be fair, unfortunate
Edmund did not know at the time that she was a witch, but he might have
reasoned as much based on the fact that she conjured his treats from a potion!
For my own sake, I never even knew what Turkish Delight was until I moved
to Scotland many years later to take on graduate work. From the way that it
was written about, and judging by what it seemed to do to Edmund, I assumed
it must be the most delicious thing that a human being had ever put to tongue.
It was not.

Yet there is clearly something else quite a bit more insidious about C.S.
Lewis's White Witch than her vending of (what at least I consider to be)
dodgy treats. There is also the fact that her target prey in *The Lion, the Witch
and the Wardrobe* are children. What compounds even further this twisted
fact is the manner in which she entices them and lures them into her trap.
The White Witch is in fact the classic honey pot, made all the more symbolically obvious by the fact that she is actually using sweets in *The Lion, The
Witch and the Wardrobe* in order to entrap and coerce young Edmund. A
witch who uses enchanted food to trick and trap a visitor to her realm is fairly
standard as far as fairy tale villainy goes. Still, the White Witch of Lewis's
Narnia tales breaks and exceeds this type in one important way: where hags
are supposed to look like hags, Jadis is, dare I say, sexy. She is a popular figure
for the psychoanalytical school of literary criticism to expose for this reason.

Yet the purpose of this small essay is not to psychoanalyze Lewis's writings, but rather to examine broadly the spiritual dynamic resulting from our psychological interactions with Lewis's plots and characters. I want to find out why the White Witch is so easily and prevalently identified with evil and indeed the nature of that evil, not to enumerate potential psychological causes influencing the imagery in which she appears to us in print. And while her posturing as an Oedipal-themed dominatrix who preys on children certainly adds a thick, revolting layer of perversity to her malfeasance, what I want to talk about is the White Witch as evil itself— not just as *a really bad person*.

I am operating out of a Christian theological tradition in which evil exists not only as a way of characterizing anti-social actions, postures and behaviors, but also as a force or an anti-force within the cosmos. Yet for many Christian thinkers over the past two millennia, notably Augustine, it is not simply the existence of evil — troubling enough — but the human compliance and cooperation with it that predicates its nature and significance as a catastrophe. This brings me to address the misleadingly casual tone of this essay. My contention is that to understand from a theological perspective what makes the White Witch so evil, we must understand what she does to *us* as readers. It is not enough to simply analyze and understand the ethical dimension of her behavior; we must also scrutinize our whole engagement with her character.

For this reason, I adopt the schematic of a reader's response criticism. This school of criticism — made famous by figures such as Wolfgang Iser, Roland Barthes and Stanley Fish — seeks to study reader-generated meaning from texts. Typically texts were read within a historical framework in order to try and help the reader understand what an author was trying to communicate through the text. Reader's response criticism, on the other hand, theorized that readers create meanings through their interactions with texts and that this is, in fact, a supremely important aspect of the literary encounter. That the strategy is apt has already been proven in Fish's great piece *Surprised by Sin*,[1] which examines the effect of Milton's great anti-hero, Satan, on the moral judgments of the reader. It is also a way of approaching literature with which Lewis himself might have worked had he lived and worked perhaps five years longer. His 1961 work *An Experiment in Criticism*[2] certainly laid much of the groundwork for reader's response criticism by arguing that the literary worth of a text could be better judged by how it was read than by the method and artistry of its composition. In light of this work and perhaps also because Lewis was so in the habit of using a conversational narrating *to* the reader in his Narnia books, a reader's response criticism seems an appropriate tactic for examining these works.

Now, it is worth mentioning that the way in which we interact with the White Witch will actually be deeply affected by two factors in our reading of her. First, gender/sexuality plays a significant role in how characters (and likely many readers as well) react to the White Witch. In the texts themselves, the female characters introduced to the Witch always immediately distrust her and are immune to her wiles, whereas males — from boys to men — are captivated and entranced by her. Second, for readers, it makes a difference where one first meets the White Witch. If one reads *The Magician's Nephew* first, one knows the Witch for who she is as soon as she is introduced.* The introduction takes place after two children, Digory and Polly, find themselves transported into another world by means of a set of magical rings. In that world, in a formerly great city called Charn, the children discover a vast chamber filled with facsimiles of the former rulers. They notice that the manikin-like figures at one end of the chamber — a type of Madame Tussaud's gone terribly wrong — look happy and noble, but the figures farther into the chamber look less noble, then less happy, until they are both wicked and unhappy. "They were even despairing faces: as if the people they belonged to had done dreadful things and also suffered dreadful things."[4]

At the terminus of this long, harrowing visual narrative of moral devolution stood a figure that caught their attention, "a woman even more richly dressed than the others, very tall ... with a look of such fierceness and pride that it took your breath away. Yet she was beautiful too. Years afterwards when he was an old man, Digory said he had never in all his life known a woman so beautiful."[5] This figure was that of Jadis, the White Witch, who would come to do so much evil in Narnia. The children are clearly enchanted by her, but she also pulls at the reader's imagination — an Amazonian figure in exotic surroundings. Importantly, she is suspicious-looking despite her good looks; consider her "fierceness and pride" and her place at the end of a line of increasingly cruel and unhappy visages. The narrator gives the reader an additional, gendered warning: "It is only fair to add that Polly always said she couldn't see anything specially beautiful about her."[6]

This, then, is where the White Witch's magic begins, although the reader is given a talisman of defense in Polly, who constantly rebuffs Digory's poor judgment and is able to see through Jadis's deception.[7] Yet it seems that all of her prudence is lost on Digory, who, already lost in the overwhelming allure and *womanhood* of the witch, now has no time for young girls — "I should never dream of calling a kid like you a woman,"[8] he says to Polly after

---

*The Magician's Nephew was published in 1955, five years after *The Lion, the Witch and the Wardrobe*, and was originally Book 6 in the series. The most recent editions place *The Magician's Nephew* first and deem it Book 1, with *The Lion, the Witch and the Wardrobe* as Book 2.

she rebukes his churlishness towards her. Yet while Polly can provide Digory insight and right judgment of Jadis's character, what she cannot provide is the internal moral and physical strength to resist Jadis ("the Queen") and her overwhelming presence and sexuality. Unlike her tactics in subsequent encounters with human children, here Jadis seeks not to seduce or persuade but simply to domineer: "The Queen put her other hand under his chin and forced it up so that she could see his face better. Digory tried to stare back but he soon had to let his eyes drop. There was something about hers that overpowered him."[9]

Here I sympathize with Digory and I reckon others will also. I find it easy to be overwhelmed by the White Witch, even in this tale in which she is so clearly depicted as troublesome. Yet when the moment in which she has done some horrible thing has passed, it is practically impossible not to become enamored with "her beauty, her fierceness, her wildness."[10] Digory's Uncle Andrew finds this as well when the children accidentally transport Jadis back to London with them. Upon arriving, she begins to dominate Uncle Andrew just as she had done Digory back in Charn. Uncle Andrew, a hopeless fool for women, cannot but be infatuated with her and fantasize about her despite the fact that she is quite wicked towards him: "Now that the Witch was no longer in the same room with him he was quickly forgetting how she had frightened him and thinking more and more of her wonderful beauty. He kept on saying to himself, 'A dem fine woman, sir, a dem fine woman. A superb creature.' ... You see, the foolish old man was actually beginning to imagine the Witch would fall in love with him."[11]

Again, it is hard for me not to sympathize with Uncle Andrew in this case, having experienced his same folly (well, not with a witch, you see, but a girl quite like her). And as I sympathize with him, I begin to identify with him and also identify the Witch with that long forgotten love who always so magnificently strung me along before rejecting me in a grand, public spectacle. Suddenly the Witch becomes for me like that same siren who tortured me in the tenth grade. I know she is evil. I know she is even perhaps Evil itself. Yet I cannot help being rather sentimental towards her and ultimately attracted to her as well. The experience is common; perhaps Lewis himself experienced it on occasion. Of course she is wicked, but isn't her villainy somewhat intriguing and exciting? How can one resist the image of her commandeering a London hansom cab and driving it around the city like some mad concoction of Napoleon, Jehu and Queen Elizabeth I? "On the roof— not sitting, but standing on the roof— swaying with superb balance as it came at full speed round the corner with one wheel in the air — was Jadis the Queen of Queens and the Terror of Charn. Her teeth were bared, her eyes shone like fire, and he long hair streamed out behind her like a comet's tail."[12] The image is so compelling and delightful one nearly forgets that the horrible woman is nearly beating the poor horse to death!

The ease and frequency with which Andrew or Digory, and ourselves, are seduced by the White Witch is the very foundation of reading her evilness. It is not the cold inhumanity with which she governs — she claims: "I poured out the blood of my armies like water" and then justifies the slaughter by saying "Don't you understand? ... I was the Queen. They were all *my* people"[13] — that so readily identifies her with evil. Nor is it even the residually blasphemous feel of her employment of the Deplorable Word, "a word which, if spoken with the proper ceremonies, would destroy all living things except the one who spoke it"[14] (unlike the Word of John 1, the Christ, through whom all living things were created). No, the true evil of the Queen of Charn is that she makes us like her.

When Edmund Pevensie met the White Witch for the first time, like most readers of the *Chronicles of Narnia*, he was without benefit of the prudent voice of Polly. Despite the information his sister, Lucy, had gathered earlier from the faun, Mr. Tumnus, Edmund was on his own, all alone in a snowy woodland. Meeting the White Witch in Narnia is altogether unlike meeting her in post-apocalyptic Charn, with its wasted landscape and cold, red sun. Though locked in winter when Edmund first saw it, Narnia was still a vibrant and lovely place, especially for those (like Edmund) not privy to the fact that Narnia's was an "always winter and never Christmas" sort of affair.[15] Winter has that wonderful duality like no other season. It can be either cold, barren, and hostile, or it can be refreshing, stunning, beautiful and romantic. This duality is played out in the Witch's very person. Indeed, the fact that she is the *White* Witch closely aligns her very personality (along with her telling appearance) to that enchanted season which she perpetuated over Narnia.

Children, when they come from comfortable homes where all their needs are met, are more likely to see the winter positively, as its dangers and hostility are for the most part removed from their realities. Thus winter becomes about all those lovely things frequently associated with winter: presents, Father Christmas, hot cocoa, sledding, snow angels, and holidays. For myself as a child, winter was my favorite time of year! It's just this kind of innocence and naïveté that the witch exploits in Edmund. The Jadis of Narnia is even craftier than the one that followed Polly and Digory back to London from Charn. When she meets Edmund in the wood, we see initially a good measure of that same, dominating roguishness of *The Magician's Nephew* — initially chiding Edmund for his bad manners before a queen — but now she has masked her tyrannizing with a more reassuring demeanor of chiding maternalism. Even more insidiously still, mixed in with all of this (admittedly confusing) imagery of the maternal and the tyrannical is the White Witch's sexuality, even more latent than in *The Magician's Nephew* (perhaps because Edmund is pictured as being a slightly older, slightly less childish boy than Digory?).

It almost seems that Edmund's first sight of the Witch could not have been more sexualized without regressing to the pornographic. She was

> ... a great lady, taller than any woman that Edmund had ever seen. She was also covered in white fur up to her throat and held a long straight golden wand [phallus] and wore a golden crown on her head. Her face was white — not merely pale, but white like snow or paper or icing-sugar, *except for her very red mouth*. It was a beautiful face in other respects, but proud and cold and stern [emphasis added].[16]

The sexualization of the Witch's image here appears obvious, if not intentional. Why, for instance, is her fur coat described as going "up to her throat"? It seems odd to describe clothing as coming up to one's throat and not one's chin, yet there is a clear difference. Necks are sexy, erogenous even, while chins are not. Her very paleness, her incandescently white skin is a marker for an exotic sexuality. The proliferation of cosmetic skin lightening products in Asia, Africa and North America is evidence that the ancient equating of paleness (which signifies a life of luxury and leisure out of the sun) with social standing and attractiveness still stands.[17] Combine these elements with an Amazonian stature and demeanor, a golden phallus, and one "very red mouth," and the result is one sexy witch.

Of course, a sexy witch was in no way a new creation. Lewis had, in fact, a fantastic tradition to draw from in that respect. Beginning with his classical sources for Jadis, Circe and Medusa, we can start to develop a clearer picture about her alluring and mystifying abilities. Both Circe and Medusa are lenses through which she is read. Medusa, like Jadis, is both beautiful and hideous. Originally, she was *simply* a brutish abomination, one of the three Gorgon daughters of the ancient sea monsters Phorcys and Ceto. But something interesting happens in the mythology of Medusa. She can, of course, turn men into stone just like the White Witch. Yet whereas in the beginning this trait was a result of her hideousness, as early as 490 B.C. there is evidence of a Medusa who is both beautiful and terrible.[18] Certainly, by the time of Ovid, Medusa is seen as a figure for whom power rests as much in her beauty as her frightful, supernatural deformity.[19] Because of this, today Medusa figures as a symbol of feminine power and even features on the logo of prominent fashion design firm, Versace.

The significance of all of this, of course, is that the character of Medusa evolved in a way that made her more threatening. Monsters could always be slain by feats of strength, but a being like Medusa, both monstrous and beautiful, presents unique challenges and requires a unique type of fortitude. Such beings are scary within the mythical world (and perhaps the psychological world of readers) because men know that despite whatever other feats of strength they might have accomplished, one glimpse of Medusa or one flick of Jadis's wand could turn them into stone. Indeed, many will be able to identify with this experience of paralysis induced by nothing less than the utter fearsomeness of awesome beauty. It is this kind of threatening female sexuality that has long been associated with witches. Beyond the Classical period, the Middle Ages brought about a whole spectrum of suspicion in this regard. The fifteenth-century Dominican theologian and witch hunter Heinrich Institoris describes it this way:

> So let me now say what experience tells us — that in order to satisfy this kind of filthiness, as much in themselves as in the powerful men of the age and no matter what their rank or status, [these women] leave their fingermarks all over innumerable acts of harmful magic by so changing the men's minds towards wanton passion of infatuation that no embarrassment or persuasion can make them leave off their company.[20]

This is why the "sexy witch" is evil, because by some mysterious power she seems to be able to bereft a man of his own will and reason. As Margaret Hourihan writes, "the witches, sirens, fatal enchantresses and other evil female creatures, serve the ideological purposes of myth perfectly. They are 'wild' and irrational, governed by emotions and physical hungers.... They threaten the hero's rationality, self-control and purpose."[21]

It is this very sort of "hunger" which leads Edmund towards trouble. The very food with which he is enticed is, of course, a stand-in and metaphor for something much more luscious. Why should Edmund betray his family for a snack? Anne Alston evaluates the scene thus:

> The reader is forewarned of the witch's evil intent by the sensuous description of the food; it is sweet, foamy, creamy, light and delicious. Edmund is seduced by the White Witch's promise of plenty, of "rooms full of Turkish Delight": food leads to the downfall of Edmund as surely as it did for Eve and for Hansel and Gretel. Almost immediately the enchanted food results in Edmund forgetting his manners: he is losing his purity as a child as he lusts over the sweet forbidden food and begins to lose control.[22]

The combination of food and sex seems a natural one; at least within the Greco-Roman philosophical discourse, they both represent the passions of the flesh. St. Paul, in a famous passage from 1 Corinthians in which he declares the body a temple of the Holy Spirit, combines the issues of morality in sex and eating by saying that, with regard to both, one should honor God with his body.[23] Both sex and food are enjoyed with the body, and both can affect the body both positively and negatively. St. Paul seems concerned with helping the Corinthian church enjoy both sex and food in ways that are healthy for both soul and body.

For Edmund, sex and food are clearly confounded in this instance. If the change in his demeanor is any indication, the experience is every bit the loss of innocence that Alston suggests it is. Hourihan confirms this much: "While this clearly symbolic sweetmeat suggests the effect of an addictive drug Edmund's response to the Turkish Delight is also strongly suggestive of sexual arousal."[24]

Lewis himself once addressed the issue of food and sex in Edmund's temptation. He writes:

> In my own first story I had described at great length what I thought a rather fine high tea given by a hospitable faun to the little girl who was my heroine. A man, who has children of his own, said, 'Ah, I see how you got that. If you want to please grown-up readers you give them sex, so you thought to yourself, "that won't do for children, what shall I give them instead? I know! The little blighters like plenty of good eating." ' In reality, however, I myself like eating and drinking. I put in what I would like to have read when I was a child and what I still like reading now that I am in my fifties.[25]

For Lewis, the perpetual bachelor at this point in his life, food was actually the most sensuous thing in his experience. Even a complete amateur at psychoanalysis (and I include myself in this category) could easily see what Lewis could not know about himself: his love and enjoyment of food was a proxy for unsatisfied sexual drive.

So, should the Narnia books be kept from children because of their lewdness? No, that reaction would be a bit extreme. Hourihan's conclusion: "While children are extremely unlikely to pick up these suggestions at a conscious level the whole scene with the Witch evokes the excitement of forbidden, secret things."[26] That is, children are unfamiliar with the kind of sexual discourse which is going on between Edmund and the White Witch and are likely incapable of reading the scene in that manner. What they do get a sense of is the transgression, if for no other reason than that Edmund breaks two of the cardinal rules taught to children from a young age: (1) Don't talk to strangers; and (2) Never take food from a stranger.

Alston describes how this culinary temptation affects children readers in particular:

> Traditionally, in children's literature and in reality, the family, especially the mother, controls food and implicitly desire. In Lewis' text, Edmund's seduction by and subsequent allegiance to the White Witch parodies the traditional norm as he succumbs to the temptations offered by the sexualized female figure.[27]

Essentially, the White Witch perverts the traditional role of family and entices Edmund to betray his proper loyalties and abandon his position within the familial scheme. Indeed, when his actions come to be revealed to all, he is not treated as a glutton or a prurient lout, but as a traitor: " 'You have a traitor there, Aslan,' said the Witch. Of course everyone present knew she meant Edmund."[28] This, then, is where Lewis's moralizing becomes abruptly, intensely theological, for Aslan responds to the Witch: "His offense was not against you."[29] The implication is that neither was it against his family, that part of it already having been resolved when Aslan told his siblings, "Here is your brother ... there is no need to talk to him about what is past."[30] This response suggests that in betraying his familial loyalties, Edmund actually transgresses something much greater, whether it was the "Deep Magic" which the Witch seeks to enforce, or Aslan, or even the Emperor Beyond the Sea for whom Aslan acts as a proxy.

In this way, Edmund's encounter with the White Witch serves as a moral education not just for himself but also for readers. For the youngest readers, the experience seems to be quite scary, simply conveying that terrible, unintended things can happen when rules are broken. I will leave it to others to discuss whether or not it is appropriate to try and educate children in this way. I will simply confine myself to two observations. First, this is how fairy tales have always worked, from "Little Red Riding Hood" to "Goldilocks and the Three Bears" to "Hansel and Gretel" and of course many others. Second, I've never known any children to be seriously damaged by the fright they might get from a fairy tale. Not only are they perfectly capable of distinguishing fantasy from reality, but the fact that these stories always end happily, or comically or absurdly, goes the rest of the distance in terms of dissolving any fright. I myself always loved fairy tales and still do, which is likely the reason why I am writing this essay; and, ultimately, your own love of fairy tales is also probably why you reading it.

For readers who can be roughly defined as adolescent, like Edmund, experiencing the loss of innocence and the beginnings of moral adulthood, the White Witch stands as a terrible warning about how things can go wrongly when one indulges one's desires without regard to potential consequences. One of the lessons that Edmund learns is that one never grows too old from rules (a lesson which, I am afraid, will be terribly unpopular with many). Rules not only protect us from things we know about, they also protect us from things we do not know about. Edmund reckons that he is old enough, and wise enough, to handle himself in the woods. He thinks that he is good enough a judge of things to be able to keep himself out of harm's way. Why shouldn't he have some Turkish Delight? He wants it, and what's the worst thing that could happen? He's not a kid, after all. He does not know how terrible his new mistress truly is, or that the food he eats is enchanted and will harm him in ways he would have avoided if only he had known. In the end, he is really the same as Lucy, whose own actions led to Mr. Tumnus's betraying her, then crossing sides and being turned to stone by the White Witch. The difference between himself and his younger sister is that he indeed was old enough to know better. It was Edmund who became the traitor and not Lucy because Edmund chose his path whereas Lucy was acted upon. Edmund was tempted; Lucy was duped.

For adult readers, there will likely be plenty of lessons to retain which have already been enumerated. I suppose myself to be like many other readers of the Narnia series. I have experienced the White Witch at every stage of my development. As a child I found her horrid, repugnant, and vicious. I thought at that time that Edmund was a bit maltreated, but I was glad that things worked out well in the end. As an adolescent I felt drawn to the Witch without really knowing why. I also seemed to understand on an instinctual basis why Edmund's actions were both important and reprehensible. I was impacted, viscerally — not theologically — by Aslan's death on his behalf. As an adult, my interaction with the White Witch has changed almost completely. I am delighted and mystified, and I find myself inexorably attracted to her. As a student of literature, I am fascinated by her character and its mystique. I am impressed, technically, with the range of emotions that she is able to elicit.

Yet this is not an essay evaluating the literary merit of the White Witch as a character, but one that endeavors to respond to her as evil, to deal with her morally. What makes her evil is not only that she does evil things, but also that she makes us like her even while she's doing it. My biggest problem with the White Witch is that I, like uncle Andrew, find it all too easy to think of her as a "dem fine woman" when I'm not being immediately confronted with her terribleness.

I am well aware that there are plenty of readers who are more than happy to read with moral abandon. They will be, perhaps, unconcerned with a certain puritanical worrying and wringing of hands over what is, after all, a fictional encounter. Maybe they have a point. Can it be important to take such a stern approach to a fanciful villain from a children's book? My contention is that if a character as deliciously *bad* as the White Witch can entice us to check our ethics at the door, then this is a demonstration of exactly what makes her evil.

NOTES

1. Stanley Fish, *Surprised by Sin: The Reader in Paradise Lost*, 2nd ed. (Cambridge, MA: Harvard University Press, 1998).

2. C.S. Lewis, *An Experiment in Criticism (Canto)* (Cambridge: Cambridge University Press, 1992).

3. Digory will grow up to be the old bachelor professor with whom the Pevensie children go to stay during the London bombings in *The Lion, the Witch and the Wardrobe*.

4. C.S. Lewis, *The Magician's Nephew* (London: HarperCollins, 2001), 34.
5. Ibid.
6. Ibid.
7. Upon meeting the White Witch for the first time, Polly's immediate reaction is to think, "This is a terrible woman" (*The Magician's Nephew*, 39).
8. *The Magician's Nephew*, 38.
9. Ibid., 38–39.
10. Ibid., 45. As it is written, "As a dog returns to its vomit, so a fool repeats his folly" (Proverbs 26:11).
11. *The Magician's Nephew*, 49.
12. Ibid., 54.
13. Ibid., 41–42.
14. Ibid.
15. C.S. Lewis, *The Lion, the Witch and the Wardrobe* (London: HarperCollins, 2001), 118.
16. Ibid., 123.
17. Bonnie Berry, *Beauty Bias: Discrimination and Social Power* (Westport, CT: Praeger, 2007), 66–67.
18. In "Pythian Ode 12," Pindar speaks of "fair-cheeked Medusa." *The Olympian and Pythian Odes of Pindar*, available at http://www.archive.org/stream/olympianpythitra00pindu oft/olympianpythitra00pinduoft_djvu.txt (retrieved 21 June 2010).
19. Ovid, *Metamorphoses*, trans. David Raeburn (New York: Penguin Classics, 2004), 4.769–4.777.
20. Heinrich Institoris, *Malleus Maleficarum*, trans. P.G. Maxwell-Stuart (Manchester: Manchester University Press, 2007), 78.
21. Margaret Hourihan, *Deconstructing the Hero: Literary Theory and Children's Literature* (London: Routledge, 1997), 175.
22. Anne Alston, *The Family in English Children's Literature* (New York: Routledge, 2008), 115.
23. 1 Corinthians 6:12–20.
24. Hourihan, 183.
25. Quoted in Elizabeth Baird Hardy, *Milton, Spenser and the Chronicles of Narnia: Literary Sources for the C.S. Lewis Novels* (Jefferson, NC: McFarland, 2007), 9.
26. Hourihan, 183.
27. Alston, 115.
28. *The Lion, the Witch and the Wardrobe*, 175.
29. Ibid.
30. Ibid., 174.

BIBLIOGRAPHY

Alston, Anne. *The Family in English Children's Literature*. New York: Routledge, 2008.
Berry, Bonnie. *Beauty Bias: Discrimination and Social Power*. Westport, CT: Praeger, 2007.
Breuer, Heidi. *Crafting the Witch*. London: Routledge, 2009.
Fish, Stanley. *Surprised by Sin: The Reader in Paradise Lost*. 2nd ed. Cambridge, MA: Harvard University Press, 1998.
Hardy, Elizabeth Baird. *Milton, Spenser and the Chronicles of Narnia: Literary Sources for the C.S. Lewis Novels*. Jefferson, NC: McFarland, 2007.
Hourihan, Margaret. *Deconstructing the Hero: Literary Theory and Children's Literature*. London: Routledge, 1997.
Institoris, Heinrich. *Malleus Maleficarum*. Trans. P.G. Maxwell-Stuart. Manchester: Manchester University Press, 2007.
Levack, Brian P., ed. *Articles on Witchcraft, Magic and Demonology*. Vol. 10. "Witchcraft, Women and Society." New York: Garland, 1992.
Lewis, C.S. *The Chronicles of Narnia*. London: HarperCollins, 2001.

_____. *An Experiment in Criticism (Canto)*. Cambridge: Cambridge University Press, 1992.

Pindar. *The Olympian and Pythian Odes of Pindar*. Available at http://www.archive.org/stream/olympianpythitra00pinduoft/olympianpythitra00pinduoft_djvu.txt. Retrieved 21 June 2010.

Stephens, Walter. *Demon Lovers*. Chicago: University of Chicago Press, 2002.

8

Paradise Inverted:
Philip Pullman's Use of
High Fantasy and
Epic Poetry to Portray
Evil in *His Dark Materials*

E. Quinn Fox

In April 2003 the BBC set out to establish the best-loved novel in Britain. The results were at once predictable and surprising. Behind expected winners like J.R.R. Tolkien's *Lord of the Rings* trilogy and Jane Austen's *Pride and Prejudice*, in third place — ahead of Harry Potter — was Philip Pullman's *His Dark Materials*! For most North Americans, Pullman's high rank still comes as something of a surprise.[1] The appeal of *His Dark Materials* is unexpected considering that many of its key ideas are based on the 17th-century poetry of John Milton (and the 18th-century work of William Blake).[2] "His dark materials" is a line from Book II of Milton's *Paradise Lost*, a Pullman favorite.[3] Pullman has set out to retell Milton's classic, for teenagers, with a different outcome. Who would have thought such obscure stuff would be at the root of a publishing phenomenon?

Pullman's compelling prose, his highly imaginative storytelling, the breathtaking pace of the action, and a big marketing budget have thrust his narrative work into the spotlight of popular culture, even if he does love old poetry. Of course he is not the first fantasy author to combine classical themes and literature with vivid imagination to transport the reader into what Tolkien called "secondary worlds."[4] In addition to Tolkien and Rowling, C.S. Lewis did this in his *Narnia* and quasi–science fiction books on interplanetary space travel.

Pullman has not just created another world like Tolkien's Middle-earth; he has created multiple worlds, populated by magnificently imaginative characters, uniquely creative technologies and fantastic equipment.[5] Moreover, Pullman juxtaposes the telling of a classical story with uncommon and unanticipated developments. He gives us such time-honored elements as juvenile heroes who undertake a life-threatening and character-defining quest, an epic struggle between good and evil that results in a coming of age and saves the world in the process. But there is more.

Fantasy literature nearly always depends on a conflict with evil, and *His Dark Materials* is no exception. Yet Pullman tells this aspect of his story and develops his plot in unexpected and unorthodox ways: everything even remotely *associated* with Christendom (conventionally considered a force for good) is profoundly and irredeemably evil. Its institutions — principally the Church,[6] its servants, its angelic heavenly host, and *especially* God — are the "bad guys." On the other hand, most that *oppose* God and the Church — including such iconic symbols of evil as rebel angels and witches — are overwhelmingly on the side of good. Pullman is not just retelling John Milton's 17th-century epic poem. He inverts the story, offering an alternative "sequel" that revises the traditional Christian interpretation. As Mrs. Coulter tells Sir Charles Latrom: "Lord Asriel is gathering an army, with the purpose of completing the war that was fought in heaven eons ago."[7]

In spite of his arresting *in*version of the conventional icons of good and evil, Pullman does not subvert a traditional understanding of Western (Judeo-Christian shaped) morality. Violations of traditional codes of behavior (e.g., the Golden Rule and Ten Commandments)[8] remain immoral. Murder, kidnapping, stealing, lying and selfish abuse of power are wrong, even when they are the actions of an attractive character. Honesty, sacrifice, and courage, are virtuous. As we will explore in detail below, Lyra is a liar who learns to tell the truth, Will is a murderer who comes to hate violence, Lord Asriel is a ruthless Machiavellian who eventually sacrifices his ambition to enable his illegitimate daughter to fulfill her destiny, and Mrs. Coulter is a viperous *femme fatale* who learns to love. Perhaps Mary Malone is the only thoroughly virtuous central character — and she plays the role of the Tempter! And witches are viewed completely differently than in traditional fantasy stories, such as Narnia's evil White Witch under whose spell it is "always winter but never Christmas."[9] These various juxtapositions pose a complex question about how evil is understood by Pullman in *His Dark Materials* and ultimately catapult his work well beyond the province of children's or young adult fantasy literature. We will also find that this dynamic complicates his overall narrative development in very significant ways.

Overview

His Dark Materials is a trilogy. Each book's title names a particularly creative tool that is used by the protagonist introduced in that book. In *The Golden Compass*, young Lyra Belacqua is given an alethiometer. This "truth-meter" helps her to discern what is good and evil because (unlike Lyra) it never lies, and it reflects classical morality in its discernment. This "golden compass" guides her quest to rescue her best friend, Roger, and other boys and girls who have been kidnapped and taken to the North for horrendous experiments by the "Gobblers." All of this takes place in "a universe like ours, but different in many ways."[10]

In *The Subtle Knife*, Will Parry — who lives in our world and is roughly the same age as Lyra — encounters her in a third universe. There Will comes upon a uniquely powerful knife, created by a guild of alchemists 300 years ago. One side of this double-edged blade can slice through absolutely anything, like a proverbial hot knife through butter; the other edge, in the hands of a proper knife-bearer, can cut the fabric of the universe, opening entryways into other worlds. Use of this special tool, we learn, has ramifications that are not immediately apparent. Among these is its potential as a weapon that can tip the balance of power, attaining victory and salvation in an imminent cosmic conflict.[11]

In *The Amber Spyglass*, Dr. Mary Malone, a former nun turned Oxford physicist from Will's (our) world, invents a monocular device that enables her to detect the flow of elementary particles called Dust. This longest of the three volumes, more or less successfully, brings the trilogy's various themes, ideas and plots to their spectacular conclusion. Will and Lyra descend to the Underworld to release the dead from their prison. Mary Malone comprehends the severity of Dust's disappearance. Lord Asriel prepares to do battle with The Authority and his forces. The Church's Consistorial Court of Discipline launches a deadly comprehensive strategy to prevent Lyra from becoming the new Eve. Mary (as Satan-type) tells her story of sensual awakening, which in turn "tempts" Will and Lyra to explore their adolescent sexuality in the context of the love they have developed for each other.

Dramatis Personae, Themes and Ideas

Lyra and Will

Readers of *The Golden Compass* immediately meet the story's female protagonist, Lyra Belacqua, an orphaned aristocrat on the cusp of early adolescence. Central to Lyra's character, and to the plot of the trilogy, is the power of stories — including her sheer joy in telling and hearing them (even if they are not completely true). As the story develops, a growing awareness of her sexuality drives the heart of the story line as we learn of the prophecy that foretells her destiny to be the Second Eve. Will Parry, the epitome of responsible behavior, is introduced in *The Subtle Knife*. He is a serious boy, an only child looking after his mentally disturbed single mother. He embodies his name: determined and resourceful — a consistent moral voice who insists on making his own decisions. He is a "good boy," modeling manners and morals, and strives for honesty and uprightness even when no one is looking.[12] Will is intense — a fierce opponent and skilled combatant against malevolence of any sort, particularly when it threatens those whom he loves (his mother, and increasingly Lyra). Although he has killed, he abhors violence. He is compassionate and perceptive. During the course of their quest, these two characters fall in love, positioning Will as Adam to Lyra's Eve.

Lord Asriel

This swash-buckling archetype of the classic Byronic hero-figure is introduced as Lyra's paternal uncle. "Lord Asriel was a tall man with powerful shoulders, a fierce dark face, and eyes that seemed to flash and glitter with savage laughter. It was a face to be dominated by, or to fight: never a face to patronize or pity."[13] He evokes a panoply of strong emotions from everyone he encounters. A man of ruthless ambition and extraordinary vision, his goals reach beyond the comprehension of all but a few: "He dares to do what men and women don't even dare to think ... he's torn open the sky, he's opened the way to another world. Who else has ever done that? Who else could think of it? ... he's not like other men."[14] We learn Asriel is Lyra's father through an adulterous love affair with Marisa Coulter. He is focused on the heretical phenomenon called "Dust" and wants to "build a bridge between this world and the world beyond."[15] This puts him in conflict with the Church, which he disdains. His full-blown Promethean vision includes overthrowing the Authority (God), defeating death, ending the Church's centuries-long tyranny, and creating a purely democratic "Republic of Heaven." He is the partial embodiment of Milton's Satan.

Mrs. Coulter

The epitome of the *femme fatale*, she can perhaps best be characterized as a dangerous woman. "She was beautiful and young. Her sleek black hair framed her cheeks, and her dæmon was a golden monkey.... Mrs. Coulter had such an air of glamour that Lyra was entranced."[16] Dangerously pretty, dangerously manipulative, dangerously seductive and dangerously powerful in a man's world, Marisa Coulter is the most enigmatic and unpredictable character in the trilogy. Clearly evil in the first two books, she has a utilitarian alliance with the Church, heading a special ecclesiastical order that conducts terrible experiments on children. Her feminine wiles devastate men and children ... even angels. Beneath the seductive surface of her beauty and charisma she is callous and brutal. Torture is second nature to her. Even evil Specters respect her! If ever a character was beyond redemption, it is Mrs. Coulter. Yet as the narrative evolves, maternal instincts emerge; feelings for her daughter Lyra lead her to abandon her alliance with the Church and ally herself to Asriel's cause.

Dæmons

One of the most ingenious narrative devices ever imagined, dæmons are uniquely personal physical, symbiotic animal manifestations of a person's alter ego; they are something like a person's "soul." While dæmons are not physically attached, they are connected in every other conceivable way: psychologically, intellectually, morally and spiritually. Prior to adolescence, a dæmon's shape remains dynamic. At puberty dæmons stop shape-shifting and "settle" into their permanent form (this represents how a maturing adult mind moves away from the more easily distracted attention span of the child).

Dust

Dust (always capitalized) is Pullman's other terrifically creative concept. It is the "dark material" in the title of the trilogy, and is at the heart of the plot. Dust is *not* attracted to people *until* adolescence, when dæmons settle. In ignorance the Church sees Dust as the physical evidence for original sin.[17] Mrs. Coulter tells Lyra: "Dust is something bad, something wrong, something evil and wicked. Grownups and their dæmons are infected with Dust so deeply that it's too late for them."[18] Because it sees Dust as evil the Church gives Mrs. Coulter *carte blanche* to establish the General Oblation Board (Gobblers), which operates the Experimental Station at Bolvangar. There, kidnapped children from the margins of society are subjected to "intercision,"[19] which severs the metaphysical connection between human and dæmon, yielding a soulless zombie. Since Dust is not attracted to "severed" children, the Church reasons, intercision must neutralize the fall and original sin. Although the Church is afraid of Dust, their solution(s) are mistaken (not to mention lethal). The central conflict of *His Dark Materials* is not the presence of Dust, but its disappearance.

When Lyra and Will meet Dr. Mary Malone, an unorthodox Oxford University physicist researching "shadow particles," she is amazed at Lyra's relationship to this "dark material," or as Lyra calls it, Dust. These "shadows" lead Mary into the world of the Mulefa through an opening created by the subtle knife. There she learns that Dust, the byproduct of conscious activity, has caused the delicate ecology of human consciousness to evolve. But for some 300 years it has been disappearing. Every time the subtle knife cuts windows between the worlds, Dust can vanish into the emptiness. Cuts from the knife have another unintended consequence, foreshadowed by Iorek Byrnison's visceral misgivings concerning the blade: "With it you can do strange things. What you don't know is what the knife does on its own. Your intentions may be good. *The knife has intentions, too*" (emphasis added).[20]

With each cut, part of the void between the universes "leaks out" in the form of a Specter (always capitalized, like Dust). These "children of the abyss" feed unchecked on Dust and people's dæmons, threatening to zombify the worlds. Mary discovers that Dust is hemorrhaging into oblivion through two enormous holes, one made by Asriel, the other blasted by a powerful bomb the Magisterium detonated in their failed attempt to assassinate Lyra. This creates the metaphysical equivalent of an environmental catastrophe. Mary is stymied as to how to solve the problem. Can anything be done to save the world(s)? In Mary's story we find the answer.

True Stories and Redemption[21]

On their journey to the land of the dead to find Roger, Lyra learns the liberating power of truth-telling. Harpies, there to torment the residents of the land of the dead, look for the worst in every ghost. In a showdown with the harpy leader, Lyra has barely embarked on a monstrous fiction when the harpy starts screaming: "Liar! Liar! Liar!" Soon *liar* sounds like *Lyra*. Harpies learn they have an appetite for truth and agree to free a person's ghost from the land of the dead in exchange for true stories. Truth sets these captives free and undoes the Authority's cruel punishment, realizing Asriel's pledge to "destroy death."[22]

Mary's story leads Will and Lyra to explore sexually their growing love for each other. Her feelings for Will combined with her budding adolescent sexuality culminate in a tender scene in a pristine, second "Garden of Eden," where Lyra gives Will the fruit provided by Mary.[23] Lyra thus fulfills her destiny as the new Eve; the propitious event staunches the flood of Dust and saves the world. The retold "fall" of *Paradise Lost* is celebrated this time, and the knowledge gained is virtuous.

At the plot's climax there is considerable sacrifice. Asriel and Coulter forfeit their lives and his dream of setting up a Republic of Heaven, in order to bring down heaven's regent Metatron, making it possible for Lyra to fulfill her destiny to re-enact Eden. As the story ends, Will and Lyra realize that to control Dust loss and Specter creation they must live in separate worlds. They sacrifice their newfound love for each other, agreeing to seal the openings in the worlds — meaning that they will never see each other again.

Intertextuality: "Stealing" from Milton, Blake, Tolkien and Lewis

Pullman's trilogy richly draws upon and plays off of stories written by others.[24] He acknowledges: "I have stolen ideas from every book I have ever read. My principle in researching for a novel is 'Read like a butterfly, write like a bee.'"[25] Most important for *His Dark Materials* is *Paradise Lost*, Milton's epic retelling of the landmark ancient biblical poem (Genesis 1–3)[26] of how Adam and Eve succumbed to the serpent's temptation. *Paradise Lost* opens in hell, where fallen Lucifer and his rebel angels regroup following their failed rebellion. Unable to match the power of Almighty God, they resolve to sabotage Paradise (Genesis 1–2). Satan slithers into Eden (Book IX) and corrupts Eve and Adam (Genesis 3).[27]

There are three "Miltonic" streams to consider. The primary tributary is the work of William Blake. Next is C.S. Lewis, a leading 20th-century interpreter of Milton. Finally, Tolkien's *Lord of the Rings*, though not a direct interpretation of Milton *per se*, represents the Christian worldview Milton presupposed; Pullman uses its quest trilogy genre, even as he modifies it.

Blake thought Milton's characterization of Satan was (unwittingly) more sympathetic than his depiction of God, asserting that Milton was "of the devil's party without knowing it."[28] Pullman is fond of playing off of Blake's line to state his own position: "I am of the Devil's party, and I know it."[29] By inverting the traditional telling of the Genesis story, giving Satan victory in his rebellion against God, and having Eve's fall result in the world's salvation, Pullman aligns himself with Blake's romantic reading. This challenges Lewis's classically Christian interpretation of *Paradise Lost*.[30] The confrontation becomes even more apparent when one considers that, like Lewis's first Narnian chronicle, *The Golden Compass* also begins with an overly curious girl hiding in a wardrobe that eventually leads her to discover another world. One of Pullman's particular dislikes in Lewis's *Narnia* series is Susan's exclusion from "heaven" in *The Last Battle*: "Susan, like Cinderella, is undergoing a transition from one phase of her life to another. Lewis didn't approve of that.

He didn't like women in general, or sexuality at all, at least at the stage of his life when he wrote the Narnia books. He was frightened and appalled at the notion of wanting to grow up."[31]

In his quasi–science fiction novel *Perelandra*,[32] Lewis also retells *Paradise Lost* with an alternative outcome to Milton's. But in *Perelandra*, "Eve" successfully resists the Tempter. In *His Dark Materials* Pullman intentionally contrasts Lewis's alleged "distaste for adolescent sexuality"[33]; his heroine embraces her sexuality, resulting in the world's salvation, rather than (with Milton and Lewis) its sin and condemnation. It is worth noting that *Paradise Lost* and *His Dark Materials* reflect a later tradition in which "Eve's" temptation involves sexuality; in Genesis (and *Perelandra*) the temptation concerns a mundane act of obedience.

Pullman has thus built on the narrative traditions of Genesis and Virgil to create a "quest trilogy" in the genre of "high fantasy" literature[34] resulting in a new kind of "secular humanist fantasy."[35] To put an even sharper point on it, in print and on screen, Pullman has taken aim at the work, worldview and even the moral integrity of Lewis (and to a lesser extent Tolkien), unequivocally rejecting their Christian worldview.[36]

Good and Evil Inverted in His Dark Materials

In traditional fantasy literature evil is easy to identify. There is nothing subtle about Darth Vader or Voldemort, a serpent or a dragon. Fantasy is typically driven by the protagonist's attempt to defeat the villain(s): the "good guys" oppose evil. In *The Lion, the Witch and the Wardrobe* the Lion Aslan comes to "put all to rights." He redeems Edmund's life, and kills the Witch. In *The Hobbit* Bilbo Baggins recaptures the Lonely Mountain gold from the evil dragon Smaug. In these stories good characters perform heroic, courageous, and virtuous deeds; evil characters perpetrate wicked, malevolent actions. In *Paradise Lost* we see a similar dynamic. God's vastly superior forces victoriously cast Satan and his followers out of heaven, even as Satan persists in rebellion.

In *The Lord of the Rings* the stereotypical dragon and his hoard, front and center in *The Hobbit*, are missing in action. They are superseded by a more subtle, and sinister, evil: the One Ring. Initially little more than a one-dimensional invisibility charm, the Ring eventually manifests the deceitful intention of its maker Sauron. It overwhelms whoever wears it: hobbit or human, elf or wizard. The end of Frodo's quest[37] is surely a disappointment to those who prize free will and human potential. He does not heroically hurl the Ring into the primeval fire in triumph over the powers of darkness. In fact, his own resources fail him. In the end the Ring destroys itself, fortuitously (a theological word for which is *providentially*). As Ralph Wood insightfully observes, had the story ended in a triumphal way, it "would have provided us with a traditional hero whom we could have exalted and acclaimed as one of our own. It would have also assured us that evil can be defeated by dint of human and hobbitic effort. Tolkien refuses such illusions."[38]

In retelling *Paradise Lost*, on the one hand Pullman reverses the roles. The traditional protagonists (God and his party) are evil while the antagonists (Satan and his tribe) are heroic. Yet he makes this alteration without significantly changing a conventional (Western, Judeo-Christian) understanding of moral order. So deceit (Satan's activity) is not suddenly good. Rather, it is "God" who behaves badly (e.g., deceitfully); indeed the deceit begins with the Authority falsely claiming to be the Creator.[39] To say it in more technical language, in *His Dark Materials* Philip Pullman inverts traditional Western metaphysics without altering traditional Western ethics. This change is captured in Mary Malone's reply to Will:

> "When you stopped believing in God [Will asked Mary], "did you stop believing in good and evil?" "No [said Mary]. But I stopped believing there was a power of good and a power of evil that were outside us. And I came to believe that good and evil are names for what people do, not for what they are. All we can say is that this is a good deed, because it helps someone, or that's an evil one, because it hurts them. People are too complicated to have simple labels."[40]

A critical question arises in any good vs. evil story: Where does evil come from? In *Paradise Lost*, Satan chooses to revolt; in Middle-earth Melkor rebels.[41] Milton, Lewis and Tolkien, as orthodox Christians, held a classic Augustinian view of evil,[42] seeing it as a perversion of something originally good by nature. Tolkien refers to evil as "shadow." As a cast shadow means light's absence, so evil is the absence or privation of something good.

To drive home the point that "people are too complicated to have simple labels," Pullman portrays his characters with considerable moral ambiguity. Lyra lies; Will kills. Lord Asriel (Lyra's father) appears to be a full-on hero. Then he turns Machiavellian, sacrificing her best friend Roger, and proves to be a poor father. Furthermore, he jeopardizes both the physical and metaphysical environments of the cosmos! But he remains a protagonist because he opposes the story's evil forces, embodied in the Church. Mrs. Coulter is a power-hungry seducer with maternal instincts. Gypsies ("gyptians" in the book), stereotypical thieves and swindlers, rescue Lyra and the children from the Gobblers. These archetypal deceivers tell Lyra the truth about her family of origin, and explain that *they* cared for her in her illegitimate infancy. Although both Lyra's parents betray her, the gyptians nurture, care for and rescue her. Pullman's witches are neither evil nor ugly; they are ageless, sensual and virtuous. Tempter Mary is a former nun. God is a fraudulent imposter, and the Church is more terrible than the worst nightmare of any French *philosophe*. Nearly all of our presuppositions about what constitutes good and evil characters in fantasy literature are capsized by Pullman's story, even as a traditional understanding of good and evil remains on an even keel. Burton Hatlen captures what Pullman is up to: "Every time we imagine that we've sorted out the good guys and the bad guys, Pullman pulls the rug out from under us."[43]

The Church's actions become increasingly suspect as the narrative unfolds. It is the font for most of the trilogy's evil characters and images: Father MacPhail orders Father Gomez to assassinate Lyra. The vulgar Russian priest, Semyon Borisovitch, spouts apocalyptic bigotry while touching Will inappropriately and forcing him to drink vodka. The Consistorial Court is the ultimate in utilitarian pragmatism, eager to compromise with Mrs. Coulter — even witches. Their ends always justify the means, even murder. Bolvangar, eerily reminiscent of Nazi death camps, is the most evil place in *His Dark Materials*. By the time Pullman is finished describing these revolting people, we despise them and their Church.[44]

Unlike William Blake who despised the church but did not abandon commitment to (or at least reverence for) God, for Pullman the Church is a simple reflection of its fraudulent deity. This leads to perhaps the greatest surprise in the book: God's death. Dying gods are a common enough theme in mythology and theology: Hercules, Orpheus and Balder are murdered; Christ is crucified. But no god dies of old age. Here Pullman follows Nietzsche. Near the end of *The Amber Spyglass*, Will comes upon a senile and decrepit angel in a crystal sedan chair, deserted by his porters in the face of an onslaught from cliff-ghasts. Will's rescue inadvertently exposes the fragile Authority to blustery wind, and euthanizes him. This scene graphically portrays secular modernism's verdict on God. Once the indisputable and unquestioned center of all reality, God has increasingly failed to account for the exigencies of modern life. This view is expressed by Mrs. Coulter, in a soliloquy before Father MacPhail in Geneva:

> "Well, where is God ... if he's alive? And why doesn't he speak anymore? At the beginning of the world, God walked in the Garden and spoke with Adam and Eve. Then he began to withdraw, and he forbade Moses to look at his face. Later, in the time of Daniel, he was aged — he was the Ancient of Days. Where is he now? Is he still alive, at some inconceivable age, decrepit and demented, unable to think or act or speak and unable to die, a rotten hulk? And if that is his condition, wouldn't it be the most merciful thing, the truest proof of our love for God, to seek him out and give him the gift of death?"[45]

Will's and Lyra's journey into the land of the dead offers empirical proof that there is no such thing as heaven, further evidence of God's non-existence. Indeed, the afterlife is a never-ending prison sentence — a morbid hoax perpetrated by the cruel Authority. Two "fallen angels" clarify precisely how the Church, its servants and its God can be thoroughly and completely evil.

Lyra is not the only liar! The Authority committed primordial perjury, misleading the angelic host, deceitfully subjecting them to his authority and delighting in the manipulation of human creatures, well, just for the hell of it; this includes their torment by harpies in the land of the dead when they die. The Authority is a fraud and, at least by the defining standards of the Bible and Christian theology, he is no God at all. This totalitarian manipulation and deceit actually describe Milton's fallen angel Lucifer. Here we have the most significant inversion imaginable. Not only are God and the Church the primary source of evil and falsehood, God behaves like, and thus according to Pullman's criteria is, Satan.

While we have focused on the complex nature of good and evil in Pullman's trilogy, there are some whose actions are not based on choice. The terrifying Specters of Indifference constitute the most virulent evil in *His Dark Materials*. They consume Dust and dæmons, threatening the ecology of consciousness. And there is no defense against them. Specters are the devastating consequence of ignorant choices involving the subtle knife. Whether or not it can be said that it was a "good idea" to create the blade in the first place, using it to cut holes between the worlds, in retrospect, is bad because it allows Dust to leak and produces Specters. The loss of Dust and the presence of Specters are manifestations of a type of "original sin" committed by knife use; it must be redeemed in order to save the world(s). How the trilogy resolves this plot conflict constitutes a serious flaw in Pullman's story.

Critical Analysis

Two distinct conflicts drive the plot of *His Dark Materials*: the Satan narrative and the Dust narrative. The Authority, like Satan or Sauron, engages in a deceitful power play in order to become God. Heroic Asriel sets out to destroy the Authority, but finds his deputy Metatron a more fitting opponent. With the aid of Marisa Coulter, Asriel defeats him, even as the fierce combat requires them to sacrifice their lives.[46] Will and Lyra complete the resolution of this conflict when they despoil the land of the dead ("death dies") and they become the hope for realizing Asriel's Republic of Heaven.

The Dust conflict turns the traditional Christian sin and salvation typology on its head. The impact of 300 years of human carelessness (knife cuts), compounded by Asriel's opening and the Magisterium's bomb, has jeopardized consciousness. Resolution comes when the new Eve becomes savior, and her fall the new salvation event. Connected to the loss of Dust are Specters. Produced every time a cut is made by the subtle knife (and far more from Asriel's hole and the abyss created by the blast), Specters grow stronger as they consume more dæmons and Dust. Worse, there is (for most of the story at least) no defense against them (every other entity appears at least to have a lifespan). Is this conflict then irresolvable?

There are aspects of the resolution of these two conflicts that are not clear, raising significant questions. First, how is Lyra's and Will's act of carnal knowing salvific? What causal transaction reverses Dust's departure into the void? We are only told that this is the case. Neither are reasons given for Lyra's role as prophesied elect savior of the worlds. These find coherence only in the context of *Paradise Lost*: if "Eve I" caused the race to fall, an inversion means "Eve II" brings salvation. Fantasy fiction often requires the willing suspension of disbelief.

Second, and of much greater consequence, is the issue of Specters — the most powerful, fearsome malevolent force in the trilogy. Why is it that every time the subtle knife opens a window to a new universe, "a little bit of the abyss ... floats out and enters the world,"[47] creating a Specter? How can "nothingness" materialize into something? In one sense this would be a vivid way to depict an Augustinian view of evil — a literal incarnation of what Tolkien described as the shadow side of reality, the unintended consequence of physically violating the universe(s). Unlike Augustine, however, Pullman's evolutionary metaphysics cannot account for the sudden production of beings with the capacity to consume dæmons and the sentience to make distinctions. Explaining evil solely by human actions inadequately accounts for Specters.

In the final pages of the trilogy the angel Xaphania assures Will that once 300 years of left-open windows between the worlds have been closed by the angels, they will also "take care of the Specters." Really? Where were these angels when Specters were devouring dæmons and creating entire populations of "Specter orphans?" Given all the creative complexity with which Pullman portrays his characters, such a facile *deus ex machina* solution to the most potent evil in the book is disappointing to say the least. It is, in fact, unbelievable. Pullman has painted himself into a metaphysical corner, having created an evil for which his narrative cannot account. In spite of the fact that Mary (Pullman) denies "a power of evil ... outside us," Specters are precisely that! Pullman has given us a world with supernatural evil, but no supernatural good to combat it. This is a significant narrative deficiency.

After this simplistic and abrupt dispatch of the story's most relentless malevolence, the only evil that remains is the Church. Within Pullman's story the Church is the main antagonist, and it is no secret that it is the author's favorite target. Pullman's treatment of church, religion and God now needs to be addressed because it is clear that a didactic hostility has overtaken his storytelling and, while not ruining it, has compromised its brilliance.

Pullman's Mis-telling of the Christian Story

As an author, Philip Pullman claims not to want to preach or even teach, yet he has an overt agenda at work. Given his well-known personal antipathies, it is no surprise to find Christianity the brunt of his narrative inversion. But in pursuing his agenda he mis-tells the church's story, creating a monochrome caricature. In *His Dark Materials* readers encounter neither congregations nor sanctuaries; no one worships, hears sermons or sings hymns (not even bad ones!). The hungry are not fed nor the poor clothed. There is only manipulative political hierarchy; this church is devoid of congregants and life together. We encounter only one parish minister, and apparently all he does is smoke, eat, and drink to excess. Not a single Church character captures our imagination longer than is necessary simply to turn our stomachs. Pullman thinks Satan is the most interesting character in *Paradise Lost*. Asriel and Mrs. Coulter are Pullman's most compelling characters because we don't know until the end (if then!) whether they are good or evil. Yet not one of Pullman's Church characters is afforded the least nuance. The personalities, convictions and actions of the various protagonists reflect the moral ambiguity present in real life. Virtually every single character in the trilogy has a chance at redemption, and in most cases realizes it — even the harpies! But not the Church. There is not so much as a pang of conscience on the part of a single character for a single action. Church characters consistently choose evil. Indeed, they are incapable of good actions, and thus beyond redemption.

Pullman has taken some of the most extreme, egregious faults of the Christian church and personified them. Some of his criticism is misapplied to actual Christian practice (e.g., genital mutilation and castration).[48] He is subversive in places, blending fact and fiction so that his allegations of the Magisterium are similar to, if not identical with, non-fictional historical realities.[49] The criticisms expressed by the witch Ruta Skadi overlap considerably, especially in tone, with comments Pullman has made in various interviews and articles: "I thought of the Bolvangar children, and the other terrible mutilations I have seen done in our own south-lands ... of many more hideous cruelties dealt out in the Authority's name — of how they capture witches, in some worlds, and burn them alive ... cruelties and horrors all committed in the name of the Authority...."[50]

Of course some of his criticism is true, and there is no defense for such things as the horrendous violence of the witch craze in early modern Europe. Not mentioned specifically are the Crusades and other religious wars, particularly at the time of the Reformation. Pullman has clarified his criticism of "organized religion:

> churches and priesthoods have set themselves up to rule people's lives in the name of some invisible god ... and done terrible damage.... They have burned, hanged, tortured, maimed, robbed, violated, and enslaved millions of their fellow-creatures ... with the happy conviction that they were doing the will of God, and they would go to Heaven for it. That is the religion I hate, and I'm happy to be known as its enemy.[51]

What can a Christian say to such withering criticism? I hate that religion too! But I can't identify a continuous (Christian) ecclesial structure that has ever existed to hold accountable for all these accusations. Insofar as it does exist, I'm with Philip Pullman. I would, however, like to see some warrant for his glib assertions.

There is much more to be said. The Christian church over a period of some 1700 years transformed the violent barbarian ruins of the post–Classical world into a Renaissance culture that embodied civilized life, invented modern science, and prepared the soil for the very Enlightenment critique that Pullman and many others are wont to level. Moreover, the martial means of feudal society were no invention of the church. It is a grim reality that the church conformed to societal norms at times, and even on occasion excelled at them. But from the very beginning of what became civilized Western Europe there were consistent reform movements to call the church away from power politics, a game it was never very good at and lost in the end amidst the rise of nation states. Indeed the church led the way in trying to control violence (e.g., the medieval Peace and Truce of God movements) and eventually developed the pacifist traditions. It is also important to remember the many social reform movements rooted in Christian values as expressed by structures of the church, such as Wilberforce's abolition of the slave trade.

Furthermore, whatever the evil for which Christianity and the church are responsible in the history of the world, there is plenty of secular violence to account for as well.[52] The misguided reformers combined could not begin to have created such wholesale slaughter. This is to say nothing of the repressive, atheistic totalitarian regimes under which millions more have been "made to live in constant fear of violating the oppressive system and thus bringing its terror upon them."[53] Pullman's anti–Christian chauvinism notwithstanding, the historical reality of the church is one of significant complexity — there is both good and evil and, like the wheat and tares of the parable,[54] it is impossible to separate them.

Critique

Of all the ways to portray the church, the simplistic monochrome is both uncreative and a willful ignorance of historical reality. Indeed, Pullman's pre-occupying antipathy for Christianity has distracted him from engaging evil in its systemic, "demonic" and atheistic (in addition to its ecclesial) expressions. He missed an important opportunity to grapple with the complex aspects of evil that Specters might represent, the way Tolkien has in *Lord of the Rings*.[55]

Pullman has also re-told much of the Christian gospel story even as he has mis-told it. His trilogy ends sounding strong soteriological notes of redemption. Although Lyra's fall mitigates the Dust disaster, the completion of this salvific act is to close up all the openings between the various worlds, and not to create new ones. Because a dæmon cannot survive for long in a world other than its own, Lyra and Will make the most painful decision imaginable: they separate, never to be together again. The world's salvation is made complete by Will and Lyra sacrificing their love. We come to care so much for these two in the course of the trilogy. Their love is described in such tender, almost mystical language.[56] Their sacrifice is at once stunning and consequential. And so the world of *His Dark Materials* is saved through the selfless act of personal sacrifice, rooted in love for the other. Even more paradoxically, Lord Asriel, the partial manifestation of the Blakean Satan figure, sacrifices his life and vision so Lyra can fulfill her destiny to save the worlds. The theme of sacrificial love (*agape*) has Isaiah's suffering servant (a type for Israel) and the crucified Lord of the Christian tradition written all over it. One would expect Pullman's evolutionary metaphysics to yield a very different, much less redemptive, survival-of-the-fittest story instead. There is an irony here. In spite of all of his harsh criticism and dismissal of Christian faith, the underlying beliefs, attitudes and values of *His Dark Materials* are (Pullman's narrative *content* notwithstanding) rather Christian. He may have retold *Paradise Lost* by inverting the roles, but he (obviously) has not inverted the story's overall narrative structure. This, ironically, is the Christian meta-narrative, like it or not.

Throughout the story, readers are confronted by decisions and choices: Is Asriel a "bad guy" because he sacrifices Roger, or is he good because he defeats the villain Metatron? Is Mrs. Coulter evil for her role in Bolvangar? What about her torture of the poor witch? The children in Cittàgazze, orphaned by Specters — are they victims or villains? It is up to the individual reader to decide, and Pullman is committed to allowing such choices, just as his protagonists must choose, proving by their actions whether they are good or evil. But there is no such choice where the Authority, Metatron, President

MacPhail, Father Gomez and Semyon Borisovitch are concerned. They have no choices to make; nor do we the readers. The author(ity) has made up our minds for us! In terms of narrative, this may be the worst evil of all. This is surely the ultimate irony: that the behavior of the most bullying, arbitrary and deceitful (read evil) characters in the book — the Authority and his celestial and terrestrial servants — is exhibited by Philip Pullman in his portrayal of evil in *His Dark Materials*.

NOTES

1. "Top 21," available at www.bbc.co.uk/arts/bigread/vote/ (retrieved 21 June 2010). The result may be a bit misleading, since voters only had the option of Pullman's and Tolkien's trilogies, while J.K. Rowling's Harry Potter books, not yet complete in their now-7 volume set, were voted on individually (*Harry Potter and the Goblet of Fire* came in fifth place, and was arguably the most well-written of the series at the time of the poll). Sales figures for Tolkien, Pullman and Rowling regularly reported the 2 trilogies combined, and the Harry Potter books as discrete titles. Regardless, Pullman's rank is impressive, even if the statistics are somewhat dated. A summary of the many awards from the publishing guild recognizing Pullman's remarkable work can be found in Claire Squires, *Philip Pullman, Master Storyteller: A Guide to the Worlds of* His Dark Materials (New York: Continuum, 2006), 4ff.

2. Philip Pullman, "Acknowledgments," *The Amber Spyglass* (New York: Alfred A. Knopf, 2000), 521. Among Blake's poems, most important for further insight into *His Dark Materials* are an epic poem with Milton as hero (*Milton: A Poem*), which inverts the Calvinist doctrine of election, and *Marriage of Heaven and Hell*, which views hell as a place of virtuous energy. Both can be found in William Blake, *The Complete Poetry and Prose of William Blake*, ed. David V. Erdman (New York: Anchor, 1995).

3. Pullman's admiration and enjoyment of Milton is articulated in the introductions (of the book and each chapter of the poem) he wrote for a new edition of the Oxford World Classics edition of John Milton, *Paradise Lost* (Oxford: Oxford University Press, 2005).

4. J.R.R. Tolkien, "On Fairy Stories," in *Essays Presented to Charles Williams*, ed. C.S. Lewis (Grand Rapids: Eerdmans, 1947).

5. Pullman's vast imagination has spawned dozens of reference-based websites and at least one encyclopedic guide for the thousands of new "facts" that he has invented in his story. The most comprehensive reference of which I'm aware is Laurie Frost, *The Definitive Guide to Philip Pullman's* His Dark Materials (London: Scholastic, 2008).

6. The American edition of *His Dark Materials* capitalizes Church (church in the UK editions), and I have sought to be consistent with this practice. When I use the word *Church* it is to specify the institution in Lyra's world, or in the books more broadly. When church is spelled in lower case, I am differentiating the broader Christian theological concept of Christians worldwide in their manifold universal non-fiction communal expression.

7. Philip Pullman, *The Subtle Knife* (New York: Alfred A. Knopf, 1997), 198.

8. See Luke 6:31 and Matthew 7:12. For the Ten Commandments see Exodus 20 and Deuteronomy 5.

9. C.S. Lewis, *The Lion, the Witch and the Wardrobe* (London: Macmillan, 1950), 14.

10. From the second prefatory epigraph, Philip Pullman, *The Golden Compass* (New York: Alfred A. Knopf, 2002).

11. There are similarities and differences between the subtle knife and Tolkien's One Ring that are beyond the scope of this essay to explore. Similarities include the object's (initially unknown) power for evil, the fact that it chooses a "bearer," and the fact that in spite of its potential for good it must finally be destroyed. The main difference is that the One Ring was created from deceit, while the subtle knife was created out of a desire to learn about "the deepest

nature of things ... the bonds that held the smallest particles of matter together" (*The Subtle Knife*, 187).

12. In Cittàgazze he tells Lyra literally to clean up her act before going to a clothing store because "in my world people are clean" (*The Subtle Knife*, 62). Although the store is abandoned, Will insists upon leaving money because it is the "right thing" to pay for merchandise, in spite of the fact that Lyra is certain they could take anything they wanted from the deserted city without paying for it. We see that Lyra has learned this lesson when she justifies Will's payment for some foodstuff they take, articulating her acquired sense of morality: "you should always pay for what you take" (*The Amber Spyglass*, 244).

13. *The Golden Compass*, 13.

14. *The Subtle Knife*, 47.

15. *The Golden Compass*, 189.

16. Ibid., 65ff.

17. Ibid., 370ff. Asriel informs Lyra that the name "Dust" comes from the Bible, pointing to Genesis 3:19, where God says to Adam: "from dust you have come, to dust you shall return."

18. *The Golden Compass*, 283.

19. The term "intercision" appears to be an allusion to the Judeo-Christian practice of circumcision, the surgical removal of the male foreskin (usually in the hours following birth). At other points the narrative suggests that intercision is similar to genital mutilation (*The Subtle Knife*, 50) and castration (*The Golden Compass*, 374).

20. *The Amber Spyglass*, 180ff.

21. John 8:32 (KJV), "And ye shall know the truth and the truth shall make you free," provides the epigraph to Chapter Twenty-three of *The Amber Spyglass*.

22. *The Golden Compass*, 377. This release of the dead is a retelling of the medieval tradition's "harrowing of hell," which suggests that during the three days between his crucifixion and resurrection Jesus went to preach to the dead and raise the faithful. This is seen in Christian tradition as a victory over Satan.

23. *The Amber Spyglass*, 465ff.

24. Claire Squires discusses Pullman's appropriation of others' work. See Squires, 115–137.

25. Philip Pullman, "Acknowledgements," *The Amber Spyglass*, 521.

26. It is interesting to realize that Genesis 1–3, itself Hebrew poetry, was written in intertextual dialogue with ancient Babylonian creation mythology — the primordial battle between Tiamat and Marduk as told in the *Enuma elish* (e.g., in Genesis 1:2 — "darkness covered the face of the deep"— the Hebrew word for "deep" is *tehom*, a Semitic cognate of *tiamat*). Milton knew Hebrew, Greek and Latin, along with four modern languages. A consideration of the whether he appreciated the implications of the Hebrew poetic genre for his appropriation of the Genesis material in *Paradise Lost* is beyond the scope of this project.

27. There is no direct mention of Satan in the Genesis 3 temptation narrative, only of a serpent, which later tradition understood to be the devil.

28. Philip Pullman, "Introduction," in Milton, *Paradise Lost*, 8.

29. This quote is frequently cited by Pullman's critics. See, for example, Alan Jacobs, "The Devil's Party: Philip Pullman's Bestselling Fantasy Series Retells the Story of Creation — With Satan as the Hero," *The Weekly Standard*, 23 October 2000, available at www.weeklystandard.com/content/public/articles/000/000/001/746hxukk.asp (retrieved 21 June 2010).

30. See C.S. Lewis, *A Preface to Paradise Lost* (Oxford: Oxford University Press, 1942).

31. Burton Hatlen, "Pullman's *His Dark Materials*, a Challenge to the Fantasies of J.R.R. Tolkien and C.S. Lewis, with an Epilogue on Pullman's Neo-Romantic Reading of *Paradise Lost*," in His Dark Materials *Illuminated: Critical Essays on Philip Pullman's Trilogy*, ed. Millicent Lenz with Carole Scott (Detroit: Wayne State University Press, 2005), 82.

32. See C.S. Lewis, *Perelandra* (New York: Scribner, 2003).

33. Squires, 100.

34. High fantasy denotes those epic good-vs.-evil narratives that take place in what Tolkien called secondary worlds (such as those written by Lewis, Tolkien and Pullman). It is worth noting that Lewis and Tolkien were professors and close friends at Oxford University. Pullman, an Oxford graduate, studied in the generation after their tenure; he still resides in that city.

35. In the spirit of John Dewey's descriptive coinage of the term, not Jerry Falwell's polemical appropriation of it. See Hatlen, 76, 91n2.

36. "I would propose that rather than simply rejecting Lewis as a model, Pullman has, in *His Dark Materials*, offered a kind of inverted homage to his predecessor, deliberately composing a kind of 'anti–Narnia,' a secular humanist alternative to Lewis's Christian fantasy" (Hatlen, 82). Squires takes up Pullman's dislike for Lewis and his work, and some of the controversy that has resulted. See Squires, 99ff.

37. Ralph Wood draws a helpful distinction between an adventure and a quest, using the work of Tolkien to illustrate. An adventure is a story of "there and back again," like *The Hobbit*. A quest is a journey, as in *The Lord of the Rings*, from which you may not return, and if you do, you are inalterably transformed and shaped by it ("Three Kinds of Christian Witness," one of Wood's three Midwinter Lectures, presented in February 2000 at Austin Presbyterian Theological Seminary). Wood makes a similar distinction in "Frodo's Faith," *The Christian Century*, 6 September 2003, 21–23.

38. Ralph Wood, *The Gospel According to Tolkien* (Louisville, KY: Westminster John Knox Press, 2003), 73.

39. Had Pullman's narrative been a complete inversion of good and evil, it would be reflected in the way narrative functions. Vices would become virtues and so on. Deceit and murder would be praised, while truth-telling and self-sacrifice would be condemned. The sexual encounter between Will and Lyra would have been violent rape or a meaningless hook-up, rather than the tender, subtle and discreet account of carnal knowledge.

40. *The Amber Spyglass*, 447.

41. Like Satan in *Paradise Lost*, Melkor seduces those around him. Sauron and other demiurges take Melkor's side in rebellion against Ilúvatar (literally "Father of All"). See J.R.R. Tolkien, *The Silmarillion*, ed. Christopher Tolkien (New York: Houghton Mifflin, 2001), 16.

42. For a summary of Augustine's view on evil, see G.R. Evans, "Evil," in *Augustine through the Ages: An Encyclopedia*, ed. Allan D. Fitzgerald (Grand Rapids: Eerdmans, 1999), 340–344.

43. Hatlen, 79.

44. For the most part, the Church that is criticized in the course of Pullman's story is an institution in Lyra's world. However, the boundaries do tend to blur, especially given the ever-growing body of interviews and articles in which Philip Pullman criticizes the church and religion generally in our "real" world.

45. *The Amber Spyglass*, 328.

46. This scene compares and contrasts with the destruction of the One Ring in *Lord of the Rings*. Just as Gollum's lust for the Ring is manifest in him over time, so Metatron's personal lust is his own undoing. On the other hand, Asriel's and Coulter's heroic sacrificial plunge into the abyss is precisely the kind of illusion that Tolkien refuses to allow in his resolution of evil.

47. *The Amber Spyglass*, 486.

48. Genital mutilation (which is different from male circumcision) is not taught in the Bible or the Koran. Rather, it is a practice of folk religion in Africa and Asia that predates Christianity and Islam. Religious castration was practiced only rarely, by a few early Christians (e.g., Origen and Melito of Sardis). The well-known *castrati* mentioned in 16th-century Italian church records resulted from clandestine violation of canon law.

49. For example, Pullman makes a reference to "Pope John Calvin in Geneva" (*The Golden Compass*, 30). The actual John Calvin (1509–1564) was a leading second-generation Reformation theologian in Geneva, Switzerland. This French refugee spent most of his adult life as a Genevan pastor. He became an influential Protestant thinker, second only to Martin Luther. Calvin is perhaps still the leading figure of the Reformed theological tradition, which includes Presbyterianism, Dutch and German Reformed churches and the main denominations in the Baptist tradition. Calvin is much maligned and was a favorite target of critics during the Enlightenment and afterwards. The execution in Geneva of heretic Michael Servetus, often cited as evidence of Calvin's religious excess, could have taken place anywhere; he was wanted for heresy by both Roman Catholics and Protestants. Servetus singled out Geneva because of his obsession to confront the best Protestant mind: Calvin (Luther was no longer living). But it was secular courts

that condemned and burned Servetus, not the church or Calvin. It can all read about in the city archives of Geneva. To be sure, Calvin had a very intentional vision for moral discipline in the city of Geneva. However, his considerable French tone caused many (especially Genevan citizens) to resent a foreign influence. Indeed, Calvin was not a citizen, but rather one of a large number of religious refugees who were fleeing the very kinds of persecution over which he is alleged to have presided, with no vote in elections, much less a role on the city council. Persuasion was his only power. Popular notions that Calvin established a Genevan theocracy tend to lack adequate understanding of historical context and ecclesiastical background to appreciate what such a statement would mean, let alone that it could not possibly be true. Allegations (by Balzac and Huxley) that Calvin initiated executions, conducted a "religious reign of terror," and even had a child decapitated have absolutely no historical support in a city that has kept extraordinary archival records. Pullman seems intent on continuing Huxley's slanderous (fabricated) legacy that Calvin was responsible for the execution of a child (Pullman makes it plural). See Bruce Hall, "The Calvin Legend," in *John Calvin: A Collection of Distinguished Essays*, ed. G.E. Duffield (Grand Rapids: Eerdmans, 1966), 10. Hall's entire 16-page essay gives important context for understanding the myriad misunderstandings, mischaracterizations and "phrase-making prejudice" that have been carelessly (if not libelously) directed at the Genevan reformer. Apparently Claire Squires (61ff.) has uncritically appropriated some of this anti–Calvin propaganda.

50. *The Subtle Knife*, 271ff.

51. Philip Pullman, "Religion," available at www.philip-pullman.com/pages/content/index.asp?PageID=110 (retrieved 21 June 2010).

52. One thinks of Stalin's purges, Hitler's Holocaust, Mao's Cultural Revolution, Japanese Emperor Tojo's murder of millions of Chinese, Korean, Filipino and Southeast Asian civilians, the Killing Fields of Cambodia's Pol Pot, and the purges of North Korea's Kim Il Sung, to name some of the worst slaughters.

53. Wood, 73ff.

54. Matthew 13:24–29.

55. The closer Frodo comes to Mount Doom, the heavier the burden of the Ring. Like Bilbo before him, Frodo finds the Ring increasingly irresistible. Even his pure-in-heart companion Samwise Gamgee comes perilously close to succumbing to the Ring. In the most surprising and anti-climactic turn of Tolkien's plot, the Quest is completed "not by Frodo the brave [who ends up totally seduced by the Ring's power] but by the greed-maddened Gollum" (Wood, 73). Biting the Ring off of Frodo's finger (as Isildur did to Sauron ages ago), the withered, no-longer-hobbit gloats too near the edge of the Cracks of Doom. Intoxicated with desire, Gollum stumbles and plummets, returning the evil talisman to the blazing abyss from which it was forged.

56. Pullman allows readers to draw their own conclusions about whether these two young teenagers "go all the way." Given the under-development of popular culture in Lyra's world — there are no movies, so presumably no television — and Will's unrelenting task of caring for his mother, it is difficult to imagine that either would have the requisite background knowledge to engage in intercourse during their first sexual encounter. But I am entitled to my interpretation, just as others have concluded that intercourse did take place.

57. By using the terms "narrative structure" and "meta-narrative" (not metanarrative) I wish not to make universal implications about structuralism vs. post-structuralism. I am using the terms within the limited context of Milton, Pullman and the Judeo-Christian tradition.

Bibliography

Blake, William. *The Complete Poetry and Prose of William Blake*. Rev. ed. Ed. David V. Erdman. Commentary by David Bloom. New York: Anchor, 1995.

Bruner, Kurt, and Jim Ware. *Shedding Light on* His Dark Materials. Carol Stream, IL: SaltRiver/Tyndale House, 2007.

Cavanaugh, William T. *The Myth of Religious Violence*. Oxford: Oxford University Press, 2009.

Evans, G.R. "Evil." In *Augustine through the Ages: An Encyclopedia.* Edited by Allan D. Fitzgerald. Grand Rapids: Eerdmans, 1999. 340–344.

Forsyth, Neil. *The Satanic Epic.* Princeton, NJ: Princeton University Press, 1987.

Frost, Laurie. *The Definitive Guide to Philip Pullman's* His Dark Materials. London: Scholastic, 2008.

Gribbin, Mary, and Gribbin, John. *The Science of Philip Pullman's* His Dark Materials. Introduction by Philip Pullman. New York: Random House/Laurel Leaf Books, 2005.

Hall, Bruce. "The Calvin Legend." In *John Calvin: A Collection of Distinguished Essays.* Ed. G.E. Duffield. Grand Rapids: Eerdmans, 1966.

Hatlen, Burton. "Pullman's *His Dark Materials,* a Challenge to the Fantasies of J.R.R. Tolkien and C.S. Lewis, with an Epilogue on Pullman's Neo-Romantic Reading of *Paradise Lost.*" His Dark Materials *Illuminated: Critical Essays on Philip Pullman's Trilogy.* Ed. Millicent Lenz, with Carole Scott. Detroit: Wayne State University Press, 2005. 75–94.

Jacobs, Alan. "The Devil's Party: Philip Pullman's Bestselling Fantasy Series Retells the Story of Creation — With Satan as the Hero." *The Weekly Standard,* 23 October 2000. Available at www.weeklystandard.com/content/public/articles/000/000/001/746hxukk.asp. Retrieved 21 June 2010.

Lenz, Millicent, ed., with Carole Scott. His Dark Materials *Illuminated: Critical Essays on Philip Pullman's Trilogy.* Detroit: Wayne State University Press, 2005.

Lewis, C.S. *The Lion, the Witch and the Wardrobe.* London: Macmillan, 1950.

_____. *The Magician's Nephew.* London: Macmillan, 1955.

_____. *Perelandra: A Novel.* New York: Scribner, 2003.

_____. *A Preface to Paradise Lost.* Oxford: Oxford University Press, 1942.

Milton, John. *Paradise Lost.* Introduction by Philip Pullman. Oxford World Classics. Oxford: Oxford University Press, 2005.

Pullman, Philip. *The Amber Spyglass.* New York: Alfred A. Knopf, 2000.

_____. *The Golden Compass.* New York: Alfred A. Knopf, 1995.

_____. "Religion." Available at www.philip-pullman.com/pages/content/index.asp?PageID=110. Retrieved 21 June 2010.

_____. *The Subtle Knife.* New York: Alfred A. Knopf, 1997.

Squires, Claire. *Philip Pullman, Master Storyteller: A Guide to the Worlds of* His Dark Materials. New York: Continuum, 2006.

Tolkien, J.R.R. "On Fairy Stories." In *Essays Presented to Charles Williams.* Reprint ed. Ed. C.S. Lewis. 1947. Grand Rapids: Eerdmans, 1966.

_____. *The Silmarillion.* Ed. Christopher Tolkien. New York: Houghton Mifflin, 2001.

"Top 21." Available at www.bbc.co.uk/arts/bigread/vote/. Retrieved 21 June 2010.

Wood, Ralph. "Frodo's Faith." *The Christian Century,* 6 September 2003, 21–23.

_____. *The Gospel According to Tolkien.* Louisville, KY: Westminster John Knox Press, 2003.

9

Sim Evil: Avatars and the Ethical Game Mechanic

Kelly Kelleway

You are in darkness. Distinct noises surround you: breathing; the heavy rustling of canvas; zippers opening or closing; the metallic clacking unmistakable to the initiated as the sound of ammunition magazines slapped into gun receivers. Suddenly there is light, a widening vertical gap that — along with a familiar "ping!" — lets you know you are in an elevator. As the view coalesces outside the open elevator doors, you see you are in the company of several heavily armed men encased in military-grade, hard body armor. You have just enough time to register that your elevator has delivered you to an airport security checkpoint, clogged with air travelers, before you and your companions ready yourselves to step out and the level title fades in: "No Russian." The people in line — civilians, families — have no time to react. Your companions raise their machine guns and fire into the crowd at point-blank range.

So begins the fourth and most controversial level of the recent first-person shooter video game *Call of Duty: Modern Warfare 2*. While controversial, it took this game only two months of release to earn $1 billion, making it one of the most financially successful media products — including motion pictures, music, and books — of all time.[1] While the roots of its success are beyond the scope of this discussion, the underpinnings of one of its controversies are a convenient entry point into an examination of the appeal of "evil" in popular recent video games.

In the "No Russian" level of the game, the player assumes the role of Private Joseph Allen, a U.S. Army Ranger, who is told by his military commanders that their main objective is to plant someone close to Vladimir Makarov, the game's Russian terrorist adversary, in order to prevent an unspecified but catastrophic attack. Thus "you," as Pvt. Allen and disguised as Alexei Borodin, are sent to infiltrate Makarov's terrorist group. The terrorists' mission, as you soon learn, is to massacre innocent civilians at the fictitious Zakhaev International Airport in Moscow. Once you have exited the elevator, you and your computer-controlled companions begin to fire your weapons. Realistically modeled civilians start to react as the massacre begins. As you move through the level, you may notice that your participation in the mass murder is voluntary; the AI-controlled terrorists fail to notice if you do not take an active part in the killing. However, if you attempt to engage one of the terrorists with your weapon, to try to prevent the massacre from happening (and for many, to avoid playing an "evil" role), you will be immediately killed by the terrorists and earn an unsuccessful game ending. You will not be allowed to progress past this point and play the rest of the game. At minimum the level enforces your complicity in the carnage.

Towards the end of the level, after the sweep through the airport terminal is finished and every human being in view has been killed, your terrorist group moves outside to the tarmac to engage the counterterrorist police forces awaiting you. At this point, the player's active participation *is* required; the AI-controlled terrorists cannot seem to hit their targets, and you will find yourself stuck in a perpetual gun battle until your ammunition runs out and you are killed. Game over. The player must fire upon and kill at least some of the police officers in order to move to the final area of the level where there is a double cross and you, the player character, are killed by Makarov.

While there are many interesting aspects to this level, perhaps the most interesting was the gaming community's reaction. Several influential and widely read gaming commentators articulated what was a pervasive reaction: frustration and dissatisfaction with the level.[2] It seems that the level inspired a negative reaction, not so much due to its requirement that you, the player, play a character who in turn must play an "evil" role, but rather due to the lack of agency that the level entails and the ultimate meaninglessness of your/Pvt. Allen's/Borodin's actions in the level. No matter what the player does, only death at the end results, ironically, in a successful play-through and the ability to continue on with the rest of the game. It is a striking incongruity that the "evil" role featured in the most financially successful video game of all time engendered some of the game's harshest criticism. After all, playing as an evil character is an option common to many popular video games in the past several years and indeed an expected feature of modern role-playing games (RPGs).

There are many questions that arise when considering the phenomenon of "evil avatars" — or player character options that enable morally questionable actions like mass murder. For example, what does it mean to assert in this game — or any other, for that matter — that a character or action (or lack thereof) is "evil," to *simulate evil*, in other words? What are the ethical premises that frame such actions? And why, most importantly, do millions of gamers eagerly await their electronic opportunity to undertake such roles?

It is my contention that modern video games that enable or require players to undertake an "evil" or at least ethically questionable role are appealing for two reasons. First, they justify by rendering intelligible the morally fraught acts or choices of the player in the context of the game world itself. As we shall see, this justification can take a variety of forms, but the results are the same — "evil" as a role within the game is rationalized for the player and perhaps excused to some degree. The second reason for this appeal has to do with the ontological nature of the moral frameworks within the games themselves; in contrast with prevailing postmodern notions of moral relativism or ethical uncertainty, these sorts of video games offer moral "truths" through their programmatic and predetermined nature. Ironically, it may be the case that modern video games — eyed with suspicion by many social conservatives — offer a reassuring return to the halcyon days of unshakeable moral certainties.

In addition to making these assertions about the appeal of video games with evil avatar options, I also argue that such moral frameworks entail veiled ideologically suggestive claims about morality and the nature of evil itself. In order to lay bare these potentially taken-for-granted views and to support my interpretation of appeal, I have classified these games into three descriptive categories as detailed in Table 1 (see page 148).

While in what follows I explain each category through an analysis of exemplar games, it is important to remember that these categories should be thought of as purely descriptive and indicative of phases of a continuum; there are likely games not mentioned here that offer evil options that would best fit "between" categories. My goal in such classification is to examine the variety of mechanics and conventions used in games that feature evil player characters and to analyze the ideological foundation of the ethical structures established in the games.

Category I: Deterministic

I title this category "Deterministic" to draw attention to the ethical predetermination of the player's avatar. Games in this category afford the player little or no *agency* in terms of the avatar's goals, motivations, or choices. They necessitate that the player undertake the role of a preconstructed character who, most commonly due to some inescapable fact of birth, genetics, or cir-

	Deterministic	Binary	Embodied
Agency	Little to no choice or options	Limited to "either/ or" choices	Choices & actions may have range & consequence, simulation
World Type	Linear	Linear or open world	Usually open world
Avatar	Preconstructed	Minimal to some input	Great degree of input, esp. physicality
Ethical Mechanic	None	Clear "good vs. bad" choices, quantified	Choice & behaviors, may be gray area, may not be quantified
Examples	*Manhunt, Hitman, Overlord*	*KOTOR, GTA 3 & 4, Bioshock*	*Fallout 3, Mass Effect 1 & 2, Dragon Age*

Table 1. Categories of Games

cumstance, is already well down a path likely considered by many as at least morally fraught. For example, the player's avatar in *Manhunt* is an inmate on death row, while the avatar in *Star Wars: The Force Unleashed* is Darth Vader's secret apprentice.[3] Avatars of this type are thus static end products of any number of moral choices, actions, or structures that presumably influenced the characters in the back-story of the game, and as such they imply a programmed or "determined" view of human nature. Philosophies as diverse as the Christian concept of original sin on the one hand and Rousseau's state of innocence on the other claim that what one "is" in terms of morality is a set feature of one's nature, and the actions or influences of social context can only delimit (or debase according to Rousseau) that given moral propensity.[4] As we shall see, this sort of static character is the crux of these games' persuasive ethical arguments; not only does the fact that the player's character is *already*, say, a convicted murderer or professional assassin make any chance for redemption seem unlikely and even a bit cliché, but also the determined nature of that character's ethical being implies a lack of free will that mitigates the player's moral responsibility.

For example, this type of rationalization is evidenced in the *Hitman* series of games.[5] In these games the player controls Agent 47, an assassin for hire. From the game's back-story we learn that Agent 47 is actually genetically engineered to be the best killer possible. His shadowy creators culled DNA from world-class criminals to craft a perfect assassination tool. This premise presupposes a powerful form of genetic determinism and is typical of the "programmed" character concepts found in Category I games.

Within the scope of the game world itself, the murders for hire that Agent 47 commits (and the character himself) are not the subject of overt moralizing; indeed, the targets of assassination missions are generally not defined in ethical terms and are simply goals that must be accomplished. In the game's fiction, Agent 47 is an emotionless and remorseless killer of multiple unknowing victims, but it is up to the player's out-of-game ethical judgment to define such behavior as amoral or "evil" as the game makes only gradations of professionalism and skill. Thus the only way for an individual player to apprehend Agent 47's moral state is through a subjective ethical lens. This seems to imply, on the one hand, the necessity of some sort of ethical relativism; players must look to their own reading of the game's situations for an unambiguous moral evaluation. On the other hand, this subjective ethical evaluation is further complicated by the teleologic view implicated by both the character's back-story and the game's lack of player choice. While the player may be free to apply any ethical label to Agent 47 that he or she deems appropriate (or none at all), unhampered by overt moralizing in the game's fiction, the lack of agency Agent 47 experiences as a genetically engineered killer in some sense echoes the lack of agency experienced by the player. Agent 47 has a predetermined genetic destiny that the player must then take a hand in unfolding according to the programming established by the game's designer. As the game supports only one ending and offers no options for the player to alter the story or make significant choices — other than the method and physical route through the various levels to kill his targets — the only way to "win" (or reach the conclusion of the narrative) is to correctly perform the activities pre-established by the game's designer.

This "fate" or determinism helps to rationalize the fact that the main premise of the game is to murder human beings for gain. In the ethical structure of Category I games like *Hitman*, the actions of the player's avatar are not those of a moral agent, but rather of an individual essentially lacking free will. They are programmed, both literally by the game's designer and figuratively by the premise of the character's back-story. In this way, such determinism may offer amelioration to those players who find murder abhorrent and evil in the real world. Within the fiction of the game world, the same actions lack true intentionality and moral responsibility. The player may experience being evil in a guilt-free context.

However, while the opportunity to play as a morally fraught character — a convicted murderer, an assassin for hire — may appear titillatingly rebellious in its brassy refusal of the traditional heroic vantage point or protagonist, such games are in many ways the most hidebound narratives possible.

As we have seen, the games in Category I rely on deterministic premises for their player avatars; ethical frameworks that issue forth from such deterministic premises can wind up naturalizing the status quo and quashing change or rebellion. After all, if one's moral behavior is a result of one's DNA, if people are programmed to be good or bad, then any impetus to alleviate socio-cultural causes of crime or unrest becomes a non-starter. Deterministic frame-works, especially those that purport to explain how and why people act the way they do, do one thing very well: they prop up the power paradigm in current ascendancy with the suggestion that those "on top" — economically, socially, politically — are meant to be there.

Category II: Binary

Games in this category, unlike those in Category I, do offer players some (albeit often minor) degree of choice. This choice typically takes the form of an occasional forking path in the game's narrative, one where the choice of either path is clearly demarcated and often ethically charged. Thus the "either/or" choice is also often a "good or evil" choice. The term "Binary" refers to this bifurcating path and the conflicting nature of the choices. Diver-gence from the prescribed flow of the narrative is thus given illusory life through the occasional forking-path moment. Players may be able to select options from pairs of choices that appear diametrically opposed, but as we shall see in the following example, it is often the case that these choices create simply a veneer of agency; one player's avatar may travel down a different path from another's, but, as the endgame destination remains more or less the same, games in this category are finally "determined" in manner similar to those in Category I.

Where these games most apparently diverge from Category I is in their use of an ethical mechanic.[6] This mechanic describes and operates the binary choices mentioned previously, offering situations in the game's narrative in which players have an either/or choice to make. This situation can take various forms; for example, it may be an actual choice between accomplishing one of two distinct game missions or quests, or it may take the form of two con-trasting dialogue options players can explore. These choices are often arranged in a simplistic moral register — they are either stereotypically good or bad. The range of the moral choice is often dependent on the deterministic nature of the player's avatar; neither option may be obviously "good" if the player's avatar has been set up beforehand as heavily immersed in criminal behavior.

Grand Theft Auto 4[7] demonstrates both a binary ethical mechanic and a strongly communitarian view of ethics. As the player's character — Niko

Bellic, a Serbian ex-military man — slowly advances deeper into the criminal underworld of "Liberty City," so too does the ethical context for his actions adjust to that of the new community of which he is a functionary. As we shall see, the communitarian framework that undergirds his actions serves rationalizing purpose similar to how determinism functions for Category I games.

Niko's slow descent into the criminal underworld performs a persuasive narrative function: it allows players to adjust gradually to a change in the social context that provides the rubric for Niko's ethical behavior. At the beginning of the game, Niko arrives in Liberty City at the urging of his cousin, Roman, who extols to him the reality of the "American Dream." This turns out to be a lie, and Roman is actually in deep trouble with the Russian mob. Many of the player's first missions involve helping Roman out of the predicament he is in with organized crime, and some of the first criminal acts players must commit are apparently meant to be justified by the fact that their victims are actually serious criminals themselves.

However, several hours into the game's main narrative, the character development process comes to its first major either/or ethical mechanic. Niko, tasked with killing a crime boss' associate, chases the target until the target falls on the roof of a building and leaves the player with a binary choice: do they grab his arm and save him, or stomp on his hands to let him fall to his death? At this point in the narrative the either/or fork follows a clear moral pattern: It is not reaching to suggest most players would deem letting someone fall to their death a morally questionable act at least, if not categorically evil, whereas the choice to save a hostile foe suggests mercy and forgiveness, both qualities commonly associated with good moral conduct. At this early phase, players may select either option with no real penalty; thus the game supports multiple ethical evaluations of Niko's behavior — players can make choices according to their out-of-game notions about right and wrong, or according to their assumptions about Niko's prior non-criminal social context, without concern that the game will penalize them for choosing incorrectly.[8]

However, this is not the case later in the game's narrative as the slow process of Niko's entry into a criminal community continues. Towards the midpoint of the game's narrative, he is fully a premeditated, contract killer. In one example, a corrupt deputy police commissioner has Niko undertake a number of missions, the most heinous being the murder of an attorney who is trying to marshal evidence of the commissioner's corruption. In order to successfully complete this mission, the player must kill the attorney after infiltrating his office in the guise of a job applicant. Interestingly enough, the ethical game mechanic is *not* used in this mission, whereas it *is* used in a similar mission right after (players may kill their innocent victim or let him escape). This measured implementation of the ethical mechanic makes possible the reframing of Niko's social context; players do not have opportunities to derail the pivotal points on their journey into the criminal underworld. The player as Niko may be able to perform the occasional charitable act, but increasingly these become mere digressions from the narrative impetus towards Niko's new community context, a criminal underworld that supports an ethical structure quite different from mainstream society.

In a communitarian ethical view, it is the moral code of the social group that is predominant and provides the foundation for each individual's moral judgment. In Niko's new social context, his actions have some social legitimacy; he is a part of a byzantine system of criminal checks and balances, and there are definitely "dos and don'ts" to which he adheres. For example, he does have *some* sort of ethical code, a code that by and large depends on loyalty to charismatic criminal leadership. It seems as though the narrative requires the player/Niko to perform an act mainstream society would consider as evil (murdering of non-criminals such as police officers, attorneys, conducting major drug operations, and so on) only when it is motivated by the command of someone higher up the criminal food chain. In Niko's social code and context, he is operating according to legible rules, and the most important of those seem to focus on the maintenance of a hierarchical criminal power structure; most of the main mission-givers in the game use Niko to keep their powerbase consolidated in one way or another. Niko's violence is thus not random or chaotic, but directed to the accomplishment of tasks designed to keep order in the criminal world of which he is a part. Even within the relentless action of gun battles and power shifts, Niko's deeds strengthen his new criminal community; his ethics are thus contextualized within the community of which he is a functionary, and even cold-blooded murder may be labeled the "right" thing to do within this new community. In this way *GTA 4* suggests the local, rather than universal, nature of morality, while at the same time offering the player a rationale for behaviors in-game that out-of-game would result in long prison terms. The slow process of this social context shift avoids abrupt transitions that would otherwise exacerbate the dissonance between the player's ethical judgment and Niko's.

However, this narrative implication of the local nature of ethical judgment is surmounted ultimately by the programmed quality of the game itself. As indicated earlier, while the binary ethical game mechanic creates a veneer of agency and choice, the reality is that either choice has been predetermined by the game's designers and factored in to their construct of a criminal underworld. As a game, *GTA 4* is a closed system that depends on the authorial intent of its creator, and, by so doing, provides in the end the same sense of ethical certainty and clarity found in deterministic Category I games.

Category III: Embodied

I term this final category "Embodied" to call attention to its crucial distinctions from the prior two categories: the player's ability to create and modify the physical appearance of his or her avatar, and the complex mechanisms in place for the player to craft that avatar's characteristics, both in terms of skills and personality. As we shall see, this broad range of options and input helps games in this category to function as *simulations* and, by so doing, to potentially veil the ethical implications of their narratives.

In order to introduce the concept of simulation, let's look at one of the most successful examples, the long-running game series *The Sims*. As an asserted simulation of "real life," *The Sims* games have been repeatedly the focus of academic analysis. For some commentators, it is the games' very nature as simulation that makes them worthy of critical inquiry. Gonzalo Frasca writes:

> Videogames like *The Sims* are introducing to the masses a different form of representation — simulation — which has always been present in our culture through games, but that now can dare to start modeling more complex systems, such as human life. Even if *The Sims* is a very limited model of human relationships, it is a harbinger of videogames as a mature communicational and artistic form.[9]

This view argues that, compared to presumably less "real" game simulations, *The Sims* is more directly relevant to the player's own life, and thus more transparently pedagogical in terms of the ethical lessons, dilemmas, and choices it offers. As Frasca asserts, "the fact that it portrays people, and not aliens, results in players asking questions about the game's ideology. Is it okay to let a Sim starve to death?"[10] For Frasca and others, simulations have an educational potential that goes beyond simple rote and reactionary training to the realm of self-aware critical considerations of player actions and consequences.

While there are surface dissimilarities between *The Sims* games and other game genres like RPGs, there are also fundamental similarities. To varying degrees, many modern video games are "simulations." This means primarily that they procedurally model systems with which players interact.[11] Games in Category III are rightly considered "sim-like" in their extensive player character creation tools. Does this mean they foster player reflection on their ethical frameworks? In seemingly direct conflict with the hopeful evaluation of the critical inquiry spurred by simulations espoused by Frasca, Simon Penny and many others have argued an invidious power of simulation resulting from its perceived "realism" and the façade of player agency thereby created.[12] Simply put, computer simulations' semblance of reality can obscure their basic ideological premises.[13] This question of ideological transparency most definitely comes into play in the exemplar game for this category, *Mass Effect 2*, a complex RPG that offers players a deep "sim" for their avatar creation and features an ethical mechanic whose premises imply a surprisingly metaphysical moral absolutism.[14]

In *Mass Effect 2 (ME2)*, players undertake the role of Commander Shepard. As is common to games in this category, players have a great deal of input into their avatar. In *ME2*, players can craft the look of "their" Shepard through a complex set of design tools. In addition to the choice of gender, there are "sliders" or inputs for things like eye color and shape, mouth and lip size and depth, hair styles and colors, and so forth. These tools are so detailed it is possible to recreate a facsimile of one's favorite celebrity or even oneself. In addition to this physical creation control, players can select their avatar's background or origin story, their character class, and their recent public reputation, all of which have consequences in the game, in addition to allocating points in skills that moderate what may and may not be accomplished during the game. Other game genres rely on this type of detailed creation control to help establish their identity as simulations — racing games, for example, are classified as "sims" when they allow players to select and modify elements of their vehicles like tires, shocks, spoilers, and so on, and this range of choice has an impact on the vehicle's performance on the track. Typically this is tied to an evaluation of the level of "realism" the game demonstrates. If we apply this idea to *ME2* and the other complex RPGs in Category III, it is suggestive of the power such simulation or "realism" may have in naturalizing the suppositions inherent in such games regarding morality. The player has some degree of control — in terms of physical appearance, voice, inherent skill sets, and so forth — over his or her vantage point or marker in the game, and this implied agency suggests a stronger player "presence" in the game; it helps to draw closed the fourth wall, and, as Penny reminds us, "In simulation ... one is encouraged to believe there is no 'outside.' The desire is for complete enveloping illusion."[15]

In addition to "sim" avatar creation, games in Category III use ethical mechanics more extensively than those in Category II. Generally, these mechanics are more complex and integral to the unfolding of the narrative due to their impact on the player's avatar. In *ME2*, the ethical mechanic follows a binary pattern — as it did in *GTA 4*— but it differs greatly from that game and others in Category II primarily due to the specific and concrete manner of its implementation and the consequences for the player's avatar. As is typical for Category III games, morality in *ME2* is *quantified* by way of the ethical mechanic.[16] In the game, players have continual ethical choices to make, and the results of these choices allow players to accrue "morality points," which in turn fill up either of two "morality meters" found on the character information screen; one meter is blue and labeled "Paragon," and the other is red and labeled "Renegade." Extremely violent or callous actions, or rude or threatening dialogue choices, earn Renegade points, while self-effacement and ensuring the safety of innocents earn Paragon points. Because of this precise system, players can decide from the outset to what degree "their Shepard" will be a Paragon or Renegade, and they can measure their progress as the game unfolds. In this way *ME2* suggests that morality is a "something" as abstractions cannot be measured or indexed in any meaningful way. The idea that morality is substantive is metaphysical in nature and harkens back to classical views of ethics.

However, what is even more metaphysical in its implications is the way in which the ethical mechanic in *ME2* actually works. For example, while dialogue in the game is handled via "dialogue trees," a mechanic common to the RPG genre, the descriptions of the choices players are offered are deliberately vague and reductive.[17] The choices in a scenario are arrayed in an oval, called the "dialogue wheel," and blue Paragon options are located at the top of the wheel while red Renegade options are at the bottom. Players thus know, without question, that by selecting the red dialogue at the bottom of the wheel they will earn Renegade morality points and move their avatar a few increments closer to fully realizing their chosen ethical direction. However, the choice itself is only *suggestive* of what their avatar will actually do. The actual lines of dialogue delivered in the scene, for example, are usually much longer, can vary significantly from the short "guesstimate" listed as the choice, and often are accompanied by physical acts on the part of the avatar. This phenomenon is also evidenced via the game's system of "interrupts," which are moments during cinematic sequences wherein players who have accrued enough morality points in one of the meters are offered — through a quick flashing icon at the bottom of the screen — a chance to interrupt the cinematic and perform an action keyed to the moral pole most developed by the player.

For example, early in the narrative, players (as Shepard) confront an armored mercenary in a tower after a long combat sequence. This computer-controlled character is caught unawares, and a cinematic ensues in which the player/Shepard questions the mercenary. If the player has a high enough Renegade score, a flashing red icon at the bottom of the screen appears, and players quick enough to hit the right trigger on the gamepad are rewarded with a new cinematic wherein Shepard strikes the mercenary and sends him smashing through a window to his death many stories below. What is crucial here is that while hitting the trigger players *don't know* what their avatar will do in the ensuing sequences; they only know that the action is classified within the game's parameters as Renegade. Thus the player goes by his or her intent to role play a "good guy" or Paragon, or a "bad guy" or Renegade, and leaves the definition and description of just what that good or bad behavior may be up to the game's designers. In this way the ethical mechanic in *ME2* undermines the player's role as a moral agent; the predominance of moral judgment is placed in the hands of the game's creators and morality becomes *absolute* as those creators define and bring to life the specifics of ethical practice.

The metaphysical nature of the ethical framework of the game is further demonstrated by the physical manifestation of morality on the player's avatar; within *ME2*, morality is written on the body. *ME2* is a sequel to *Mass Effect*, and players can "import" their Commander Shepard from the prior installment. At the beginning of *ME2*, it is established that Shepard was killed right after events concluded in the first game and has now been reconstructed by a mysterious interstellar group to help to save the galaxy. The reconstruction leaves Shepard with some facial scarring; the more players fill up their Paragon meter, the more that scarring fades. The greater the Renegade score, the more the scarring spreads and deepens, resulting in a faint glow from subdermal cybernetics implanted to assist in Shepard's resurrection.

While non-player character (NPC) reaction to extreme moral actions (excessively altruistic *or* profoundly vicious) is minimal, the way such choices are marked on the body of the avatar suggests that morality itself is embodied, that one's ethics are a material part of one's existence, and that the Platonic notion of essence has made an unusual reappearance. The metaphysical implications of this view of morality as substance are in keeping with the obviation of moral responsibility implied by the ethical mechanic; the player *had* agency in the sim-like creation of the avatar, but that agency is dismissed as morality is inscribed upon that avatar's body. Morality as a "thing" or substance suggests it is an embedded property of the physical universe and necessitates an absolutist framework that presupposes the *a priori* truth and existence of moral values. Add to this the idea that only the game's creators' know the details and definitions of these values, and the result is an ethical structure in keeping with traditional religious frameworks wherein good and evil are a part of the fabric of reality — not the misguided result of language bewitchment — and believers "go on faith" or "leave it up to God" to sort out the specific details.

As with the determinism of Category I and the communitarian implications of *GTA4*, this metaphysical moral absolutism may minimize players' perceived complicity in extremely vicious gameplay. In addition to this amelioration, the ethical framework undergirding the game suggests a bedrock certainty to morality that avoids the postmodern vacuity of the term. When "being evil" is *inscribed* on the body, there are no worries about ethical legibility. However, does the sim-like nature of the player avatar indeed obscure these metaphysical implications? Perhaps, but is it also possible that these implications are a part of the game's appeal as a reassuring return to moral "truth." After all, the game's narrative takes minimal pains to mask its nature as a Christian allegory — the main character, Shepard, is a newly resurrected "shepherd" of humankind who saves the galaxy. In an intriguing "ends justifying means" way, players can be a fully developed Renegade Shepard and still be the savior, which suggests, among other things, a twisted deontological view in which duty is the final ethical arbiter.[18]

Some Conclusions

The popularity of games that feature "evil" avatars is undeniable. Complex RPGs with options to develop an anti-heroic, morally murky, or just plain sociopathic player character continue to sell well, as well as games that pre-establish the murderous presence of the player's avatar.[19] While there may be any number of reasons for this popularity, certainly the shared characteristic of the preceding categories — a game world and mechanics that suggest moral fixity and clarity — may go some way in explaining the trend.

In particular, however, the construction of evil in these games may also do something else. It may create a certain (for lack of a better term) *reassurance* granted the player, both that his or her "bad" behavior is either motivated or unavoidable, and that the game provides what Huizinga calls a "magic circle," a safe place removed from real world consequence and *inexplicability*, wherein an *explicable* evil may be encountered and experienced.[20] If we borrow a bit from Hegel and his notion that the goal of knowledge is to remove the "strangeness" of the world and thus decrease our feelings of alienation,[21] we can imagine that an immersive interactive experience that enables an individual to come to grips with representations of real-world events, actions, or behaviors — albeit oftentimes unrealistic versions of these things veiled in the metaphoric trappings of other worlds or fantastic scenarios — would facilitate a sort of dealienation. By playing through a game *deliberately* as what we feel to be an evil character, we can, in Hegel's terms, "find ourselves at home" in our world, a place in which even fantastical evil has an analogue. We may find that such a world stands just a little less "opposed" to us.

Finally, let us return to the game that opened this discussion with perhaps a better understanding of the consternation raised by the "No Russian" level. Unlike the powerful determinism of Category I games like *Hitman*, *Modern Warfare 2* offers no motivating personality rationalization for your character's actions (or inaction); "you" are actually a heroic soldier. Unlike the strong structural limitations enforced by the binary ethical mechanics of Category

II games and specifically the communitarian implications of *GTA 4*, *MW2* offers no narrative plausibility or contextualized legibility for your actions or inaction; if the aim of the mission is to get close enough to Makarov the terrorist to stop some other greater catastrophe, why not kill him there, at the airport, and stop both events? Finally, without the metaphysical moral absolutism of a game like *Mass Effect 2*, *MW2* cannot establish an exculpatory moral role for the player; while players, as Pvt. Allen, are ultimately "just following orders," the meaninglessness of Allen's sacrifice and the human slaughter create moral *chaos* rather than moral clarity and certainty.

It is important to remember that depictions of good or evil are always ideological as ethics and morality are socio-cultural constructs, dependent upon historic and geographic context, and that other media representations with moral overtones haul their own ideological freight. There's no way of knowing either the critical capacity or interest of most gamers, or the analytic nature of their play, but it would be a mistake to argue simply that players lack insight; after all, something rang hollow in many gamers' experience with the "No Russian" level of *Modern Warfare 2*. For these gamers, the opportunity to slaughter innocents, to be most starkly "evil," lacked the appeal evidenced by many other evil avatars. The "No Russian" controversy suggests that — perhaps — simulated evil cannot rely solely on shock or spectacle, but must also provide a sort of ethical escapism, a departure from the potentially disturbing murkiness of twenty-first century ethical realities.

NOTES

1. Jodie Humphries, "Avatar Vs Modern Warfare 2: The Billion Dollar Behemoths," *Business Management*, available at http://www.bme.eu.com/news/avatar-vs-modern-warfare-2/ (retrieved 22 February 2010). *Call of Duty: Modern Warfare 2* is the 2009 sequel to the 2007 game *Call of Duty 4: Modern Warfare*. As is the case with the first game, *MW2* depicts modern, 21st century combat operations from a first-person perspective. Players undertake various predetermined character roles — a U.S. Army Ranger, an elite commando, a captain in the British Special Air Service, and so on — and navigate their way through linear, obstacle-packed combat environments, engaging enemies with a variety of real-world and experimental military weapons. All of these vignettes are tied together by a convoluted military thriller plot perhaps more indebted to Tom Clancy than Dexter Filkins of the *New York Times*. In every level aside from the one under discussion here, the player assumes a stereotypically "heroic" Western vantage point, battling terrorists and defending the U.S. and her allies from various foes.

2. For example: Tom Chick, "Is *Modern Warfare 2* the Most Disgusting Game of the Year?" *Fidgit*, available at http://www.fidgit.com/archives/2009/11/is_modern_warfare_2_the_most_d.php (retrieved 24 February 2010).

3. *Manhunt* (Edinburgh: Rockstar North, 2003), console and PC video game. *Star Wars: The Force Unleashed* (San Francisco: LucasArts, 2008), console video game.

4. For more on the Romantic view of human nature see Jean-Jacques Rousseau, *The Social Contract and Discourses* (1761), trans. G.D.H. Cole (London and Toronto: J.M. Dent, 1923), available at http://oll.libertyfund.org/title/638 (retrieved 19 May 2010).

5. *Hitman* (Copenhagen: IO Interactive, 2000 to 2006), console and PC video game.

6. An ethical mechanic is a rule set and set of possible player actions that describe, depict, and enable choices and actions in a game that have moral significance. I use the term "ethical mechanic" rather than "moral" to draw attention to the systematic and evaluative nature of the mechanic. All games, not just video games, have mechanics. For example, a board game may have — among a number of other mechanics — a card mechanic that describes the actual set of cards included for use in the game and their use in play. Players must understand the rules that guide the use of the cards, and they must interact within the bounds of the mechanic in order for the game to unfold in a coherent manner. The results of drawing the "Get out of jail free!" card in *Monopoly*, for example, assist in driving the game to its conclusion and add an element of randomness and excitement to the play. In the same vein, an ethical mechanic has a structure and rules, and while players must understand that selecting the clearly "evil" option — assist the merchant, or kill him and take his goods? — will move their avatar further along in its evil development, the interaction with such mechanics adds a great deal to the entertainment and play afforded by the game.

7. *Grand Theft Auto 4* (Edinburgh: Rockstar North, 2008), console and PC video game.

8. Games like *GTA 4* are often called "sandbox" games, meaning that they present from the outset a large, open game world that the player can explore. These sandboxes, in turn, often include a procedural "law enforcement" system wherein wanton acts like the murder of a person on the street or vehicular mayhem attract the attention of the police. Players are free to attempt to escape the police — in the case of *GTA 4* upping their "wanted level" — but failure to surrender can result in the avatar's death in a hail of bullets. When arrested in *GTA*, players are punished by the confiscation of weapons on the person of their avatar and the levying of fines in the game's currency. Other types of games have different ways to punish players for choosing incorrectly; for example, in *Mass Effect 2* (discussed in Category III), players who choose to dawdle after they are assigned the final mission of the game will see a non-player character (NPC) — with whom they may have even cultivated a romance — horrifically killed in a non-interactive cut scene later in the game. If they immediately embark on the final mission this NPC is spared.

9. Gonzalo Frasca, "Videogames of the Oppressed," in *First Person: New Media as Story, Performance, and Game,* ed. Noah Wardrip-Fruin and Pat Harrigan (Cambridge, MA: MIT Press, 2004), 85.

10. Frasca, 91.

11. For the purposes of this analysis, I use the term "simulation" as a catch-all label for games and parts of games that claim to offer in-game a procedural representation of an out-of-game event or phenomenon. Simulations differ from simple representation in the degree of process or progress implied by the procedural generation of events. Players start with a set of initial conditions and options, and through a series of inputs direct the flow of events and consequences to some degree. In complex simulations like the various *Sims* games, players can set up the initial conditions of something like a city or household, and then let the simulation run to see what may happen over time. Games are considered more "sim" and less "arcade" the more input players have into the manipulation and set-up of in-game icons and processes, and the more complex the ensuing interactions become. A game like *Mario Power Tennis*, for example, is considered an "arcade" tennis game due to its reductive play options and simple conditions, whereas *Top Spin 3* is a tennis "sim" due to its great variety and depth of player avatar control and creation, and its adherence to "realistic" matters such as varying weather and career tournament progress.

12. See Simon Penny, "Representation, Enaction, and the Ethics of Simulation" in *First Person: New Media as Story, Performance, and Game,* ed. Noah Wardrip-Fruin and Pat Harrigan (Cambridge, MA: MIT Press, 2004).

13. Paul Starr, "Seductions of Sim: Policy as Simulation Game," *The American Prospect* (21 March 1994), available at http://www.prospect.org (retrieved 1 June 2010). I am indebted to video game scholar and creator Ian Bogost, whose insightful analysis of games, *Unit Operations,* drew my attention to Paul Starr's seminal article focusing on the "black box" nature of simulations and our tendency as players to leave unexamined the founding presumptions of models depending on how realistic we perceive them to be — the more realistic, the less examined.

Starr cautions that the premises of models must be examined, not just in popular entertainments such as *SimCity*, but in the economic and social computer models used help to guide political decision making. See also Bogost.

14. *Mass Effect 2* (Edmonton, Alberta: BioWare, 2010), console and PC video game.

15. Penny, 81.

16. While the majority of RPGs in Category III evince this quantification, how that atomization and measurement takes place in certain games can be subtle. For example, another recent game eschews an outright "morality meter" in favor of strong reactions from the player avatar's group of NPCs. Players can gauge their ethical state by the "reaction meters" located on the information screens for these NPCs. A few of these characters are established as strongly "good" via their selfless actions and defense of the innocent, while a few are established as "bad" via their selfishness and viciousness. While this ethical mechanic suggests the "relational" nature of ethics and the social construction of moral judgment, it is also another form of measurement, in this case outsourced to the NPCs. See *Dragon Age: Origins*.

17. Dialogue "trees" are so named because the arrangement of dialogue options through the course of a conversation can be visualized much like a tree. Games often present a first set of options — for example, perhaps two or three separate lines of dialogue the player can choose from — and then the options "branch off" from there according to the player's choices. This means, in theory, that once a player has selected a certain branch of the conversation, branches from earlier in the conversation are no longer available. The reality is that games often "reset" NPCs after conversations so that players can return to the same character and explore the other branches. However, some games, like *Mass Effect 2*, do not allow this return to options for crucial or plot-significant conversations. Players must be careful to save their progress before any such interaction if they want to revisit or "fix" a conversation mistake.

18. I say "twisted" because many of the Renegade Shepard/player's choices, if "universalized" à la Kant, would result in galaxy-wide mayhem.

19. The recent Category III game *Fallout 3*, for example, while not quite reaching the blockbuster appeal of *Modern Warfare 2*, is still a huge success. A Bethesda Softworks press release reports that the game made $300 million in its first week of release, with 4.7 million copies of the game shipped, as reported in *Kotaku*, available at http://www.kotaku.com/5078237/fallout-3-moves-47-million-copies (retrieved 1 June 2010).

20. Johan Huizinga, *Homo Ludens: A Study of the Play-Element in Culture* (Boston: Beacon, 1955).

21. Georg Wilhelm Friedrich Hegel, *Hegel's Logic*, trans. William Wallace (Oxford: Clarendon, 1975), available at http://www.marxists.org/reference/archive/hegel/works/sl/slobject.htm (retrieved 3 May 2010). The entire line is: "The aim of knowledge is to divest the objective world that stands opposed to us of its strangeness, and, as the phrase is, to find ourselves at home in it."

Bibliography

Aarseth, Espen. *Cybertext: Perspectives on Ergodic Literature*. Baltimore: Johns Hopkins University Press, 1997.

Bogost, Ian. *Unit Operations: An Approach to Videogame Criticism*. Cambridge, MA: MIT Press, 2008.

Chick, Tom. "Is *Modern Warfare 2* the Most Disgusting Game of the Year?" *Fidgit*, 10 November 2009. http://www.fidit.com/archives/2009/11/is_modern_warfare_2_the_most_d.php. Retrieved 24 February 2010.

Dragon Age: Origins. Edmonton, Alberta: BioWare, 2009, console and PC video game.

Frasca, Gonzalo. "Videogames of the Oppressed." In *First Person: New Media as Story, Performance, and Game*, ed. Noah Wardrip-Fruin and Pat Harrigan. Cambridge, MA: MIT Press, 2004. 85–93.

Gee, James Paul. *What Video Games Have to Teach Us About Learning and Literacy*. New York: Palgrave Macmillan, 2007.

Hegel, Georg Wilhelm Friedrich. *Hegel's Logic.* Trans. William Wallace. Oxford: Clarendon, 1975. http://www.marxists.org/reference/archive/hegel/works/sl/Slobject.htm. Retrieved 3 May 2010.

Hitman. Copenhagen: IO Interactive, 2000–2006, console and PC video game series.

Huizinga, Johan. *A Study of the Play-Element in Culture.* Boston: Beacon, 1955.

Humphries, Jodie. "Avatar Vs. Modern Warfare 2: The Billion Dollar Behemoths." *Business Management,* 14 January 2010. http://www.bme.eu.com/news/avatar-vs-modern-warfare-2. Retrieved 22 February 2010.

Manhunt. Edinburgh: Rockstar North, 2003, console and PC video game.

Mass Effect 2. Edmonton, Alberta: BioWare, 2010, console and PC video game.

Penny, Simon. "Representation, Enaction, and the Ethics of Simulation." In *First Person: New Media as Story, Performance, and Game.* Ed Noah Wardrip-Fruin and Pat Harrigan. Cambridge, MA: MIT Press, 2004. 73–83.

Star Wars: The Force Unleashed. San Francisco: LucasArts, 2008, console video game.

Starr, Paul. "Policy as a Simulation Game." *American Prospect* 5, no. 17 (1994). http://www.Prospect.org/print/V5/17/starr-p.html. Retrieved 1 June 2010.

10

Making Modern Evil:
Terrorism, Torture, and
the Creation of Evil in *24*

Michael J. Lewis

On December 25, 2009, Umar Farouk Abdulmutallab attempted to detonate an explosive device on Northwest Airlines Flight 253. Abdulmutallab had smuggled explosive chemicals in packages sewn into his underwear. The chemicals failed to explode, and Abdulmutallab was left with burns on his legs and groin. As with other attempted mid-flight terror attacks, the passengers and flight crew worked together to limit the damage.

Within hours, conservative pundits and politicians began to use the failed attack to criticize the Obama administration, saying that President Obama did not take the threat of terrorism seriously and that his administration had not done enough to prevent attacks. One question that quickly became a focus of debate was whether the United States was doing enough to extract information from terrorists. Pundits called for broader use of "enhanced interrogation" — techniques that others called torture.

Christmas holiday notwithstanding, cable news networks in the United States ramped the debate up into high gear. On the December 29, 2009, edition of *Morning Joe* on MSNBC, Pat Buchanan argued, "Frankly, if that means you have to deny him pain medication because he's badly burned, I think you go ahead and do that. I'm not arguing for torture.... Nobody is, but I am arguing for hostile interrogations of this fellow, because our job is to protect American lives. It's not to make sure his Miranda rights haven't been violated."[1] In response, Spencer Ackerman, the national security correspondent for the *Washington Independent*, pointed out that Abdulmutallab began talking immediately after the attack failed — even though he was twice reminded of his right to remain silent. He informed the passengers on Flight 253 that he was a member of al-Qaeda. Then, after being taken into custody at the Detroit Airport, he began cooperating with law enforcement. Ackerman said, "I mean, the fact is, al-Qaeda is a dangerous and really important threat, but ... it's ludicrous to think that we should inflate how dangerous they are because that's exactly what they want."[2]

The disagreement between Ackerman and Buchanan is more than just a public policy debate. They disagree at a deep ideological level. The goal of Buchanan, and his ideological allies, is to reframe the debate over the United States' terrorism policy by defining terrorists as evil. This allows them to gloss over both the contexts out of which terrorism grows, and the human rights violations manifest in the use of torture by the CIA and military contractors. Buchanan wants the viewers to believe that Abdulmutallab is an evil person, pure and simple. Ackerman believes that the story of Abdulmutallab is far more complex. Abdulmutallab came from a well-off family, but was frustrated by the disconnect he saw between his religion and the culture. This disconnect was exploited by the people Abdulmutallab looked up to. In the end, Abdulmutallab committed himself to being a solider, or pawn, for a cause far greater than he understood. If Buchanan and his ilk were to acknowledge the complexities of Abdulmutallab's motivations, they would be forced to deal with issues at the root of terrorism.

The debate underlying this dispute is an example of how the broader ideology flattens the argument and hides the more complicated issues driving terrorism. Buchanan sets up a good/evil dichotomy that is easy to explain and plays to our base understanding of the world. His rhetoric is an example of how the media seek to shape the public's ideological understanding of terrorism.

This chapter focuses specifically on one of the most popular media representations of terrorism and terrorists: the television show *24*. I will particularly focus on how the producers of this series differentiate "good" characters from "evil" characters, when the actions of these characters are often quite similar. This line of analysis demonstrates the role that the producers' political ideology plays in the creation of *24*. Of particular interest is the way *24*'s producers frame representations of torture as a means of delineating good and evil.

When *24* premiered on Fox in November 2001 it represented an experiment in American television production for two reasons. The first was the way it was narratively constructed. The show was billed as a "real time" drama: the hour of television was an hour in real time. (To show simultaneous events, the producers employed split screens showing what was happening in multiple storylines.) The second reason was that *24* premiered only months after the

September 11 terror attacks in New York and Washington. This moment in history marks a transition in the way many Americans felt about terrorism. No longer was terrorism relegated to movie screens and special effects sequences. Terrorism was something real that could happen at any moment, anywhere. In keeping with this new era, *24* focused on the randomness and realism of terrorism in a way that no other popular American television show had.

The first season tracked the attempted assassination plot against African American senator and presidential candidate David Palmer by a group of Serbian nationalists. Subsequent seasons centered on more expansive plots, from large-scale biological attacks to the detonation of tactical suitcase-sized nuclear weapons. Over the program's eight seasons, the producers of *24* were able to create a formula that mixed classic action with political intrigue.

Whatever the center of a season's plot, one element always present was the use of torture by both heroes and villains. Torture, in the world of *24*, is value neutral. Torture became a medium through which the producers define the characters' motivations.

I argue that *24*'s texts of terrorism function at two levels. The first level is the narrative of the terrorist group's political motivations for committing acts of terrorism. The second level is the personal reasons that supersede their stated political agenda. This second level of motivation is revealed not through acts of terrorism, but through acts of torture. That is, the producers use torture committed by the terrorists as a narrative device to reveal the terrorists' true motivations. These torture scenes mirror the more notable torture acts committed by *24*'s hero, Jack Bauer. When contrasted with the "enhanced interrogation" techniques used by the government or the brutal torture the program's central character, Jack Bauer, uses "for the greater good," acts of torture used by terrorists take on a selfish and sadistic tone. As we explore the political discourse of these representations, we will begin to come towards a greater understanding of how popular culture texts create and maintain cultural villains.

Defining Terrorism

Terrorism is difficult to define. A 2003 study written by Jeffrey Record for the United States War College found that there were over 109 definitions of terrorism used by different departments and agencies within the U.S. government.[3] A study conducted by Walter Laqueur in 1999 found similar results. In that paper, Laqueur argues that "the only characteristic generally agreed upon is that terrorism involves violence and the threat of violence."[4]

Record goes to great lengths to work through many of these definitions of terrorism. He begins with a definition used by the National Security Agency: "premeditated, politically motivated violence against innocents."[5] However, this definition is purposefully vague, and it could be used equally to characterize the al-Qaeda attacks on the World Trade Center, suicide bombings in Israel, the Allied Forces' firebombing of Dresden in World War II, or America's use of atomic bombs in Hiroshima and Nagasaki.

The U.S. Defense Department defines terrorism as the "calculated use of unlawful violence to inculcate fear; intended to coerce or intimidate governments or societies in pursuit of goals that are generally political, religious, or ideological."[6] Record points out that this definition privileges non-state terrorism over state sponsored terrorism, because a broader definition might inadvertently throw many allies under the bus. One constant issue is the old cliché "One man's terrorist is another man's freedom fighter."

The final definition critiqued by Record focuses on terrorism as a part of guerrilla warfare. This definition comes from *Small Wars, Their Principles and Practice*, Sir C.E. Callwell's late 19th century instruction manual for fighting wars outside of Europe. This definition privileges the uneven nature of terrorist attacks. In this definition, terrorism is a tactic used by a marginalized group to fight a more powerful entrenched group. Both guerrilla warfare and terrorism are asymmetrical in nature. An individual or small group of terrorists is able to inflict a great deal of damage with little investment of manpower or resources. Like the "freedom fighter" definition, Callwell's understanding of terrorism opens many dangerous doors. This definition could cast George Washington's revolutionary army as terrorists, or Oklahoma City bomber Timothy McVeigh as a hero fighting the tyranny of the American government.

At first glance it might seem we have reached a dead end in the analysis of representations of terrorism in post–9/11 popular culture. Without a solid definition to work from, how can we discuss the way the terrorist character functions ideologically within a popular text? In fact, however, the difficulty of defining terrorism becomes a discursive strategy that allows for ideological work on behalf of a hegemonic power. With an open definition it becomes easy to revert to a rhetorical position in which the terrorist is the ultimate Other. Due to the polysemic nature of terrorism, anyone can be a terrorist, and a terrorist strike can happen at any time and at any place.

Defining National Villains

Since the September 11 terrorist attacks, the rhetorical position of the American government has remained firm: terrorists represent the ultimate evil. In a speech given on September 14, 2001, at the National Cathedral, President George W. Bush stated, "Just three days removed from these events, Americans do not yet have the distance of history. But our responsibility to history is already clear: to answer these attacks and rid the world of evil."[7] For President Bush, terrorism and the terrorist were the new National Villains — evil itself, the antithesis of everything that America stood for.

This rhetoric, I believe, was a first move towards the transformation of the terrorist from an individual acting out of desperation, to ultimate Other, to a National Villain. Jessica Stern argues:

> If we see ourselves as fighting evil, rather than a mere threat to national security (among many such threats), we are more veiling to make sacrifices.... If a leader can persuade us that we are fighting evil itself, we are more likely to make sacrifices, and are more prone to throw caution aside with regard to new risks introduced by our action.[8]

Sacrifices in this case include nothing less than civil liberties and what might be called a moral and ethical high ground — the ceding of which is masked through a discourse of the faulty us/them binary. By standing up to terrorism and the terrorist threat, President Bush and his ideological supporters appeared to represent ultimate truth and righteousness. To challenge them was akin to siding with the terrorists that now threatened the United States.

This discursive strategy is aided by the fact that the terrorists who attacked the United States on September 11 were not Americans. The nineteen hijackers were from the Middle East, primarily from Saudi Arabia, a country and a culture dominated by an extremist branch of Islam. They had trained in Afghanistan, home to an extremely repressive government. The hijackers were quite literally Others. Public policy scholar Mathew Coleman argues, "The identification of 'terrorism' suggests the incapacity of a stratal inside/outside geography that 'usually' provides distance from such violence through, for instance, the vigorous policing of borders and the surveillance of potentially 'troublesome' domestic constituents."[9] The logic goes: if terrorists are evil and they attack the United States, the United States must be good. This clear-cut logic leaves no room for American (or Western) complicity in creation of the conditions that have led to the rise of international terrorism. By obfuscating the motivations of al-Qaeda, the global war on terrorism becomes easier to implement and easier to sell to the American public and the United States' international allies.

Coleman continues:

> [T]he naming of "terrorism" provides an alien other against and through which the shape and substance of the state is clarified and subsequently barricaded, thereby targeting and clearly defining enemy rather than the

state's complicity in creating the conditions for violent non-prone state global politicking in the first place.[10]

Coleman believes that classifying terrorists as evil accomplishes two things. First, focusing solely on the inside/outside rhetoric of international and terrorism redefines what "America" is. Second, and more importantly, it obscures the root causes of terrorism.

Terrorists are not just one evil force; they are *the* evil force in contemporary America. This is why, I argue, the figure of the terrorist has become the new National Villain.

Torture and the U.S. Government

With the American invasion of Afghanistan in October 2001, the United States set up a detention center at Guantánamo Bay, Cuba, to hold people captured by the American military, the CIA, and their allies. For many the detention center became a symbol of the Bush administration's human rights abuses and its disregard for international treaties. The administration argued that the men captured in Afghanistan did not conform to the definition of a lawful combatant as defined by the Geneva Convention, and thus were not subject to the Convention's protections.[11]

Once removed from the legal system, those held at Guantánamo Bay were exposed to torture. In February 2008, the CIA confirmed that they had waterboarded[12] three detainees who were being held at Guantánamo.[13] A year later, CIA officials told *The Washington Post* that Abu Zubaida, one of the detainees who had been tortured, gave them good intelligence on al-Qaeda's ongoing operations prior to being waterboarded. *The Washington Post* reported that once Abu Zubaida declared he had no more information, Bush administration officials began to put pressure on the CIA interrogators. An official speaking to *The Washington Post* said, "They couldn't stand the idea that there wasn't anything new. They'd say, 'You aren't working hard enough.' There was both a disbelief in what he was saying and also a desire for retribution — a feeling that 'He's going to talk, and if he doesn't talk, we'll do whatever.'"[14] Abu Zubaida *had* to have more information about al-Qaeda's ongoing operations as a matter of course. Within the administration's deeply ingrained ideology, the good guys had to be correct. There was no place in the logic of the war on terrorism for a man like Abu Zubaida not to be an inexhaustible source of information. As a result the CIA turned to waterboarding to get Abu Zubaida to talk. However, since torture does not work,[15] all the information provided by Abu Zubaida after being tortured was useless.

Others argue that torture is far from useless. Hard-core al-Qaeda members, the argument goes, cannot respond to reason or logic. Therefore, harsh interrogation techniques must be employed. This is the base reasoning at play in James Kirchick's *New York Daily News* editorial titled "Why Shouldn't We Waterboard Abdulmutallab? The Ticking Time Bomb Scenario Is Here." The editorial falsely claims that Abdulmutallab refused to talk to interrogators after he was mirandized. Kirchick argues, "[W]e ought to be using the tools at our disposal to find out the who, what, where, when, and how of the next potential mass casualty attack.... Would it be inappropriate or immoral to pour water over the face and into the nose and mouth of Abdulmutallab, thus generating a drowning sensation (but not actually drowning him) to obtain this information?"[16] The logic is clear: torture is a tool that can and should be applied to terrorist suspects. There is no ambiguity in Kirchick's version of events. Abdulmutallab is a terrorist. He does not deserve the same basic rights that are applied to everyone else in the United States. The good/evil binary is deeply ingrained in our value system.

Heroic Torture and Self-Sacrifice

The producers of *24* work throughout the series to draw a contrast between acts of torture committed by terrorists and acts of torture committed by the show's hero, Jack Bauer. This dichotomy works to close down the viewer's ability to form alternative ideological interpretations of torture. Both Bauer and terrorists employ torture as a means of interrogation or persuasion on a regular basis. The methods used by each group are also quite similar. The difference between the way terrorists torture and Jack Bauer tortures is in their motivations. This contrast exposes how the producers work to name terrorists as evil. Media scholar Douglas Kellner argues, "Media culture produces representations that attempt to induce consent to certain political positions, getting members of the society to see specific ideologies as 'the way things are.' ... Popular culture texts naturalize these positions and thus help mobilize consent to hegemonic political positions."[17] It is through this contrast, as Kellner argues, that the producers of *24* are able to naturalize the good/evil, hero/villain binary and decontextualize terrorism.

There is no question that Jack Bauer is the hero of *24*. Over the show's eight-season run, Bauer was put through one trial after another as he attempted to protect senators, presidents, and the populations of America's cities. His family and friends were targeted and killed along the way. His wife, Teri, was killed in retaliation for his preventing a group of Serbian terrorists from breaking their leader from a secret prison. He was forced to torture his brother and kill his father. He was kidnapped and tortured by the Chinese government because they believed he killed one of their diplomats. He was shot and had his bones broken more times than one could count. He did all of it in the name of America. Even when Bauer engages in questionable or illegal practices, the audience never stops viewing him as the program's hero.

Bauer has made great personal sacrifices at every turn. During the early seasons, Bauer is constantly forced to balance the pressure of family and duty. By the end of the first season, his wife is dead and Bauer's relationship with daughter Kim has taken a turn for the worse. Their relationship becomes more strained over the next few seasons. By the fourth season they are no longer on speaking terms. They do come in contact again during the show's fifth season. When they reunite, the CTU office is hit with a massive terrorist attack, the traumas of Kim's past come flooding back, and Kim tells Bauer that she never wants to see him again because everyone around him always dies.

This self-sacrifice works to frame Bauer as a victim of his own circumstances. His inability to maintain ties to his family in the face of overwhelming odds continuously reinforces the idea that Bauer is a tragic hero. This victimhood motivates Bauer to do what he does. It also becomes a way of absolving him for his actions: he is not acting for himself, but for a greater good. For example, in the sixth season of *24*, Bauer and CTU are attempting to stop a group of Islamist terrorists from exploding small suitcase nuclear bombs in Los Angeles. They discover that the terrorists obtained the nuclear weapons from a Russian general and an American defense contractor hired to safely dispose of the weapons. It turns out that the Russian involved had worked with Bauer's brother, Graem. When evidence emerges that Graem Bauer is directly involved in the smuggling of the nuclear weapons, Bauer and CTU arrest Graem in his family's home. CTU decides that it would be too dangerous to transport Graem to their offices, and instead they set up an interrogation suite in the home.

Because the terrorists have threatened to use more nuclear weapons, time is of the essence in this interrogation. CTU opts to use a (fictional) drug called hyoscine-pentothal. Hyoscine-pentothal is a "truth" drug like hyoscine and sodium pentothal. Unlike those real drugs, hyoscine-pentothal causes extreme pain. Too much of the drug can trigger a heart attack. In order to ensure the long-term health of Graem, a CTU official named Rick Burke administers the drug and monitors Graem's health. When a low dose of the drug does not break Graem, Bauer pushes Burke to inject more. Burke reluctantly complies. Graem's health begins to fail, but he does not give Bauer any information about the nuclear weapons. Again, Bauer instructs Burke to increase the hyoscine-pentothal level, but he refuses, saying that it would kill Graem. Bauer threatens Burke and he complies. The effect on Graem is immediate.

With the third dose of hyoscine-pentothal, Graem's body begins to shut down. In one last push for information Bauer embraces Graem, and with tears running down his face, he begs Graem to tell him what he knows. It is clear that Bauer does not want to torture his brother, but torture is the only way that he is going to get the information that he and CTU need to stop the terrorists from killing more people. Bauer knows what he is doing is wrong. He has deep empathy for the pain he is causing his brother. But Graem left him no other option. It was Graem's fault that he got involved with terrorists.

By framing acts of torture committed by Jack Bauer as acts of heroic self-sacrifice, 24's producers are making a broader statement about the role torture ought to play in United States policy. Torture, when viewed through this lens, becomes not a policy, but a tool of last resort that can be used by American interrogators. The government, like Bauer, does not want to torture anyone, but sometimes one has to put aside personal morality to protect the greater good. Bauer takes on this burden reluctantly, but does so because he knows what has to be done. These sorts of representations of torture work to reinforce the larger good/evil binary that is central to 24's ideological discourse. When the program's hero engages in acts of torture like its villains, viewers have a point of comparison.

Sadistic Torture and Personal Gain

The contrast between acts of torture committed by terrorists and by Bauer is stark. While Bauer is portrayed as a reluctant hero, terrorists are consistently portrayed as selfish, interested only in personal gain and revenge. By building these representations of torture this way the producers work to erase the primary causes of terrorism and replace them with broad caricature. The result of this rhetorical strategy is to portray terrorists as wholly evil.

The motivations of terrorists on 24 are twofold. First, acts of terrorism are motivated by the individual or group's desire for political change. This fits the definition of terrorism. By engaging in acts of mass violence, a subaltern or subjected group tries to change its situation. For example, at the opening of season 6 of 24, the United States has been racked with eleven weeks of suicide bombings. The unnamed terrorist group led by two uneasy allies, Hamri Al-Assad and Abu Fayed, has been calling for attacks on the United States and Americans abroad since the end of the Gulf War. They believe that the United States entered that conflict in order to further its own colonial interests in the region. They are placing pressure on the government of the United States and its citizens with the goal of getting their policies in the Middle East changed. If the United States does not change those policies, they have sent a clear message. However, this first level of motivation only seems to act as a simple narrative device. The second level of motivation is the true reason for committed acts of terrorism. The calls for policy change are nothing more than an excuse to commit acts of terrorism.

The second level of motivation behind these terrorist attacks surfaces very quickly. By emphasizing the terrorists' selfish motivations, as well as the sadism in the acts of torture, the producers of *24* are drawing a clear delineation between Bauer and the terrorists. Abu Fayed demands the American government turn over Jack Bauer. Once he has Bauer in his custody, Fayed's true motivation becomes clear: he wants to take revenge on Bauer for killing his brother. Terrorizing Americans is a satisfying byproduct of the pleasure Fayed will get from torturing and killing Bauer. Fayed's goal is to subject Bauer to the same suffering his brother experienced at Bauer's hands before his death. Fayed does not want information about the government's plan to stop the attacks; he wants to punish, and ultimately kill, Bauer for what was done to his brother. Fayed directs his men to attack the Americans on buses and trains because *he* wants an opportunity to take revenge on a single man. Fayed uses his men's trust in him, their faith in the cause, and their religion to persuade them to sacrifice themselves. Fayed's cult of personality drives his men to commit self-destructive acts of terrorism so that he may have a chance to take revenge on Bauer. By portraying Fayed as an opportunistic and selfish leader taking advantage of his followers, the producers are, in turn, portraying low-level terrorists as mindless slaves to a cult of personality. The show ignores the complex socio-economic and socio-political conditions that lead to the radicalization of the majority of the young men who find themselves wearing suicide vests.

The other way that the producers of *24* draw a contrast between Bauer and terrorists like Fayed is by comparing and contrasting their methods of torture. In order for Fayed to get the most effective revenge on Bauer, he must make the pain last as long as possible and be as intense as possible. To do this, he hooks Bauer up to an EKG machine to make sure he does not die too quickly. Fayed also uses crude medical instruments as means of causing pain. Throughout the torture scene, he makes sure Bauer knows exactly why he is being tortured. It is in the discourse of this scene and others like it that the producers of *24* are able to transform their terrorists into monomaniacal, hand-rubbing Bond villains. Fayed reveals he is driven by vengeance alone. He is not attempting to uphold ideals or correct the wrongs of generations of subjugation at the hands of a faceless hegemony. Fayed is simply a convenient caricature that hides the complex reality of modern global terrorism.

There are similarities between this scene and the one where Bauer tortures his brother. Both scenes use monitoring equipment and medical tools to inflict pain. Torture becomes shorthand that the producers can use to emphasize the dichotomy between Bauer and terrorists, between good and evil. The difference is in the intent and the goals. Fayed perverts the use of the EKG by using it to make sure Bauer does not die too quickly. Fayed's tools appear to be crude and rusted, again perverting their intended use. Instead of being tools of healing they are tools of pain. By comparison, the medical equipment used by Bauer and CTU is top of the line. There is no real difference between the acts of torture committed by Bauer and Fayed, but the ways that the producers represent each signals to the viewer that there is a difference in how one ought to feel about what is going on onscreen.

The Creation of Evil

Popular representations such as those detailed in this chapter work to lead the viewer to a specific understanding of terrorism. The transfer of ideology via television is complex. John Fiske argues, "We can thus call television an essentially realistic medium because of its ability to carry a social convincing sense of the real. Realism is not a matter of any fidelity to an empirical reality, but of discursive conventions by which and for which reality is constructed."[18] Thus the average viewer of a program like *24* is being exposed only to the good/evil dichotomy. The root causes of terrorism are downplayed and erased.

Our culture takes as a given that terrorists are evil. We take for granted that the people who commit mass acts of violence must be villains. How else can it be explained? Yet dismissing terrorists as villains, and therefore evil, ignores the causes of terrorism by explaining symptoms. Such a narrative reinforces a prevailing wisdom without anyone's having to think too much about it.

The discursive strategy deployed by the producers of *24* mirrors Pat Buchanan's attempt, mentioned earlier in this chapter, to hide the root causes of terrorism in order to bolster his ideological beliefs. Whatever one thinks about imperialism and globalization, it is hard to ignore their impact on the world. Simply portraying terrorists as evil glosses over the context in which they became radicalized. Such rhetoric works towards a single end: to render the figure of the terrorist and terrorism as a generic idea onto which anything can be applied. Naming terrorists as evil implicitly means that those who oppose terrorism are good. In *24*, this means that the program's hero, Jack Bauer, is allowed to torture without consequences or rejection from the viewers.

For Bauer and CTU the complex circumstances that drive someone to commit an act of terrorism never enter the equation. Their goal is law enforcement — and while the bomb is ticking away waiting to be disarmed, there is no time for a philosophical discussion about the natural consequences of globalization and the rise of the military industrial complex. Terrorists are evil. Period. End of discussion. Framing Bauer and CTU's response to terrorism as one of law enforcement provides them with an excuse for their actions, and strips them of responsibility for the outcomes. By extension, torture becomes merely an essential tool to do their job.

This logic is a mirror image of the larger debate happening about terrorism. It should be no surprise that so many talking heads on cable television were quick to name Umar Farouk Abdulmutallab as an evil terrorist. Abdulmutallab is declared evil; therefore he is evil. The circumstances of his upbringing are irrelevant; whatever might have brought him to the point at which he was willing to blow himself up in order to kill hundreds of people on a plane, it does not matter. It only matters that he tried. Abdulmutallab is evil by virtue of his actions.

Discussion of terrorism and terrorists in these stark binary terms pushes complex issues aside in favor of empty rhetoric. When newspaper columnists and talking heads on cable news vilify and passively dismiss terrorists as evil, there is no room for a discussion about the motivation or causes of terrorism. But those things do not really matter. Terrorists are evil. It is as simple as that.

NOTES

1. John Amato, "Pat Buchanan's Torture American Style: Withhold Meds from Would-Be Flight 253 Bomber," 29 December 2009, available at http://crooksandliars.com/john-amato/pat-buchanan-torture-american-style-wit (retrieved 12 January 2010).

2. Ibid.

3. Jeffrey Record, "Bounding the Global War on Terrorism," December 2003, available at http://www.globalsecurity.org/military/library/report/2003/record_bounding.pdf (retrieved 20 June 2010), 6.

4. Walter Laqueur, *The New Terrorism: Fanaticism and the Arms of Mass Destruction* (New York: Oxford University Press, 1999), 6.

5. Record, 6.

6. Ibid., 8.

7. George W. Bush, "The National Security Strategy of the United States of America," 14 September 2001, available at http://www.informationclearinghouse.info/article2320.htmp (retrieved 20 June 2010), 5.

8. Jessica Stern, "Fearing Evil," *Social Research* 71.4 (2004), 116.

9. Matthew Coleman, "The Naming of 'Terrorism' and Evil 'Outlaws': Geopolitical Place-Making after 11 September," *Geopolitics* 8.3 (2003), 91.

10. Ibid., 92.

11. Former Bush administration lawyer John Yoo argues the point in an essay, "The U.S. Military Need Not Obey the Geneva Conventions When Dealing with Suspected Terrorists," in *Is Torture Ever Justified?* ed. Tom Head (Detroit: Thomas Gale, 2005), 28.

12. Waterboarding is a method of torture that can be broadly defined as simulated drowning. A suspect is laid on his back with his legs elevated. Water is then poured onto his nose and mouth.

13. Caitlin Price, "CIA Chief Confirms Use of Waterboarding on 3 Terror Detainees," *The Jurist*, 5 February 2008, available at http://jurist.law.pitt.edu/paperchase/2008/02/cia-chief-confirms-use-of-waterboarding.php (retrieved 3 March 2009).

14. Peter Finn and Joby Warrick, "Detainee's Harsh Treatment Foiled No Plots," *The Washington Post*, 29 March 2009, A01.

15. See Elaine Scarry, *The Body in Pain: The Making and Unmaking of the World* (New York: Oxford University Press, 1985); and Elaine Scarry, "Five Errors in the Reasoning of Alan Dershowitz," in *Torture: A Collection*, ed. Sanford Levinson (Oxford: Oxford University Press, 2004), 281–90.

16. James Kirchick, "Why Shouldn't We Waterboard Abdulmutallab? The Ticking Time Bomb Scenario Is Here," *New York Daily News*, 3 January 2010, available at http://www.nydailynews.com/opinions/2010/01/03/2010-01-03_why_shouldnt_we_waterboard_abdulmutallab_the_ticking_time_bomb_scenario_is_here.html (retrieved 22 February 2010).

17. Douglas Kellner, *Media Culture: Cultural Studies, Identity and Politics between the Modern and Post Modern* (London: Routledge, 1995), 59.

18. John Fiske, *Television Culture* (London: Routledge, 1987), 24.

BIBLIOGRAPHY

Amato, John. "Pat Buchanan's Torture American Style: Withhold Meds from Would-Be Flight 253 Bomber." 29 December 2009. Available at http://crooksandliars.com/john-amato/pat-buchanan-torture-american-style-wit. Retrieved 12 January 2010.

Bush, George W. "The National Security Strategy of the United States of America." 14 September 2001. Available at http://www.informationclearinghouse.info/article2320.htm. Retrieved 20 June 2010.

Coleman, Mathew. "The Naming of 'Terrorism' and Evil 'Outlaws': Geopolitical Place-Making after 11 September." *Geopolitics* 8.3 (2003), 87–104.

Finn, Peter, and Joby Warrick. "Detainee's Harsh Treatment Foiled No Plots." *The Washington Post*, 29 March 2009, A01.

Fiske, John. *Television Culture*. London: Routledge, 1987.

Kellner, Douglas. *Media Culture: Cultural Studies, Identity and Politics between the Modern and Post Modern*. London: Routledge, 1995.

Kirchick, James. "Why Shouldn't We Waterboard Abdulmutallab? The Ticking Time Bomb Scenario Is Here." *New York Daily News*, 3 January 2010. Available at http://www.nydailynews.com/opinions/2010/01/03/2010-01-03_why_shouldnt_we_waterboard_abdulmutallab_the_ticking_time_bomb_scenario_is_here.html. Retrieved 22 February 2010.

Laqueur, Walter. *The New Terrorism: Fanaticism and the Arms of Mass Destruction*. New York: Oxford University Press, 1999.

Price, Caitlin. "CIA Chief Confirms Use of Waterboarding on 3 Terror Detainees." *The Jurist*, 5 February 2008. Available at http://jurist.law.pitt.edu/paperchase/2008/02/cia-chief-confirms-use-of-waterboarding.php. Retrieved 3 March 2009.

Record, Jeffrey. "Bounding the Global War on Terrorism." December 2003. Available at http://www.globalsecurity.org/military/library/report/2003/record_bounding.pdf. Retrieved 20 June 2010.

Scarry, Elaine. *The Body in Pain: The Making and Unmaking of the World*. New York: Oxford University Press, 1985.

_____. "Five Errors in the Reasoning of Alan Dershowitz." In *Torture: A Collection*. Ed. Sanford Levinson. Oxford: Oxford University Press, 2004. 281–90.

Stern, Jessica. "Fearing Evil." *Social Research* 71.4 (2004): 111–26.

Yoo, John. "The U.S. Military Need Not Obey the Geneva Conventions When Dealing with Suspected Terrorists." In *Is Torture Ever Justified?* Ed. Tom Head. Detroit: Thomas Gale, 2005.

11

No Laughing Matter: The Joker as a Nietzschean Critique of Morality

Jamey Heit

In the movies, mobsters make good bad guys. The trope frequently entails a mob boss or crime lord whose grip on a city causes the populace to watch over their collective shoulder as they go about their daily lives. Robberies and murders tend to ratchet up the tension[1] until a protagonist who embodies the virtues our society expects from its good heroes appears to accomplish what no one else can: eliminating the threat that the villain poses to the world's moral structure. Mobsters, bound within a clearly delineated definition of right or good, are readily identifiable villains; by violating the narrative world's moral framework, they identify who the good guy is, as well as why that character should be preferred to his or her evil counterpart. The mobsters permit directors to establish clear poles in the classic binary that underscores our popular culture: good versus evil, or, more specifically, how good triumphs over evil.

The Dark Knight[2] begins in a similar capacity. Gotham City has descended into chaos; its citizens have been overwhelmed by the mob's corrupt grip on the city. None of Gotham's institutions can curb the unruly mob and its godfather-esque leader, Maroni. Batman does his best by night to combat the mob's influence, but, tellingly, Batman's role as a guardian of what is good does not cohere with the simplistic paradigm described above. As the opening sequence shows, the mobsters are not going to be the real villains. A man in weird face paint robs a bank, which on the surface falls within the narrative paradigm one might expect. The twist, of course, is that this is a new breed of criminal (and not just because he shoots his fellow thieves), one who dis-

175

locates himself from the narrative's sterilized notion evil that characterizes the mobsters. The man with the painted face, Heath Ledger's Joker, steals *from* the mob.

This sequence sets the stage for two conversations at the film's beginning that frame the capacity in which *The Dark Knight* explores the notion of evil. When the Joker appears at a meeting of Gotham's crime bosses, an insightful exchange unfolds. The Joker offers to rid the city of Batman, which would ensure that the mob could continue its ways without disruption. The price for eliminating good is steep: half of the mob's collective money. One of the mobsters, Gambol, in his mistrust tells the Joker: "You're crazy." The Joker's response is crucial to understanding how he characterizes evil. He tells the room matter-of-factly: "I'm not. No, I'm not." One could easily argue that the Joker *is* crazy; he exhibits no interest in our cultural values, be they material or moral. Gambol's claim reflects an easy way to dismiss this weird person who does not cohere at all with our expectations of what constitutes evil. The extent to which the Joker subverts those expectations crystallizes at this particular moment. Everyone in the room and everyone watching knows that the Joker is telling the truth. He is decidedly not crazy; he already beat the mobsters at their own game. In this realization, the mobsters and the audience must confront a representation of evil that refuses easy explanations.

The film echoes this point in a similarly early conversation between Bruce Wayne and Alfred. In their surveillance room at Wayne Enterprises, the two men discuss who this Joker might be and how to understand him, given that he does not fit the normative definition of evil that describes the mobsters:

> WAYNE: I knew the mob wouldn't go down without a fight, but this is different. They crossed the line.
>
> ALFRED: You crossed the line first, sir. You squeezed them. You hammered them to the point of desperation. And in their desperation they turned to a man they didn't fully understand.
>
> WAYNE: Criminals aren't complicated, Alfred. You just have to figure out what he's after.
>
> ALFRED: With respect, sir, perhaps this is a man that *you* don't fully understand.

When the bad guys do not know how to categorize the Joker, one can look away; villains are prone to simple mistakes (and, frequently, poor marksmanship). Batman, however, is the hero, the one who guarantees that good will eventually triumph in the face of evil. Alfred's words capture the crucial distinction about the Joker, namely that he does not square with a definition of evil that simplifies his motives to the profiteering that otherwise defines evil in Gotham. Alfred reiterates the point when telling a story from his past about a similarly difficult reduction of a criminal to our culture's stock definition of evil. The man in Alfred's story showed no interest in the valuable thing at stake: money. Bruce Wayne cannot figure out why an evil person would not be greedy. "Because," Alfred responds, "he thought it was good sport. Because some men aren't looking for anything logical, like money. They can't be bought, bullied, reasoned or negotiated with. Some men just want to watch the world burn." The vignette underscores further how the Joker diverges from the good-versus-evil paradigm that audiences expect. Even when criminals exhibit obscure motives, one can trust in a basic, Darwinian sense they have the instinct of self-preservation and, when possible, self-aggrandizement. In addition to the Joker's disinterest in the things evil figures usually want — money and power — the Joker simply does not care. Herein one uncovers an important accent in this criminal's chosen name. Crime is a joke; the evil he perpetuates is merely a game, played for its immediacy, with little regard for its outcome. Thus, the Joker subverts yet another standard by which we determine evil, namely the consequences of our actions.

The Joker's dislocation from our cultural norms of good and evil establishes, then, two questions that this chapter will explore. First, how do we make sense of someone whose actions cannot be categorized according to our deeply rooted cultural notions of good and evil? In many ways, the Joker emerges as evil within the Judeo-Christian binary of good and evil, which only aggravates the discord that results from our inability to situate the Joker within this paradigm. This, in turn, elicits a second question: why does the Joker's evil appeal to us as an audience? The question is difficult to ask, but it cannot be ignored. Largely on the strength of Heath Ledger's performance as the Joker, *The Dark Knight* became the fourth highest grossing film of all time.[3] Clearly something about the film appeals to viewers, despite its subversive narrative structure.

To respond to these questions, this chapter will turn to the Judeo-Christian tradition's moral framework and discuss how evil comes about in a world created by a good God. As his exploits unfold, the Joker displays qualities frequently associated with the Devil. However, when analyzed through the lens of Nietzsche's thought, the Joker's evilness crystallizes when he diverges from the moral binaries that the Judeo-Christian paradigm establishes. The deviation is, in the end, precisely what makes the Joker so evil and, paradoxically, why the Joker proves to be so alluring to a culture whose narrative expectations are that villains be both defined and defeated by these normative outlines.

An important quality that characterizes the devil is his ability to manipulate others. More specifically, the devil frequently accomplishes his ends through his ability to persuade through speech in order to convince people to do something. In Genesis, one finds perhaps an example of this skill that is stitched into our cultural conscience. Even though God prohibits Adam and Eve from eating the Tree of Knowledge's fruit, the snake is able to convince them to do otherwise:

> [The serpent] said to the woman, "Did God say, 'You shall not eat from any tree in the garden'?" The woman said to the serpent, "We may eat of the fruit of the trees in the garden; but God said, 'You shall not eat of the fruit of the tree that is in the middle of the garden, nor shall you touch it, or you shall die.'" But the serpent said to the woman, "You will not die; for God knows that when you eat of it your eyes will be opened, and you will be like God, knowing good and evil."[4]

Though God defines a clear boundary in a way that ensures what is good,[5] the snake is able through language to recalibrate the prohibition as a mere limitation. The snake relies on the notion that God is good and that God values the created world in order to suggest an alternative possibility. In eating from the tree, Adam and Eve will become like God rather than die. If God is good, this seems plausible. The snake's words imply that God will not ultimately punish Adam and Eve, an argument that both Adam and Eve accept without much thought.[6] Through its speech, then, the snake subverts God by introducing a more nuanced discussion of the broad distinction between good and evil.[7]

The devil's way with words becomes a tradition that emerges frequently in texts situated within the tradition that Genesis 3 establishes.[8] In *Paradise Lost*, the ability to seduce through speech allows the devil to influence his soon-to-be-followers that their allegiance is best placed with him. Satan's speech — laced with the misdirection that characterizes Genesis 3 — summarizes the conflict between good and evil, between God and devil, that informs the standard narrative structure in our popular culture:

> What though the field be lost?
> All is not lost; the unconquerable Will,
> And study of revenge, immortal hate,
> And courage never to submit or yield:
> And what is else not to be overcome?
> That Glory never shall his wrath or might
> Extort from me.[9]

Satan sounds a rebellion against God, which in turn indicates the eternal conflict between good and evil that results when Satan is expelled from heaven. Satan blames God obliquely; in his free (and hateful) will he will scheme in order to get his revenge. Milton's Satan not only establishes the classical fault line between good and evil from the very beginning; Milton also affords Satan a power of speech that those around him cannot resist. Satan's speech casts into doubt the good end of the binary by suggesting that he, not God, will be justified as this conflict plays out.

When Batman first talks with the Joker, one can recognize a similarly smooth speech in how the Joker characterizes his relationship to Gotham's supposedly good forces. When Batman attempts to fit the Joker into an accepted notion of evil, the Joker responds with an uncharacteristic passion:

> Don't talk like one of them. You're not, even if you'd like to be. To them, you're just a freak, like me. They need you right now, but when they don't, they'll cast you out, like a leper. You see, their morals, their code, it's a bad joke. Dropped at the first sign of trouble. They're only as good as the world allows them to be. I'll show you. When the chips are down, these, these civilized people, they'll eat each other. See, I'm not a monster. I'm just ahead of the curve.

Batman's language, the Joker insists, is a façade if it upholds the simplistic notion of good. The joker has a point; the institution that should uphold his right has both denied him a phone call and permitted a non-member of the force into the questioning room. The goodness with which Batman aligns himself through his language is, the Joker points out, the product of utility. Such notion of good (or, more precisely, the greatest good) should not be trusted.

This exchange captures the difficulties, aggravated through the Joker's rhetoric, of articulating just what constitutes evil in *The Dark Knight*. The Joker challenges the values that Batman upholds by questioning the implicit assumption to do so. In this capacity, the Joker echoes the snake in Genesis 3. A clear standard exists, but through the subtlety of speech the Joker presents a legitimate alternative that causes Batman's commitment to the moral paradigm's good pole to waver. The Joker taunts Batman that he might need to kill before the night is over (something Batman does not do), to which Batman responds: "I'm considering it." In a physical confrontation, the Joker, like the snake, is powerless, but through other avenues he manages to subvert the simplistic notion of good that frames the entire conflict between the hero and the villain.

One of the Joker's best tricks, then, is not to claim that evil is better than good, but, rather, to suggest that the entirely paradigm is flawed. Consequently, those who adhere to either good or evil fracture their own self-identity. Those who permit themselves to be labeled within the binary of good-versus-evil invite those in their midst to dismiss them, a condition that the Joker knows well. The alternative that the Joker suggests, to reject the paradigm altogether, links his subversive speech to a writer who famously critiqued the Christian paradigm and its notion of good: Nietzsche. In words that echo the Joker's remarks to Batman, Nietzsche claims:

> Moral judgment has this in common with religious judgment, that it
> believes in realities which do not exist. Morality is only an interpretation of
> certain phenomena, more precisely a *mis*interpretation. Moral judgment
> belongs, as does religious judgment, to a level of ignorance at which even
> the concept of the real, the distinction between the real and the imaginary,
> is lacking.... To this extent moral judgment is never to be taken literally: as
> such it never contains anything but nonsense.[10]

One can hear the Joker's insistence that he is not mad threading through
Nietzsche's claims. The institutions that affirm a good standard and, by implication, an evil, other possibility distort reality in order to justify their position.
The Joker seeks to redress such misinterpretation by subverting the paradigm
and its guardians. The Joker's very real rationality coheres with the need to
expose the institutional distinctions that Nietzsche identifies. To situate oneself
within such a paradigm is to deny reality, an idea that the Joker echoes in his
actions. It is in this capacity that the Joker claims to be ahead of the curve.
His rationality is chilling because it recognizes the point Nietzsche makes:
the rational distinctions that uphold our cultural paradigms of good and evil
are decidedly irrational in their false distinctions.

The specific moral paradigm that Nietzsche has in mind is, of course,
Christianity. While this is a significant point to note, the analysis in this chapter will focus in particular on the connection that Nietzsche establishes
between free will and rationality. In *Human, All Too Human*, Nietzsche privileges clearly human choice and indicates that misunderstanding this ability
obscures the consequences of that will: "The displeasure man feels seems to
refer to *operari* [doing], but in truth it refers to *esse* [being], which is the act
of a free will, the primary cause of an individual's existence. Man becomes
that which he *wants* to be; his volition precedes his existence."[11] Those who
are unaware of, or misconstrue, this freedom frequently and falsely understand
themselves within the simplistic moral paradigm that the Joker subverts so
clearly. Nietzsche continues: "because he thinks he is free (but not because
he is free), man feels remorse and the pangs of conscience."[12] The problem,
then, lies with the person (most of us) who chooses to subject him or herself
to a moral paradigm that reduces freedom to consequences as defined by
thinking of freedom as filtered through a particular moral framework. Those
who can excise themselves from this false condition will find, Nietzsche asserts,
that the categories of good and evil cease to apply: "No one is responsible for
his deed, no one for his nature; to judge is to be unjust."[13] Nietzsche echoes,
in order to subvert, an important moral guideline within Christianity: "'Do
not judge, so that you may not be judged. For with the judgment you make
you will be judged, and the measure you give will be the measure you get.'"[14]
The irony, as Nietzsche well knows, is that to avoid judgment one must refuse

the binaries that establish criteria for judgment. Jesus' commandment unfolds within a clear moral paradigm (a fact evident in the emergence of this statement within one of the world's great moral tracts, the Sermon on the Mount), which is the very thing Nietzsche says one must reject if one is to embrace fully one's freedom.

The logic here parallels the Joker's own thoughts. To adhere to a moral code is to cede one's freedom by submitting oneself to standards that essentially determine *a priori* whether one falls within the good or the bad category. The result of this supposed choice is, actually, to belie in the name of good the virtues that society understands to be good. In his earlier writing, Nietzsche identifies already that to privilege Christianity's normative label of good is to deny the capacity to be good: "In general, 'Surrender to the will of God' and 'humility' are often only a cloak for the timid cowardice to confront destiny with decisiveness."[15] The Joker holds steadfast to this kind of standard. When Joker rigs two ships — one with families, one with criminals — with explosives and gives each ship the detonator to the other ship, he anticipates that the chips will be down and society's instinct for self-preservation will kick in. He tells both boats that if neither destroys the other by midnight, he will detonate both boats. The experiment is designed to prove that when the chips are down, the façade of good and evil will dissolve and those involved, like those watching, will have to accept the failure of moral standards to preserve life. Surprisingly (perhaps), his social experiment ultimately fails; neither boat destroys the other by the deadline. In response, the Joker does not admit to Batman that virtue as defined within a traditional paradigm of good-versus-evil has triumphed. Rather, he mutters to himself that both boats *failed* because they clung to a flawed notion of good. The only problem that the Joker can recognize is a continued adherence to the moral standards the Nietzsche decries. In response to the boats' refusal to destroy one another, the Joker says dismissively that one "can't rely on anyone these days." From the Joker's perspective the decision to die mutually rather than to preserve oneself reflects the "timid cowardice" that Nietzsche describes. Freedom demands that one act without prohibition. It is in this capacity that the Joker reveals a Nietzschean residue. He does "not surrender" his actions to anyone in the film, regardless of the consequences that this consistency invites.

The ability to concoct these kinds of situations situates the Joker firmly within a Nietzschean perspective. In *Thus Spoke Zarathustra*, one finds a more pronounced discussion from Nietzsche concerning free will as the ability to transcend prescribed notions of good and evil. Describing a culture's obedience to such binaries, Zarathustra states: "This somnolence I disturbed when I taught: what good and evil are, *that nobody knows*— unless it be the creator!— But that is the one who creates humanity's goal and gives the earth its sense and its future: he alone *makes it that* anything is good or evil."[16] The categories that inform our cultural narratives do not reflect reality; they insist upon a dreamlike state wherein such distinctions provide certainty. Nietzsche's claim requires a particular uncertainty, namely the divestment of this false stability in favor of the opportunity one experiences in defining for oneself what these terms mean. Only the creator can determine good *through* the creator's own freedom. As he frequently does, with this idea Nietzsche inverts a hallmark of the Judeo-Christian paradigm. Whereas God creates the world (presumably as a result of God's free will), which is then considered good, Nietzsche's criticism refuses to extend that decision to affect another's freedom. God should not assert that God's creation is good for created beings who are free; they must decide what is good for themselves. The freedom to determine what is good or evil exists only when one refuses to accept another's prescribed standards. The first step in defining good and evil is to resist established definitions for these very terms.

Our culture frequently privileges reason as the basis of morality. A significant portion of the Joker's creative release from our cultural paradigms lies in his ability to devise circumstance wherein reason ceases to uphold the notion of good. A salient example of this subversive planning occurs toward the end of *The Dark Knight* when the Joker abducts both Harvey Dent, Gotham's good guardian, and Rachel Dawes, a similarly minded district attorney. To make a Nietzschean point, the Joker ties each to a chair amidst a room full of oil drums rigged to explode within a short amount of time. The Joker tells Batman where each is located, which turns out to be at opposite ends of the city. Thus, Batman must decide whom to save: the person who upholds the good for which he fights, or the woman whom he loves. This impossible moral choice undercuts the notion that reason can resolve even the most stringent dilemmas. The Joker's elaborate plan brings into focus a point that Nietzsche argues in critiquing the moral (philosophical and religious) tradition that Western culture embraces: "The most general formula at the basis of every religion and morality is: 'Do this and this, refrain from this and this — and you will be happy! Otherwise...' Every morality, every religion *is* this imperative — I call it the great original sin of reason, *immortal unreason.*"[17] The notion that there exists a specific answer for difficult moral situations affords a false sense of security. In fact, Nietzsche labels this loyalty the very opposite of its foundation. To associate happiness with adherence to a set of moral standards not only limits one's freedom, but also fractures that which provides such clarity in the first place. Like freedom, one should not take reason's ability to address issues of good and evil for granted. As the Joker's dilemma makes clear, there is no answer for Batman. Even if he applies rational thought to the dilemma, the conclusion will be costly within the good-versus-evil binary that informs the film's narrative. To emphasize the point, Batman's rational choice to save Harvey Dent — who embodies rational and moral values — exposes the irrevocable consequences that reason cannot contain. Nietzsche, then, subverts an important assumption in our culture's moral tradition and, moreover, he does so in a way that links clearly a reliance on reason with the importance of free will in establishing our cultural narrative about good and evil. As Nietzsche suggests, the original sin that condemns humanity lies not in its disobedience to God, but rather in the interpretative response to that decision. Accepting blindly that God is, in fact, good stains humanity permanently. It is only by releasing oneself from these paradigms that one can recover one's freedom.

For better or for worse, Harvey Dent survives, though not without significant burns to his face. Soon thereafter, the audience watches as he refuses medication to dull the pain (and given the extent of the burns, one can assume the amount of pain is significant). Dent's willingness to endure the pain reflects the terrible nature of disassociating oneself from the notion of good; he is now cruelly aware that the good he represents could not save Rachel. Thus, he ceases to be Harvey Dent and becomes a character whose very name indicates that he henceforward rejects the simple binary of good-versus-evil; he adopts the name Two-Face.

Dent's new identity soon receives moral instruction from an unlikely source: the Joker. While visiting Two-Face's hospital room, the Joker offers the following advice in response to Two-Face's anger over losing Rachel:

> I just did what I do best. I took your little plan and I turned it on itself. Look what I did to this city with a few drums of gas and a couple of bullets. Hmm. You know, you know what I've noticed? Nobody panics when things go "according to plan." Even if the plan is horrifying! If, tomorrow, I tell the press that, like, a gang banger will get shot, or a truckload of soldiers will be blown up, nobody panics, because it's all part of the plan. But when I say that one little old mayor will die, well then everyone loses their minds!

At this point, the Joker puts a gun in Two-Face's hands, and then positions the gun against his own head. With the gun in place, the Joker continues to describe his own lack of a moral paradigm: "Introduce a little anarchy. Upset the established order, and everything becomes chaos. I'm an agent of chaos. Oh, and you know the thing about chaos? It's fair!"

Two-Face takes the advice to heart. He pulls out the coin that he flips to make decisions. He tells the Joker that if the coin comes up heads, the Joker will live, but if the coin lands on its blackened side, he'll shoot the Joker. Without missing a beat, the Joker responds, "Now we're talking."[18]

The coin symbolizes a significant shift in how the film portrays good and evil. Previously, Dent's coin had heads on both sides, so when he appeared to leave choices to chance, he actually knew in advance the outcome. The initial coin, then, grounded Dent in the binary that the Joker encourages him to disregard. Chance is the only fair game; it is the only standard that resists the infringements that Nietzsche identifies. When Dent becomes Two-Face, he adopts the Joker's independence from a simplified moral paradigm. In so doing, Two-Face echoes a piece of advice that Zarathustra speaks. The person who leaves his or her life to chance exhibits "the yielding of the greatest, that is risk and danger, and a dice-playing for death."[19] In abandoning oneself to chance, one does not guarantee safety. In fact, one guarantees the opposite, namely that one will never be safe. Chance is morally neutral and this is the foundation upon which one can ground one's freedom. The Joker embraces and therefore embodies the paradox contained in Zarathustra's advice. He legitimately does not care whether Two-Face shoots him; his concern is whether Two-Face will abandon fully the moral framework that would inform such a decision for most people. To be free, one must accept that freedom, like chance, is morally neutral. Everyone can embrace the possibilities contained therein, but to do so is to release oneself from the false certainty — the immortal sin of reason — that Nietzsche finds in a specifically Christian moral paradigm.[20]

Within the parameters of our cultural understanding of good and evil, one can easily label the Joker as decidedly, even wholly, evil. For example, after convincing Two-Face to embrace chance, the Joker leaves the hospital room, uses the dispenser in the hall to sanitize his hands, and then detonates (as promised) a bomb that begins to destroy the hospital. As the explosions engulf the hospital, the scene shifts and the audience sees the Joker walking away. The image is absurd, particularly because the Joker is still dressed in the nurse's uniform and wig that he used to infiltrate Dent's room in the first place. As he ambles away, the explosions stop, which causes the Joker to pause. Clearly something has not worked, so he fiddles with his detonator. Eventually the final explosion sounds, the entire hospital falls to the ground, and the Joker does not seem to notice; he saunters away as he did before the interruption. The short vignette captures the extent to which we can label the Joker as evil and, at the same time, indicates the capacity of Nietzsche's thought to subvert the moral paradigm that permits us to be sure that the Joker is evil in the first place. *Clearly* his actions violate moral standards that our culture accepts (and indeed, that other cultures accept); one simply does not blow up a hospital. Aghast at what the Joker does, one can hear the question emerging in the audience members' minds: what kind of deranged person would do such a thing?

The issue at hand, which Nietzsche expresses frequently, is the assumption that informs such a question. Our collective moral compass demands that we evaluate the Joker's actions in a particular capacity, but in light of the Joker's Nietzschean character, a different question arises: how do we respond to a person who rejects completely the notion of right and wrong? The Joker's evil characteristics are perhaps most unsettling for precisely this reason. He unhinges himself completely from the standard of good and evil. As becomes apparent at the beginning of *The Dark Knight*, the audience can expect a different kind of villain, one who upsets a cultural tendency to reduce questions of good and evil to simplistic caricatures. When analyzing the Joker, one must confront the uncomfortable reality that he eludes our moral judgment because he simply does not acknowledge that his actions and the consequences that follow have *any* moral worth.[21]

This hazy moral condition echoes a problem that Hannah Arendt identifies when discussing Adolf Eichmann's trial. Her famous phrase to describe the dilemma that Eichmann poses, the banality of evil, underlines the challenges that the Joker poses for understanding how he is evil. Arendt summarizes well the intellectual problem that Eichmann creates:

> The trouble with Eichmann was precisely that so many were like him, and that the many were neither perverted nor sadistic, that they were, and still are, terribly and terrifyingly normal. From the viewpoint of our legal institutions and of our moral standards of judgment, this normality was much more terrifying than all the atrocities put together, for it implied — as had been said at Nuremberg over and over again by the defendants and their counsels — that this new type of criminal, who is in actual fact *hostis generis humani*, commits his crimes under circumstances that make it well-nigh impossible for him to know or to feel that he is doing wrong.[22]

Eichmann presents an historical counterweight to those who would dismiss what the Joker represents as narrative excess. While the Joker is fictional, his actions echo one of history's dark chapters in which cultural definitions of evil dissolved. When normality characterizes actions — and by normality I mean when something is done without cognizance of any moral implications — those who do accept cultural standards of good and evil can often only watch, not necessarily in horror, as evil unfolds. Eichmann's acts were certainly terrible, but what Arendt recognizes is the normalcy with which he was able to murder indiscriminately. The concern, then, lies not only in Eichmann's willingness to behave in an evil way, but his *ability* to do so. The banality of evil requires that others either support the evil person's actions, or, more troublingly, watch idly as that person's evil unfolds before their eyes. The Joker's alluring character parallels the point that Arendt suggests. Isolated evil can be easily dismissed, but when evil unfolds from within a culture, such a presence implicates those who permit (in whatever capacity) evil to swell unchecked. Herein lies the Joker's terribly irony. He divests himself completely of any moral framework; his doing so led to overtly horrible actions, yet audiences around the world could not help but watch the film. Objectively, one can label the Joker as evil, but his makeup, his purple suit, and his absurdity can still seduce the objectivity-minded guardians of good.

In reflecting on Eichmann's affect within the courtroom, Arendt notices a curious quality. Despite Eichmann's horrific crimes, she notes, and "[d]espite all the efforts of the prosecution, everybody could see that this man was not a 'monster.'"[23] The consequences of Eichmann's actions stretched the world's moral boundaries, not in a capacity that would justify what he did; the problem was, as Arendt explains, that "it was difficult indeed not to suspect that he was a clown. And since this suspicion would have been fatal to the entire enterprise [his trial], and was also rather hard to sustain in view of the sufferings he and his like had caused to millions of people, his worst clowneries were hardly noticed and almost never reported."[24] Clowns thrive precisely because they resist the standards that inform the rest of the circus. Their job is to divert the audience's attention, to amuse, to distract. Distractions do not usually result in untold numbers of murder victims, but the veneer of absurdity, the dislocation from a particular set of expectations and standards, can obscure a truly dark reality. Arendt may as well be describing the Joker in *The Dark Knight*. He is a clown, but when such a clown is intent on wreaking havoc, he can subvert our cultural standards with dangerous consequences.

Even Batman does not quite realize what is at stake with the Joker's Nietzschean outlook on life. What the Joker's evil exposes is this shortsightedness. Blind trust in the notion of goodness creates space for villains to exploit. In rejecting any notion of good and evil — always an important corollary to those who refuse moral standards — the Joker exposes our cultural reliance on figures or institutions to which we have entrusted guardianship of what we deem to be good. When evil refuses to conform to good's expectations, it tends to be goodness that fails. This can be paralyzing. What the Joker makes clear in *The Dark Knight* is the success evil can enjoy when we naively ignore the presence of evil.

NOTES

1. In most successful narratives, be they film, television, or book-based, it is important to note that the archetypal villain usually does not perpetrate sexually violent crimes. Moreover, the character who rules the "evil" organization in question is frequently defined by his — and it is almost always *his* — asexuality. The two most common codes to mark this erasure are an older man or a physically disfigured man. The former's age connotes that he has moved beyond sexual distraction, while the latter's physical flaw removes him from our cultural expectations that simplify virility to physical attraction. In both cases, the villain's asexuality permits a streamlined confrontation between good and evil. The protagonists (again, usually male) are able to combat

evil and uphold our culture's expectations for its heroes because the moral battle at hand brackets any sexualized competition for the heroine.

2. *The Dark Knight*, directed by Christopher Nolan (Burbank, CA: Warner Bros., 2008), DVD (Two-Disc Special Edition).

3. http://boxofficemojo.com/alltime/world/ (retrieved 19 May 2010). *Avatar* recently relegated *The Dark Knight* to fifth on the all-time gross list. The point, however, is that the Joker provides the foundation for one of only five films to earn more than one billion dollars. What's more, *The Dark Knight* is the only film in the top ten that does not privilege a storyline wherein good triumphs in the end (indeed, the film ends with Batman fleeing, with the police in hot pursuit). The Joker's role in the film's success was noted when Heath Ledger won a posthumous Oscar for his performance.

4. Genesis 3:1b-5. All biblical citations in this chapter come from the New Revised Standard Version.

5. Here I am speaking of good in broad, metaphysical terms. Specifically, prior to the snake's temptation Genesis understands the world as *wholly* good, a fact evident in God's initial evaluation of the world, which includes humans, during creation (see Genesis 1:31). This point frames a significant philosophical and theological question in our intellectual history: how can evil exist in a world that an omnipotent, good God deems to be good? A standard answer, that humans introduced evil through their own free will, keeps intact God's goodness.

6. I would like to emphasize that in the Genesis 3 text, Adam is present during the snake's conversation with Eve. (Genesis 3:6: "And she also gave some to her husband, *who was with her*, and he ate" [emphasis added].) This point is salient insofar as it resists tendencies to establish a moral distinction between men and women that is not tenable. The tendency to "blame Eve" frequently manifests significant problems when discussing issues of good and evil. The assumption that Eve is more at fault based on the Genesis 3 narrative opens space to associate women in general and their sexuality in particular with cultural conceptions of evil. Though I cannot treat this issue at length in this chapter, it is important to recognize that the binary between good and evil in our culture draws heavily on the Genesis 3 story, which, I want to stress, establishes mutual culpability between Adam and Eve in their yielding to the snake's persuasive speech.

7. In *The Trespass of the Sign: Deconstruction, Theology and Philosophy,* Kevin Hart offers a helpful analysis that links the notion of the fall in Christian theology with the ability to manipulate language. See especially pp. 3ff.

8. At this point, my analysis will assume a specifically Christian understanding of good and evil. This narrowing reflects the predominant intellectual and literary tradition that informs specifically *The Dark Knight* and, more broadly, the popular culture milieu that this volume explores.

9. John Milton, *Paradise Lost*, ed. John Leonard (London: Penguin, 2003), I.105–111.

10. Friedrich Nietzsche, *Twilight of the Idols*, "The Improvers of Mankind," §1, trans. R.J. Hollingdale (London: Penguin, 1990), 66.

11. Friedrich Nietzsche, *Human, All Too Human*, "On the History of Moral Failings," §40 from *The Nietzsche Reader*, eds. Keith Ansell Pearson and Duncan Large (Oxford: Blackwell, 2006), 174.

12. Ibid.

13. Ibid.

14. Matthew 7:1–2.

15. Friedrich Nietzsche, "Freedom of Will and Fate" (1862), *The Nietzsche Reader*, ed. Keith Ansell Pearson and Duncan Large (Oxford: Blackwell, 2006), 16.

16. Friedrich Nietzsche, *Thus Spoke Zarathustra*, "On Old and New Tablets," §2, trans. Graham Parkes (Oxford: Oxford University Press, 2005), 170.

17. *Twilight of the Idols*, "The Four Great Errors," §2, 58–59.

18. It is interesting to note that in *No Country for Old Men*, the main villain, Anton Chigurh, decides whether to kill based on a coin flip. The effect parallels the point that the Joker articulates clearly. Released from an accepted standard of good-versus-evil, Chigurh perpetuates evil with no recognition that his acts constitute as much.

19. *Thus Spoke Zarathustra,* "Of Self-Overcoming," §12, 99.

20. One can hear in the Joker's words an implicit critique of Christianity's belief structure. Specifically, by emphasizing chance as a determining factor in life, the Joker rejects the notion that there exists a divine creator and, moreover, that such a creator interacts with the world. This echoes the critique discussed above wherein Nietzsche inverts the moral tradition established in the Genesis narrative. In both cases, the salient point is clear: humans should divest themselves of the moral notions that underpin our culture, as these false frameworks only infringe upon humanity's freedom.

21. A more "positive," or perhaps optimistic, example of this dynamic occurs in *Atlas Shrugged* when Hank Reardon refuses to enter a plea when tried for breaking government regulations. Our culture expects those who live within the cultural milieu to adhere to basic assumptions concerning good, evil, and the authority of certain people or institutions to enforce those standards. What the system cannot accommodate — a fact made clear in Reardon's actions — is the person who consciously denies that such standards can or should determine an action's worth. Ayn Rand, *Atlas Shrugged* (New York: Signet, 1992), 429–460.

22. Hannah Arendt, *Eichmann in Jerusalem: A Report on the Banality of Evil* (New York: Penguin, 1994), 276.

23. Ibid., 54.

24. Ibid.

BIBLIOGRAPHY

"All Time Box Office." Available at http://boxofficemojo.com/alltime/world/. Retrieved 19 May 2010.

Arendt, Hannah. *Eichmann in Jerusalem: A Report on the Banality of Evil.* Rev. ed. New York: Penguin, 1994.

The Dark Knight. Directed by Christopher Nolan. Burbank, CA: Warner Bros., 2008. DVD. (Two-Disc Special Edition.)

Hart, Kevin. *The Trespass of the Sign: Deconstruction, Theology and Philosophy.* Cambridge: Cambridge University Press, 1989.

The Holy Bible: Containing the Old and New Testaments. New Revised Standard Version. Oxford: Oxford University Press, 1995.

Milton, John. *Paradise Lost.* Ed. John Leonard. London: Penguin, 2003.

Nietzsche, Friedrich. *The Nietzsche Reader.* Ed. Keith Ansell Pearson and Duncan Large. Oxford: Blackwell, 2006.

_____. *Thus Spoke Zarathustra.* Trans. Graham Parkes. Oxford: Oxford University Press, 2005.

_____. *Twilight of the Idols/The Anti-Christ.* Trans. R.J. Hollingdale. London: Penguin, 1990.

No Country for Old Men. Directed by Joel and Ethan Coen. Burbank, CA: Walt Disney Video, 2008. DVD.

Rand, Ayn. *Atlas Shrugged.* New York: Signet, 1992.

12

I Am Your Father:
The Villain and the Future Self

Nathaniel Van Yperen

"*I* am your father." Dave sat behind the rotating fan in the hot summer air, working on his Darth Vader impression. The spinning fan blades gave his prepubescent voice the necessary depth. Jay and I cracked up, waiting for our turns. Like many children in the 1980s, we were obsessed with the *Star Wars* phenomenon. We spent our summer vacations exploring the Adirondacks, acting out scenes from the films.[1] Imagining ourselves key members of the Rebel Alliance, we transformed the woods of upstate New York into the forest moon of Endor. An epic story, *Star Wars* appealed to our budding moral sensibilities; it engaged us in the timeless clash between the forces of good and the powers of evil. And, of course, there were the exhilarating action sequences.

In real life, the three of us were cousins, the sons of three brothers. In our own ways we looked up to our fathers and strove to emulate the men who remained not fully known to us.[2] In them we caught glimpses of our future selves, of what we might do, what we might be capable of, and who we might become. There was much excitement and not a little anxiety about our expectations for our individual futures. Like many children of the American middle class, we were each captivated, at times even frightened, by the privilege of an unarticulated sense of possibility.

These unspoken and unrealized potentialities found resonance with a film series in which a young man sets out to find himself, to discover and ultimately control his destiny. In order to achieve this destiny, the fictional Luke Skywalker must wrestle his own father, the symbol of his own potentiality. In many ways, Darth Vader, Luke's father, is the true subject of the film series. Amidst our own strivings for self-trust, the three of us boys were

189

captivated by the iconic villain in *Star Wars*. If Luke symbolizes the present self, then Darth Vader is the *future self gone bad*.

When *Star Wars* first hit the big screen in 1977, Darth Vader drew viewers in like a tractor beam.[3] On the one hand, Darth Vader is a generic villain. He is a henchmen for a tyrant. He is capable of terrible acts: murder, torture, and even genocide (the destruction of the planet of Alderaan). On the other hand, Darth Vader grasps our imagination, interest, and respect in ways that other villains in the films do not. Though clearly on the side of evil, at least for the majority of the original trilogy, he also practices key virtues: fortitude, prudence, and even the theological virtue of faith.[4] He is not debased, but rather (in a sense) is realized through his participation in the "Dark Side" of the Force. Vader successfully controls his destiny in the ways Luke strives to accomplish for himself through Jedi training. For this reason, Darth Vader resists easy categorization. That is to say, in a film series littered with "bad guys," Darth Vader occupies a special and unique status. Darth Vader is a powerful individual, a representative man oriented toward evil ends.

The other bad guys in *Star Wars* are plentiful. For example, Imperial Stormtroopers threaten the heroes of the Rebel Alliance at every turn, but they remain faceless automatons. Starship commanders and admirals largely remain in the background as they fearfully perform banal duties and responsibilities. Bounty hunters, such as Greedo[5] and Boba Fett,[6] are never developed as meaningful characters. Similarly, while the Mos Eisely bar scene in *A New Hope* portrays a literal den of iniquity, the seedy characters function only one-dimensionally. Even the powerful and debased gangster Jabba the Hutt fails to captivate the audience in any way comparable to our interest in Darth Vader. Emperor Palpatine comes closest to representing "pure" evil, but even in the climactic conflict at the end of *The Return of the Jedi* the intrigue lies with Darth Vader. All of these evil characters perform important, but largely symbolic functions: Namely, they populate the big and scary world in which Luke must find his way. These symbolic evil characters are disposable, while Darth Vader remains singular to the development of the *Star Wars* saga.

Many of the "good guys" are also, in a way, replaceable. In *A New Hope*, Leia implores Obi-Wan to come to the aid of the Rebel Alliance, her message communicating that he is their "only hope." As a character within the narrative, she perceives Obi-Wan as irreplaceable. But when Obi-Wan is killed by Darth Vader, Luke stands in as the new messiah of the Rebellion and thus the audience sees what Leia cannot: that Obi-Wan is not singular, and is not the "only hope." But lest we believe that Luke might be inimitable, later, when it is unclear whether Luke will be able to resist the seduction of the Dark Side, his teacher Yoda ruminates that another hope remains: Luke's sister Leia. All the characters that fight for good are to a certain extent symbolic; there is always hope that new goodness will rise up against the Dark Side. Darth Vader remains singular, compelling, and unique because the iconic villain blurs the lines between the heroes and the symbolic evil of the galaxy. Darth Vader problematizes the very dichotomy of good and evil that draws us into the space opera in the first place. He is able to draw us in even though we expect to be repulsed by his evil character. Darth Vader develops as an evil hero.

Throughout the trilogy, Darth Vader embodies physical and imperial strength that is both terrifying and fascinating. Vader's strength is manifested in distinctly evil ways, which is clearly demonstrated in the numerous and memorable "choking" scenes. For instance, in the first action sequence of *A New Hope*, soon after Darth Vader boards the transport ship, we see him lifting and then holding the ship's captain by the throat (with one arm no less). When the captain loses consciousness, Vader casts him to the ground in disgust. While this scene is an overt display of power, the villain conveys this intimidating message in understated ways as well. For instance, at several points in the films, Vader shows his displeasure with his counselors through the mystical power of the Force. He merely lifts his hand and the throat of his antagonist begins to close. In this way Vader undermines arrogance and administers definitive judgment. Darth Vader demands respect and commands obedience. Such power is awe-inspiring.[7] By these acts, the villain is revealed as the one who acts independently, but authoritatively, within the bureaucracy of the Empire's massive space station, the Death Star. In an interesting admixture of fealty and autonomy, "Lord" Vader answers only to the Emperor. His autonomy does not set him apart as a rogue villain, but rather as the one who imposes and preserves imperial order through terror. In the secret operations of the Empire, the villain wields tremendous power under minimal oversight. His power is boundless, but it is circumscribed by a larger story in which his tactics inspire fear. This inspired fear is not just for his person, but also for the workings of greater imperial agendas. Darth Vader is the Dick Cheney of the Galactic Empire.[8]

The character of Darth Vader is developed against the backdrop of a binary account of good and evil. To this end, *Star Wars* employs a familiar and basic cultural symbology of light versus darkness. Movie audiences first set eyes upon Darth Vader in the early scenes of *Star Wars: A New Hope*. As the scrolling introductory text disappears into outer space, the audience is immediately thrown into an action scene. A small transport ship flies into view, under fire from a massive starship in quick pursuit. This first scene introduces the disproportionate scale of the ongoing war between the Rebel Alliance and the Empire: it is David and Goliath in galactic proportions.[9]

The transport ship is captured and soldiers quickly subdue the small band of rebels. Through a veil of smoke, and fast on the heels of the Imperial Stormtroopers, the imposing figure of Darth Vader strides into view. The villain is dressed head to toe in a black spacesuit. A helmet shields his face. Each breath is an audible, mechanized labor. A few moments later, the slight figure of Princess Leia, adorned with a shining white robe, is presented before the towering figure of the "dark" knight of the Empire. The early scene sets the trajectory of the fictive metanarrative: "light shines in the darkness, and the darkness did not overcome it."[10]

Director George Lucas's symbols of light and darkness play out significantly in costuming choices. The heroes are usually dressed in white, or off-white, as in the case of Luke Skywalker and Obi-Wan Kenobi. Princess Leia is dressed in white for the entirety of *A New Hope*, signifying goodness and, presumably, virginity.[11] Han Solo, one of the good guys, but a "scoundrel" by Leia's early assessment, is dressed in a combination of light and dark. The evil Emperor Palpatine is draped in a heavy dark robe, his face always shadowed. In the last film, *The Return of the Jedi*, Luke dons an all black outfit, which serves to indicate both his likeness to his father and the possibility of his "turning" to the Dark Side. Light and darkness is also portrayed environmentally, as there is only one scene in the original trilogy where Darth Vader appears in natural light.[12] Every other scene takes place against the dark abyss of outer space, under the glare of the industrial fluorescent lights of a starship, or in dark, low-lit settings such as the Emperor's lair on the Death Star. The symbology of light and darkness is most obviously developed in Lucas's fictional cosmology, in which Jedi warriors cultivate spiritual connections to an all-pervasive and life-sustaining "Force." This power of the universe is impersonal and mystical, and it can be used for good or for evil. Because the Force is not an agent or a person, however, it resists easy comparisons to Judeo-Christian monotheism. Nevertheless, Lucas's pseudo-religious concept still capitalizes upon the biblical imagery that pervades Western cultural traditions. Moral choices in *Star Wars* come down to the decision to walk in the light or to live in darkness.[13]

Darth Vader is a powerful symbol of what it means to choose to live in darkness.[14] His workings tighten the iron grip of the Empire, while the Rebel Alliance fights against the dissolution of the Republic and the imposition of totalitarian rule. In *Star Wars* it is democracy versus dictatorship. It is therefore easy to see why these films resonated with American audiences in the era of Cold War. After Dresden, Hiroshima and Nagasaki, and Vietnam, citizens of the West were not so easily assured that America always fights as "children of the light."[15] This ambiguity draws us to a story that grants consolation in the clear, global division of good and evil. The antagonism between clearly defined sides of good and evil in *Star Wars* was, and is today, enormously successful precisely because such a binary relationship is lacking in the ordinary lives of citizens of the West.[16] The space opera has a fantastic quality that allows viewers to disengage from the complexities of real world conflict and enter a universe in which good and evil are clearly defined.

The fantastic appeal of the saga comes through in the ways that the viewers engage the characters of the films. As in any good action movie, the heroes and villains of *Star Wars* are usually, and impractically, on the front lines. Such narrative hyperbole allows the heroes to be more courageous than practical reason should allow. For instance, Han Solo and Luke Skywalker serve as exposed sentries on the frozen planet Hoth in *The Empire Strikes Back.* When the band of rebels land on Endor in *The Return of the Jedi*, Luke, Leia, and Han Solo lead the tip of the spear in a ground assault. The same is true of Darth Vader. At different points, he battles with Obi-Wan and Luke one on one. In *A New Hope,* Darth Vader personally leads a special unit of Imperial fighters against the rebel assault on the Death Star, and in *The Empire Strikes Back* he ambushes Han Solo, Leia, and Chewbacca. Like the heroes of Greek mythology, both Vader and the central rebel characters fight gloriously on the front lines, demonstrating fidelity to the cause through acts of individual courage. We are drawn to Darth Vader in similar ways as to the heroes of the Rebellion.

Despite his willingness to personally and courageously participate in battle, Darth Vader's power is characterized primarily by personal piety. Philosopher John Caputo writes that the conflict between the Rebellion and the Empire in *Star Wars* resembles a "religious war," but one in which there is no "opposition between religion and science."[17] Caputo describes the Force as a "mystico-religio-scientific structure that gives life to mystery and *unpredictability* and provides a setting for the human drama."[18] Writing of the continuing relevance of this framework, Caputo concludes, "*Star Wars* offers many young people today a high-tech religious mythology, a fairly explicit 'repetition' or appropriation of elemental religious structures outside the confines of the institutional religious faiths. Religious transcendence is beginning to transcend the traditional religions."[19] Caputo's analysis is apt, for he shows that the success of *Star Wars* points to the ongoing relevance of religious concepts such as devotion, piety, and humility, even in new, technologized contexts. In this way, George Lucas's fictional cosmology accommodates an anthropology in which people are essentially spiritual, though not necessarily religious.

It is important to note, however, that despite Caputo's observation of the alignment of religion and science in the narrative, Darth Vader's own faith is sometimes at odds with the technological spirit of his futuristic age. Darth

Vader communicates this tension memorably in *A New Hope*, when he cautions against unwarranted pride. Vader and Grand Moff Tarkin enter a conference room in which the Empire's top brass are debating the defense of the nearly completed Death Star. The following exchange ends with Darth Vader nearly choking Admiral Motti to death.

> MOTTI: This station is now the ultimate power in the universe. I suggest we use it.
>
> VADER: Don't be too proud of this technological terror you've constructed. The ability to destroy a planet is insignificant next to the power of the Force.
>
> MOTTI: Don't try to frighten us with your sorcerer's ways, Lord Vader. Your sad devotion to that ancient religion has not helped you conjure up the stolen data tapes, or given you clairvoyance enough to find the Rebel's hidden fortress....
>
> VADER: I find your lack of faith disturbing.

Against the broader narrative of the trilogy, it is clear that Admiral Motti misconstrues Darth Vader's devotion as superstition. Darth Vader is not a conjurer, but a pious observer of the ultimate power of the universe, the Force. His own power does not derive from his ability to perform tricks, but rather, from his participation in a power that is greater than himself. According to theologian Paul Tillich, "Faith is not an opinion but a state. It is the state of being grasped by the power of being which transcends everything that is and in which everything that is participates."[20] Tillich's description of faith in the Judeo-Christian tradition nicely applies to the idea of the Force. The Force is an ultimate transcendent power in which everything that is participates. Darth Vader at every point exhibits a faith that is not founded on propositions, but has its source rather in a state of being.

The theme of Darth Vader's faith is mirrored throughout the films in Luke Skywalker's own growing awareness of the power of the Force. Early in *A New Hope*, Luke trains with a light saber on the *Millennium Falcon*. Obi-Wan Kenobi teaches the young Skywalker that the Force flows through him but also follows his commands. Luke shows the fruit of this participatory training at the end of *A New Hope*, when he chooses to turn off his targeting computer in his fighter, relying instead on the power of the Force to guide his attack on the first Death Star. In this way, Luke's faith does not function as an opinion, but as a state of being. In *The Empire Strikes Back*, Yoda uses the Force to raise Luke's sunken fighter onto dry land from the bottom of the swamp in the Dagobah System. Luke runs to him amazed. "I don't believe it!" Luke exclaims. Yoda responds, "That is why you fail." For Luke and for Darth Vader, the power of the Force comes not through superstition or opinion, but in participation and trust.

Rather than acknowledging participation within a greater, transcendent reality, Admiral Motti's assertion of technological confidence instead celebrates the most recent chapter of the developing destructive power of humankind. Seen in a certain light, the Death Star is the galactic equivalent of the biblical story of the tower of Babel, in which humanity attempts to "make a name" for itself through the construction of "a tower with its top in the heavens."[21] The space-age technology of the Galactic Empire accomplished the ancient goal of inhabiting the heavens, and its architects viewed the result as the ultimate power of the universe. When Darth Vader chastens the admiral, saying, "Don't be too proud of this technological terror you've constructed," he echoes the sentiment of God's judgment in Genesis, namely, that humanity should not think of itself too highly. In *Star Wars*, as in the Bible's account of the Tower of Babel, there is a greater power that can thwart even the best of human technology. Further, the exchange between Vader and Motti illustrates the alienation from moral certainty that accompanies rapid technological progress. Seen from the perspective of modern politics, the ability to destroy a planet is the logical extension of the power of the nuclear bomb. Darth Vader's hesitancy around bald pride in technological advancement gives voice, albeit from the side of "evil," to the alienated and unsettled mood that accompanies the power to destroy whole peoples and civilizations. It is interesting to note that we *empathize* with Vader over Motti in this scene. Evil is not always clear-cut. Rather, we are able to make distinctions within it.

The question of technology implicates Darth Vader's own existence. Like the Force itself, technology in *Star Wars* is morally neutral. It can be used for good or evil. Technology, in the case of Luke's robotic prosthetic hand, ensures a full restoration of his original bodily powers. With regard to the body, the moral value of technology is essentially a question of proportionality: how much humanity remains?[22] Early in the trilogy, Obi-Wan Kenobi ruminates that Darth Vader consists of more machine than man. This tension between the human and the machine is consistently demonstrated by the audible, regulated breathing function of Darth Vader's helmet paired with the robust voice of James Earl Jones. His voice sounds human, but with distinctly technological modulations. We relate to the complex admixture of machine and man in Vader's character in a way that is different from the films' robotic droids. For example, C-3PO and R2-D2, despite their statuses as "good" characters, essentially provide comic effect through their misfortunes and successes. In several scenes, C-3PO is dismembered, either by a misstep or by violence.[23] Similarly, R2-D2 takes fire from enemy planes, falls into a swamp and is momentarily swallowed by a monster, and is shot by a blaster on Endor. In each of these scenes, the viewer always knows that the demise of the droids is temporary, and in the long term, insubstantial. They are not human, and through the patience of a Wookie, they will be eventually fully repaired. Not so with Darth Vader. Despite the fact that we do not see Vader's facial expressions, his utterances still convey emotional content, particularly anger and irritation. At the end of *Return of the Jedi*, Luke battles Vader with vehemence, driving the villain down onto his back. Deflecting a thrust, Luke wheels his own weapon around and cuts off the saber-hand of his father, revealing an intricate arrangement of severed wires. It seems as though Luke is revealing that Vader is mostly a machine. Nevertheless, we hear the humanity in his voice, in his now altered breathing, and see it represented in his defeated physical demeanor. Thus, despite the artificial components of his constitution, Darth Vader remains a decidedly human character in this moment. That is, we identify with the pathos of his suffering.

Our ability, at times, to identify with Darth Vader makes him a potent character. He represents a possible endpoint to Luke Skywalker's explorative narrative of self-trust. The greatest obstacle for the hero of *Star Wars* is himself. Luke's identity is clouded by fears, insecurities, and fantasies about his future self. He is enthusiastic and determined, but he struggles to overcome a fragile ego. As in all coming of age stories, the transition from youthful innocence to responsible adulthood is a process that is illuminated by possibility, but fraught with the anxiety. Darth Vader informs Luke's journey to self-reliance at every point. Beru, Luke's aunt, suggests that her nephew has "has too much of his father in him." Similarly, Luke's early promise, "I want to learn the ways of the Force and become a Jedi like my Father," sets the stage for his journey of self-discovery that will follow the path cut by his unknown father. Luke's exploration of self-trust requires honesty for what lies within and courage to confront what lies without. In the words of Ralph Waldo Emerson, "To believe your own thought, to believe that what is true for you in your private heart is true for all men,—that is genius."[24] Luke's Jedi training is the cultivation of his own genius, and it represents the challenge of self-trust.

One critical moment in this development comes in the midst of Luke's training with Yoda in *The Empire Strikes Back*. At one point, when Luke looks over at a dark cave, a strange feeling overwhelms him:

> YODA: A domain of evil it is. In you must go.
>
> LUKE: What's in there?
>
> YODA: Only what you take with you.

Journeying into himself in the dream-like sequence that follows, Luke explores the possible evil within. Deep in the underground cave, the figure of Darth Vader suddenly appears. Luke draws his weapon, parries a blow from Vader, and in a violent swing decapitates the villain. In slow motion, Darth Vader's helmet roles into view and the shield suddenly explodes to reveal Luke's own face. In this hallucination, Luke unconsciously kills his father, and simultaneously reveals his potential future self. Soon after this experience, Luke sees a vision of his friends in danger. Luke rushes to the aid of his allies, only to find himself the victim of an elaborate trap. Now in real life, Darth Vader confronts Luke alone. The numerous Stormtroopers that aided the capture of Leia, Han Solo, Chewbacca, and C-3PO are now curiously absent. After a series of dramatic fight sequences, Vader defeats Luke both physically and emotionally. Sensing weakness, Darth Vader appeals to the power of the Dark Side of the Force, urging Luke to join the Empire. When Luke resists, the villain issues the powerful and climatic revelation.

> DARTH VADER: Obi-Wan never told you what happened to your father.
>
> LUKE: He told me enough. He told me *you* killed him.
>
> DARTH VADER: No, *I* am your father.
>
> LUKE: No, no, that's not true. That's impossible!
>
> DARTH VADER: Search your feelings, you know it to be true.

In this moment the present and potential self come crashing together in the revelation of a frightening family relation. Luke's horror simultaneously arises from two directions. For the first time in his life, Luke meets his father. After years of absence, his father is finally before him. At the same moment, it is revealed to him what he is capable of, and what he might become. What does it mean to be the progeny of Darth Vader? Vader appeals to the "evidence" of what Luke already knows to be true for himself. The conflict between Luke and Darth Vader, of course, does not end at this moment. Instead, Luke narrowly escapes, thus deferring the resolution to the final film of the trilogy. Luke's acceptance of the revelation is the acceptance of his own capacity for evil. The capacity to turn to evil further reveals the grey area that exists between the appealing, binary account of light and darkness presented in the broad narrative of the story.

In the dramatic revelation of the father-son relation, Darth Vader's character introduces a new plot line that connects corporate liberation to individual redemption. In *A New Hope*, the narrative emphasis is the simple defeat of the Empire. The Rebel Alliance overcomes great odds right before the moment of defeat. The Death Star is destroyed and Darth Vader's fighter plane is sent spinning off into space. By the time the credits role in *The Return of the Jedi*, however, there is a decidedly different narrative emphasis: conversion. While the primary theme remains hope for victory in the face of overwhelming adversity, the story builds to incorporate an equally important theme of hope for the redemption of evil. In *The Return of the Jedi*, Luke returns to Dagobah where he first saw the vision of himself as Darth Vader. Yoda instructs Luke that only after he confronts and kills Darth Vader will the Jedi training be complete. Luke replies, "I can't kill my own father." Luke learns that Leia is his sister, thus generating another plotline of self-discovery and self-trust — albeit a stunted plotline, for Leia's own power is only apparent in a few scenes of emotive intuition. Luke's destiny remains. He must confront himself and his father. The climax of the trilogy begins in a dramatic gamble when Luke turns himself over to Darth Vader in the belief that "there is still good in him." Imprisoning Luke on the Death Star, the Emperor and Darth Vader attempt to lure Luke to the Dark Side of the Force.

This possibility of conversion dominates the last scenes of the trilogy. For a time, even in his resistance, Luke appears close to turning to the Dark Side. He battles Darth Vader vigorously, nearly giving in to anger and despair. Ultimately defeating Darth Vader in a reversal of the climactic scene in *The Empire Strikes Back,* Luke's completes his training as a Jedi and, as a result, calls forth the Emperor's vengeance. Darth Vader, the now broken villain, silently watches as Luke writhes on the floor under the power of the Emperor's Force-lightning. Emersonian themes course through these last scenes, first in Luke's embrace of self-trust, and second in Darth Vader's eventual conversion. For Emerson and, in this instance, for Darth Vader, "In every work of genius we recognize our own rejected thoughts: they come back to us with a certain alienated majesty."[25] Darth Vader recognizes himself in Luke's suffering testimony. Darth Vader sees an alternate form of his previous self, a version of his own rejected genius. Where he had capitulated to the forces of evil, his son resists, even unto death. At the critical and redemptive moment, Darth Vader intercedes with his last strength for his alienated son, thwarting the Emperor's murderous rage. The entire theme of "turning," either to the Dark Side or back to the ways of good, undergirds Darth Vader's appeal as a villain. The capacity for conversion, for good or for ill, connects deeply with the individual viewer's own sense of unrealized potential.

What makes the character of Darth Vader so compelling is that he shows what it means to turn to evil.[26] Darth Vader shows that conversion to the Dark Side brings great power, stature, and influence. In reality, given the choice, many of us would choose to be Goliath rather than David (assuming the end of the story wasn't known in advance). The New York Yankees of Major League Baseball prove this point every year: the best players depart to play in the Empire State. Not giving in may entail a good deal of giving up. Life on the imperial margins is not privileged space. Ask any minority group in the United States. In the *Star Wars* films, the liminal status of the Rebel Alliance cannot offer the privileges, benefits, and access that come with authority in the Empire. At the climactic scene in *The Empire Strikes Back,* Vader tempts Luke with the promise that together, they will "rule the galaxy as father and son." The scene recalls the temptation of Jesus in the New Testament. In the biblical text, Satan tempts Jesus with the goods of sustenance and temporal power. Satan then dares Jesus to prove his role as the Son of God. Darth Vader's appeal to Luke rings of the devil's promise regarding temporal power: "To you I will give their glory and all this authority; for it has been given over to me, and I give it to anyone I please."[27] Even in his defeated state, Luke resists the threatening promise of power, instead choosing to remain true to his mission. In the face of overwhelming odds, Luke is ready to serve as a martyr for a set of practices that define a valuable form of life. Luke's decision helps us understand Darth Vader's tragic past. We see the virtuous path Darth Vader could have chosen. Vader sees this "alienated majesty" as well, and intercedes for his son at the last moment.

At the end of the trilogy, Luke drags the broken body of his father through the faltering Death Star. In this moment, Luke's earlier hesitation, "I can't kill my own father," proves prophetic. Luke was right: there was still good in him. While Darth Vader dies, Anakin Skywalker is redeemed to the side of good. Darth Vader implores his son: "Let me look on you with my own eyes." As Vader's mask is removed, we see the villain's face for the first time. Luke is freed of the specter of his unknown father. It is a moment when both characters embrace their destinies. Good triumphs over evil. Later, the resurrection of Anakin Skywalker is made explicit when the "spiritual" bodies of the three fallen Jedi masters appear at the cremation of Darth Vader's body. Anakin appears alongside Obi-Wan and Yoda, dressed in the traditional Jedi robes. As the flames envelop the black spacesuit, so too are the anxieties for the future self consumed. In the final scene, Luke stands near the funeral pyre, a picture of self-trust, while his father and his teachers look down approvingly on the young Jedi. It is precisely this image of reconciliation (to father and self) that so appealed to my cousins and me in our childhood games.

NOTES

1. The reader is invited to recall George Michael Bluth's home video in the quirky television series *Arrested Development* (Fox Broadcasting Company, 2003–6). A running joke in the sitcom, a video of the preteen acting out scenes from the *Star Wars* films, is eventually mistaken for a terrorist training video. Multiply this image by three.

2. Referring also to Steven Spielberg, director George Lucas once commented, "Almost all of our films are about fathers and sons. Whether it's Darth Vader or E.T., I don't think you could look at any of our movies and not find that." See Anthony Breznican's article, "Father Issues Unfold on Film," *USA Today*, 21 May 2008.

3. For the purposes of this essay, I have largely confined my reflection on Darth Vader to the original *Star Wars* trilogy, episodes IV–VI. Though the "prequel" trilogy fills out the details of Anakin Skywalker's history, these later films arrived well after the establishment of Darth Vader's iconic status as one of the most memorable villains in movie history.

4. Darth Vader's semblances of virtue are distorted extensions of the "good" represented

VILLAINS: ESSAYS ON EVIL

in his childhood, a background portrayed in the first episode of the prequel trilogy, *The Phantom Menace*. In this film, his mother describes Anakin, the product of an immaculate conception (a theological theme that is never fully explained), as one "who knows nothing of greed."

5. In *A New Hope*, Greedo has a small but memorable part: Han Solo "blasts" him in the bar at Mos Eisley.

6. Boba Fett is the bounty hunter responsible for apprehending and delivering Han Solo to Jabba the Hutt in the original trilogy. In what feels like an unnecessary indulgence of the fanboy culture that surrounds the original films, George Lucas significantly expands the story of Boba Fett in Episode II, *Attack of the Clones*. Without this later character expansion, Boba Fett occupies an essentially symbolic role.

7. In the climax of the third film of the prequel trilogy, *Revenge of the Sith*, Anakin Skywalker seals his conversion to the Dark Side when he uses the Force to choke Padmé, his pregnant wife.

8. Former U.S. vice president Dick Cheney once infamously speculated that some people considered him the Darth Vader of the Bush administration. Cheney's reference came in an interview with John King on CNN's *The Situation Room*, 22 June 2006. Not surprisingly, this reference provided endless material for parody (especially for Jon Stewart and the writers of Comedy Central's *The Daily Show*).

9. Cf. 1 Samuel 17. All scriptural references are from the New Revised Standard Version. The biblical images of stones and sling versus the powerful "sword" are made explicit in the conflict between the Ewoks and the Imperial forces on Endor.

10. John 1:5.

11. Leia's purity is emphasized throughout the original trilogy. Although she is a romantic interest for both Han Solo and Luke Skywalker (until, of course, Leia and Luke discover that they are brother and sister), sexual intimacy is limited to an occasional kiss with one of the male heroes. Leia's innocence and purity of the first film, symbolized by her conservative white robe, is undermined in the final film when she is dressed as an exotic dancer bound to Jabba the Hutt by a leash. When Luke eventually rescues her, he saves more than her life — he redeems her honor. Taken together, Leia's initial innocence, captivity, and ultimate need for a male rescuer represent a tangled mess of juvenile male fantasies.

12. This scene takes place in Lando Calrissian's cloud city, Bespin, where Darth Vader ambushes Han Solo, Leia, Chewbacca and C-3PO.

13. 1 John 1:5–7. It is important to note that this biblical imagery has an extremely problematic legacy in the history of the West, whereby the language of lightness and darkness is distorted for the purpose of distinguishing whiteness and blackness. Light/white represents goodness, while dark/black signifies impurity or depravity. This employment of the biblical imagery has fueled, particularly in America, a violent history of discrimination and violence through the establishment and continuous maintenance of the "color line." While it would be difficult to show that *Star Wars* explicitly operates according to racialized categories, it does capitalize on deeply rooted symbols that have perpetuated a violent legacy of racial prejudice.

14. This choice is made explicit in Episode III of the later prequel trilogy. Chancellor Palpatine (the eventual Emperor) woos Anakin through the promise that the Dark Side will help save his young wife from death in childbirth, a premonition that occupies Skywalker's dreams. While his motivation to turn to evil is clearly directed by his love for his wife, his conversion is solidified in his own stubborn arrogance and growing anger with the Jedi council. Rejecting his training under Obi-Wan Kenobi, Anakin strives to realize his promise to Padmé in Episode II: "I will be the most powerful Jedi ever." In Episode III, the horrendous slaughter of the innocents (the young trainees at the Jedi Temple) exemplifies his *decisive* turn to the ways of evil.

15. Needless to say, the invasion of Iraq at the start of the twenty-first century has intensified this cultural sense of moral ambiguity.

16. Along this line of thinking, Richard Sennet comments that what makes our age so "peculiar" is how "uncertainty today ... exists without any looming historical disaster; instead it is woven into the everyday practices of a vigorous capitalism." Richard Sennet, *The Corrosion of Character: The Personal Consequences of Work in the New Capitalism* (New York: Norton, 1998), 31.

17. John Caputo, *On Religion* (London: Routledge, 2001), 85.
18. Ibid.
19. Ibid., 90.
20. Paul Tillich, *The Courage to Be* (New Haven: Yale University Press, 1952), 172–3.
21. Genesis 11:4.
22. This theme is captured in one of Obi-Wan's offhanded comments in Episode II, *Attack of the Clones*. He muses, "If droids could think, none of us would be here."
23. This comic emphasis is taken to a new level in Episode II, *Attack of the Clones*. In a battle scene, R2-D2 recovers C-3PO's head with a magnet and cable, dragging it through the dust.
24. Ralph Waldo Emerson, "Self-Reliance," *Essays and Lectures* (New York: Library of America, 1983), 259.
25. Ibid.
26. See note 12 above.
27. Luke 4:6. Cf. Matthew 4:1–11.

BIBLIOGRAPHY

Arrested Development. Television series. Broadcast 2 November 2003–10 February 2006. 20th Century–Fox Television.
Breznican, Anthony. "Father Issues Unfold on Film." *USA Today*, Life Section, 21 May 2008.
Caputo, John D. *On Religion*. London: Routledge, 2001.
Emerson, Ralph Waldo. *Essays and Lectures*. New York: Library of America, 1983.
The Holy Bible: Containing the Old and New Testaments. New Revised Standard Version. Oxford: Oxford University Press, 1995.
King, John. *The Situation Room*. Television interview. 22 June 2006. CNN.
Sennet, Richard. *The Corrosion of Character: The Personal Consequences of Work in the New Capitalism*. New York: Norton, 1998.
Star Wars Prequel Trilogy. Directed by George Lucas. Los Angeles: 20th Century–Fox, 2008. DVD.
Star Wars Trilogy. Directed by George Lucas. Los Angeles: 20th Century–Fox, 2008. DVD.
Tillich, Paul. *The Courage to Be*. New Haven: Yale University Press, 1952.

13

Hearts of Darkness: Voldemort and Iago, with a Little Help from Their Friends

Ken Rothman

Attractive Evil — Through Artistic Alchemy

A wise and accomplished executive mentioned the Harry Potter series. I asked him if he believed in magic. "Of course! J.K. Rowling wrote words on paper and became the richest woman in England."

The last words of Kurtz, the depraved white trader in *Heart of Darkness*, were "The horror! The horror!"[1] Like the villains in the forefront of this essay — Lord Voldemort and "honest Iago,"[2] — and like other super-scoundrels who make it to the tops of their charts, the evil Kurtz witnessed was certainly horrible, but fascinating. But what elevated these villains from creepiness, repulsiveness, to widespread salability and recognition as popular commodities and cultural icons?

Does this attractiveness of evil express the elemental joy in gawking that turns moving traffic into sludge when there are wrecked cars and people to see at the side of the road? Or was there a kind of magical genius in the art of creating Rowling's seven novels (and the films and the entire Harry Potter cult)? Both Rowling and Shakespeare succeeded in the alchemy of turning the base metal of repulsive corruption and heart-wrenching catastrophe into the gold of popular fame.

Make no mistake: Shakespeare is not a plant that grows only in schoolrooms or artistic circles. Selling and staging his plays made Shakespeare rich, and performances of the plays on stage and in film guarantee audiences to this day. From its first performance in 1604, *Othello* has had an immense and continuing appeal; and when "adapting" it for today's stage and visual media, writers rarely change a word of the original.[3]

Part of that attractiveness of the inherently repulsive is the pure evil of Iago. Another part — paralleled in the eerie connection between Harry Potter and Lord Voldemort[4] — is (for many audiences) a seemingly occult adhesion between Othello and Iago. Suggesting the depth of that adhesion (as a host of editors and other scholars have told us), many great Iagos have been great Othellos, and many pairs of actors have alternated playing the roles of hero and antihero opposite each other. Looking more deeply, in Western culture, is there (along with opposition) a kind of symbiosis between good and evil, so that the "adversary" is not only a foil for evil, but in some significant sense (as in the pre-biblically-rooted Book of Job) not only a foil but an accomplice of good/God?

Fully to examine the literary alchemy of transmuting the repulsive into the commercially and culturally (if tragically) attractive would be a labor of Sisyphus. This essay focuses on the characters through which pure evil makes itself known, on some of their similarities and differences. As one aspect, I cannot ignore the differences imposed by form (a stage play, as against seven novels which conjure virtually unlimited resources of pictures in the mind). And I choose briefly to comment on a contemporary political and philosophical lesson manifested throughout Rowling's and Shakespeare's expeditions into the heart of pure darkness. Later on, I will comment on the ontology of evil, and on darkness that is so deep that it disenables moral consciousness.

"The horror! The horror!"

Part of the recipe of commercial success — and of so much youth-cultural success that colleges and universities frequently merchandise themselves as Hogwarts-like — is a grandly horrifying villain. In Rowling's seven-volume multi-film cycle of entrancing mythology, Tom Riddle, aka Lord Voldemort, aka The Dark Lord, aka He Who Must Not Be Named, is the bad guy. Except during his periods of eclipse (sometimes the good guys fight back, and sometimes he sabotages himself), he has almost everything.

Persistently, Voldemort wants more, but rejects what he needs most. He wants — and obtains, when he is not in eclipse — great power over others, who are motivated by fear of his Dark Magic, or entranced by dreams of the glory obtainable on his coattails. Perhaps his most fanatic adherent, Beatrix Lestrange, fears him and craves his regard of her powers and loyalty, but none of his Death Eaters like him or love him. They follow him in search of advantage for themselves.[5]

More surprising is Riddle/Voldemort, who, after growing up loveless in an almost Dickensian orphanage, seems not to seek the love he never had, but rather single-mindedly to achieve dominance over others, all others, and over the principle of the good. People often seek that of which they were deprived in early life; an unloved child may be expected to dream of love. A motherless child can speculate on what it would have been like to have had a mother. But Riddle/Voldemort, even while playing nasty, hurtful tricks on his childhood contemporaries, never tried to befriend them, or to manipulate or bewitch them into adoring him. His fundamental evil, as we first observe it, is his wish to control others, most often amplified by his joy (or lack of remorse) when he harms them (usually though not always for the purpose of control).

This departure from the love-seeking quest of the unloved can be attributed in part to an unspecified compound of biological nature, choice, and fate or predestination. The Marvolo family, stunningly depraved,[6] provided him with aptitudes and a heritage of dark powers and motives which he discovered as much as learned or invented. Tom Riddle renamed himself Voldemort, and despite warnings chose to travel to learn all the dark magic he could find.

Some of the Dark Lord's qualities can be understood as derived from his catastrophic defeat and dismemberment by primordial matriarchal powers when he tried to kill the infant Harry Potter but was foiled by Harry's mother's self-sacrifice. The evil-doer was left without effective powers, though still in possession of the dark knowledge which seemed to have come to him through inheritance, choice, and fortune. At his low ebb he was virtually without a body, and without most of the appetites, which for better or worse make us human.

But even before Voldemort "blew up" the Potters and their house, he had no interest in food, drink, sex, affiliation, or constructive achievement. He showed only a death-and-destruction-loving will to power and thirst for vengeance against anyone believed to have thwarted him. We can think of him as a pure instantiation of Thanatos, the personification of death which sometimes appears in classical Greek drama, and which Freud popularized as a death instinct, a Freudian conceptualization of an urge toward dissolution and death.

In such a joyless, indeed a lifeless, life as Voldemort's, we see not just evil, but Milton's understanding of hell, the place and condition which evil treats as home:

> Which way I fly is Hell; myself am Hell;
> And in the lowest deep a lower deep
> Still threat'ning to devour me opens wide,
> To which the Hell I suffer seems a Heav'n.[7]

But even if we learn from Milton, as from Marlowe and Goethe and others, that hell exists first in this life, do we learn why Voldemort, with his great powers, desired so small a portion of the (some say God-given) benefits which earthly life affords? In Native American tradition, as in Judaic scripture, life is hard, but at least it is life in the sunshine; while death is a realm of darkness. Voldemort seems impervious, oblivious, to the benefits of life in the sunshine. And in this dark hell, this Shell or Pit of Semitic tradition, one is not only beyond light, but beyond choice. Dumbledore repeatedly offered Tom Riddle the choice of a better life; Harry did so as well, dramatically in their final duel.

The depiction of Voldemort helps us to understand a particular strand of Western thinking about evil. From Plato through the Neoplatonists through Deuteronomy, through Jesus' anguished words on the cross and through Augustine, evil is understood in part as a privation, a lack of knowledge. Jesus makes this clear in the midst of his suffering: "Forgive them, for they do not know what they are doing."[8] Voldemort has no knowledge, no inkling, of the harm he has done and intended. Both Dumbledore and, in the end, Harry Potter invite him to achieve redemption through remorse, or at least a desire for reconciliation. But he is blind to, unknowing of, the light of knowledge of the good. He rejects it as a choice. Already in hell, he lacks the comprehension, the capacity, that would enable a choice. He cannot plead to escape his fate because he lacks the ability to distinguish good from evil. He does not need to be judged and sentenced and sent to hell, for he has already placed himself in it: "Hell hath no limits, nor is circumscribed / In one self place, for where we are is hell, / And where hell is there must we ever be."[9]

Voldemort rejects the opportunities he is offered for redemption. He ends up an inconsolable, infinitely suffering splinter of his former self, in a private hell of his own engineering. As Dumbledore tells Harry in the place pictured as King's Cross railroad station (ironically, also locus of Platform 9¾), Voldemort's soul-splinters (pictured as something like a writhing abandoned baby) are beyond help, to be left to eternal unbounded agony.[10]

Voldemort's own fate aside, can evil as profound as his serve the purposes of good? Since Voldemort can validly be seen as living in a self-constructed hell on earth, his situation can provide a warning to those who can identify good and evil choices but find the choosing to be difficult. For Voldemort, it appears as if he never understood the possibility of choosing between good and evil. Someone else, capable of making the distinction, and understanding that he or she might be attracted to the evil choice, may nevertheless learn from experience and admonition, and even with difficulty make the "good" choice — as did Remus Lupin, when he was overcome by self-hate (as a human tainted by a werewolf attack) and ready to abandon wife and child, but was persuaded not to.

Without a vision of good, and without any ability to attach himself affectively to other human beings and recognize their intrinsic worth, Voldemort went beyond using human beings as means toward ends. There was no plan of tragically sacrificing some for a greater good. The individuals lacked reality; they lacked value; they were experienced as objects. When Voldemort kills Snape, his regret is coldly calculative; he is losing a valued tool. When Voldemort orders Cedric Diggory's death, he does not name him, but uses a term from the factory floor, "the spare."[11] In moral blindness, can one go further?

The closest that Voldemort came to moral awareness and therefore to conscious choice was in his killing of Snape.[12] The Dark Lord lacked the power to kill Harry with his own wand, because the magical core of both wands was a feather from the same enchanted phoenix. Nor was he able to murder Harry with the wand he ordered a Death Eater, Lucius Malfoy, to surrender. A wand works best for its owner, and ownership passes through defeat. Voldemort tells Snape that he needs his wand, and that he must kill Snape to obtain its power. He says to Snape, "I regret it," in his trademark "cold, high voice," and pronounces the killing curse.[13] Was Voldemort at that point a moral personality, choosing to cast Snape into death, for the sake of a better weapon? Perhaps, since he took Snape's life in order to acquire a tool. More in character for Voldemort, Snape too was used as a tool, and Voldemort's passionless regret was for the loss of one tool (albeit a lesser) to gain another tool. Killing Snape provides further evidence of moral unconsciousness. Voldemort knew (or, as a capable wizard, should have known) that he could have acquired the wand and its full power by disarming Snape in a duel (using the *Expelliarmus* jinx). And in the end, Voldemort is defeated by another failure of knowledge. He blasts open Dumbledore's tomb and takes his wand. He had neither killed nor disarmed a living Dumbledore. As a result, in Voldemort's final confrontation with Harry, the stolen wand backfired and undid Voldemort.

Voldemort, in fact, left a trail of apparent failures of knowledge, which point to moral vacuity rather than a straightforward lack of information or skill. He failed to appreciate the power of Lily Potter to protect her baby — failed to appreciate both the primordial magic of the Mothers and the power of love; he failed in awareness that a house elf has magical powers different from those of a human wizard; he failed to see that Snape, disappointed in love, might maintain his attachment to his beloved, rather than just choosing a substitute. But for Voldemort, humans were but objects, tools for his use. Thus he used the vocabulary of a machine shop when ordering Cedric Diggory to be killed.

In contrast, Snape related to humans as beings, not things. As a result of Snape's enduring love for Lily, Snape's loyalty was to Dumbledore, not Voldemort. Because of that ineradicable attachment to Lily, he was able to function as a double agent, while convincingly appearing loyal to the Dark Lord. The latter was not only blind to love and morality, but to any form of attachment. Everything was a means toward his ill-guided purpose of divine immortality for himself. That deformed, demonic man who wanted to be God had no regard for the creation and creatures he wished to dominate. Voldemort was alone, unattached, in a radical way, and in that way he ends.

These vignettes are all examples of evil as a privation, a paucity of knowledge. This knowledge, however, is not a compendium of disembodied facts. Morally significant knowledge, in the Platonic and Judeo-Christian traditions, is knowledge which can be applied to moral choices, i.e., to determining the presence of good and evil in alternative actions, and behaving accordingly. Voldemort did not lack the relevant knowledge in the examples just cited — but he "forgot" it. His moral unsightedness resulted in part from a failure to value sexuality, , love, house elves, and human life in every particular — and in part from a failure to engage in moral choice, weighing and if necessary choosing between values. These and other failures of awareness resulted, in the constructed theater of battles between embodiments of good and evil, in a dramatically convincing destruction of the man who would be God.

The question of whether Voldemort possessed the capacity to diagnose and assay goods and evils, and the capacity to make choices when those determinations were made, leads to two other questions. First, should persons without the capacity to recognize and weigh values be held responsible for the consequences of their actions? In the moral universe that Rowling creates, the answer has some subtlety. An act of killing damages — fragments — the human soul.[14] The consequence is intrinsic to the act, and does not require a separate moment of judgment. Apart from issues of crime, justice, and punishment, capital punishment is arguably harmful to the persons and society that administer it. The executioner becomes a person who kills, and the society becomes one which condones avoidable killing. These consequences are seen as intrinsic to the judicially sanctioned killing. Voldemort, when as Tom Riddle he manipulated Slughorn into revealing the nature of the Horcrux, contemplated the normally unthinkable, creating seven horcruxes. With each murder, subsequently, he blasted away a part of his soul, a result immediate and intrinsic to each act of murder.[15]

The other issue to which this discussion leads is the interrelation between good and evil. As the editor's introduction argues, we need not think of our moral universe in binary terms — let's wipe out evil, or let's just pen it up in some hinterland. Rather, is there a good in the continuing existence of evil? The preceding discussion suggests that the existence of evil helps maintain our vitality as moral creatures. In Western traditions, one says that our free will makes our actions morally meaningful, since if we automatically always did good, we would be robots. Put differently — and quite clearly presented in the Harry Potter cycle — the presence of evil alternatives requires us to make choices unless we lack the capacity to do so. Lily Potter could have saved her own life when Voldemort came for Harry. Harry could have accepted Draco Malfoy's offer of comradeship. The Sorting Hat tried to tempt Harry with the advantages of joining Slytherin House. Less desirable alternatives, seen as such, do more than passively act as foils for the better. Within or outside of our awareness at particular moments, alternative possibilities more than allow acts of choice. Choice, if only by default, becomes required. Simultaneously, each act of choice affects who we are — who we will be as we confront the next moment of choice.

Rowling makes sure that we notice that Voldemort, like Harry and others, is offered choices, but her depiction of Voldemort, emerging from Tom Riddle and his apparent genealogical predestination, portrays a person incapable of knowing, recognizing, choosing good. To Tom Marvolo Riddle, good is literally an absurdity.

There are many contrasts available between Voldemort and the quintessentially villainous Shakespearean staple, Iago. We are given so few clues about Iago! He is envious of Cassio's promotion, he may have loved Desdemona, and he may have loved as well as hated Othello. He has succeeded in deception — his wife Emelia has no suspicion when he first asks her to steal Desdemona's handkerchief. Othello and others call him "honest Iago."[16] But Shakespeare, while tantalizing us by having Iago swear perpetual silence as to his motives, suggests through that very promise that Iago is conscious of his guilt, and therefore capable of making a moral accounting and a moral choice. Voldemort, in comparison, has no consciousness of guilt. (Harry has ambition and purpose, but also moral awareness).

Voldemort expertly harnesses inherently destructive forces, including ambition, envy, hatred, fear, dementia, depression, and the worst of the English weather. His successes frighten us; friends we come to love fall in battle. There are terrible setbacks for the forces of good, many occasions when the Dark Mark appears in the sky. Is the sheer magnitude of Darkness in the world the key to the horror of the abyss? Or is there something more? Voldemort and his followers may be quite like the entirely demonic Iblis and his sons. But neither Harry nor his friends and followers are entirely angelic. As humans we are inherently imperfect. Our capacity for evil, and for most of us our awareness of that capacity, tell us that Darkness is within, not just "out there."

The most profound horror of Voldemort lies not in his expertise in the darkest of dark magic. Nor does it lie in his agenda for a new world order. Nor does it lie in the training, organization, and discipline of his followers, or in their sheer numbers. Does it perhaps lie in other folks' self-deceiving willingness to deny his power when it is on the rise?[17] The depth of horror reflects the dark zeniths of other destructive leaders, free apparently of conscience and of the valuation of the individual human life. Hitler, Stalin, Genghis Khan, and other masters of genocide, liquidation, induced plague, or disappearances in every hemisphere come to mind.

But, as in *Heart of Darkness* and *Othello*, have we yet plumbed the final depth? No. The ultimate depth of hell in life can be revealed quietly or theatrically. Marlow in Conrad hears of the evil up the river. He reaches the end point of his Congo quest to discover that one man, Kurtz, was able to build a small empire of depravity with the help of a relative few who followed and adored him. Iago, fueled by disappointment, envy, and other emotions, was able to fool his own wife as to his intentions and — more important — able to recruit his sycophantic friend Roderigo into his plot to madden Othello and kill him and others.

The true depth of Voldemort's horror is unveiled gradually and quietly. As in Elizabethan drama (and Marlow's long quest for Kurtz), crucial happenings occur offstage (or onstage in a manner which belies their depth). Before Harry's first term at the Hogwarts School of Witchcraft Wizardry, he encounters Draco Malfoy, the equally young scion of a Dark family. Malfoy asks Harry to join him, to ally with the right people, those with power in this world and hegemony to come in the new world order. Harry knows himself, and declines.

Likewise, soon after, when the magical Sorting Hat is placed on Harry's head, to determine to which House and which ethos he shall belong, it seeks to tempt him with the earthly rewards and superiority which Slytherin House purports to offer. Harry chooses the path of morally intact bravery, Gryffindor. The Hat respects his wish. Harry may have made the most important decision in his life. But the temptation had been real.

Harry, like all of us, was faced with choices. As an influential New Englander wrote for Victorian congregations:

> Once to every man and nation
> Comes the moment to decide.
> In the strife of truth with falsehood,
> For the good or evil side....
>
> Though the cause of evil prosper,
> Yet 'tis truth alone is strong.
> Truth forever on the scaffold,
> Wrong forever on the throne....[18]

It takes Rowling seven novels (and there will be eight long films) to mac-
erate the Dark Lord — with his own help, for each murder he commits rips
and weakens his soul. But even that self-depredation — a measure of Voldemort's practical and moral tunnel vision, and in a sense incompetence — is
not the deepest chamber in the heart of Voldemort's darkness.

Although the darkness lies within the hearts of Voldemort, Iago, Kurtz,
and countless merchants of death and destruction of body and soul, theirs
may not be the deepest darkness. Nor does the inherent destructiveness within
the individual human heart reveal the full darkness of our morally burdened
species. History reveals that the Stalins, Hitlers, Tojos, and fanatic leaders on
every continent do not work alone. Even today, it takes thousands to destroy
or dispossess millions. Effective evil is collective (Malfoy would have needed
lots of plastic surgery, were it not for Crabbe and Goyle). And though in philosophy we tend to compartmentalize our sub-disciplines, our greatest thinkers
have been aware that the political process, beyond its theatricality, is a moral
process.

The deepest darkness may therefore be that which resides in the hearts
of followers and facilitators. Voldemort needed his armies of Death Eaters
and Dementors. Iago could never succeeded without Roderigo to ply Cassio
with drink he could not handle, and lure him into a forbidden fight. Kurtz
could not have ruled a principality of cruelty without substantial help. Vast
numbers of people seem willing to follow, to kill, maim, rape, enslave, pillage,
destroy, humiliate, and more.

To peer into the heart of darkness is to see that the most capable monsters
accomplish nothing on their own. Ordinary people must follow them and do
their work. One's good neighbor may one night kill one's children and burn
one's house — it has happened far too often. The benign neighbor may appear
to be transformed, when part of a group, even a mob.

That the neighbor is (or can be) us, individually and more horribly with
others, is the darkest horror in the deepest chamber of the heart of darkness.
The Dark Lord may in the end be defeated, but the dark horror poses an
everlasting challenge. The truth in the hymn reaches beyond its Victorian
provenance. It sparked a new phase in the American antiwar movement when
draft cards were burned in the Yale University Chapel as it was sung:

> New occasions teach new duties,
> Time makes ancient good uncouth,
> They must upward still and onward,
> Who would keep abreast of truth.[19]

Whether the enemy is us, depends on our choice. If pressed, we can choose
to die, rather than do wrong. Our deepest darkness is that we yield far short
of that end point.

These remarks reflect some of the many meanings of original sin, seen here aside from theology as an inherent element of human nature. We contribute to human destructiveness whether we conceive and lead its manifestations, actively contribute, or facilitate by silence or other means. Sometimes resistance or non-cooperation is futile. But one never knows. Did James or Lily Potter consider that their apparently futile resistance and deaths would be the first link in a chain of causes of Voldemort's destruction? They could not have seen the future in any detail. They made a moral, not a calculative, choice. And if at the moments of their deaths they could look upon their actions, they would not have cried out (as did Mr. Kurtz) against their own choices.[20]

Nurture, Nature, Genre, and End

We are given almost too much information about Tom Riddle, who came to create himself Lord Voldemort. Through the skill of Harry's mentor Dumbledore, the greatest magician, we see the ancestors and machinations of the Dark Lord. We see that Tom's childhood of ill-tempered destructiveness, in that cruel orphanage and then at Hogwarts, seems virtually pre-ordained. Early on, Dumbledore tries kindly to lead him into better ways; and both Dumbledore and Harry try to kindle a spark of humanity in the twisted soul, but to no avail.

In the end, Voldemort is destroyed, or appears to be. His wand has been attained in contravention of wizarding principles, and Voldemort's death curse turns back on himself. (In traditions throughout the world, an unjust curse often boomerangs.) But the Götterdämmerung might have proceeded more favorably for the Dark Side if not for the momentary desertion of one of Voldemort's staunchest and most powerful followers (bound to her leader by fear, not love). When in the penultimate duel Harry is knocked down, Draco Malfoy's mother is sent to see if Harry is dead. He looks dead, but is breathing — barely. She surreptitiously asks Harry if Draco is still alive, and Harry whispers yes, he is in the castle. In gratitude she tells Voldemort that Harry is dead, which spares Harry a coup de grace. Then Voldemort and the Death Eaters advance to their ultimate defeat, encountering a very live Harry inside the castle.

In that way Voldemort, self-sufficient though he believed himself to be, was dependent on a follower, and, betrayed, went to his doom: "Once to every man and nation / Comes the moment to decide."[21] Draco's mother decided for her son, and for a moment of good. Voldemort again was oblivious to the power of the Mother protecting her son (and to the possibility that she had turned against Voldemort's ways). Though the deepest darkness — the fear which we ordinary people should most fear — may be the proclivity of ordinary persons to follow the devilish leader, the generalissimos of evil may not be able to count on unyielding loyalty from their followers.

That Iago's moral genealogy — in contrast with Tom Riddle's — is missing is in part a product of genre. Within the limits of a normal-length stage play, subject at least in spirit to the doctrine of the three unities (time, place, and action)[22] and to any audience's *Sitzfleisch*, it can be impracticable to explore an antihero's foul ancestry. It may even be impracticable to portray all of the motives of the actors.[23] For example, there is a case to be made that Iago was erotically attracted to Othello and jealous not only of Cassio's prefer-ment, but also of Desdemona's admiration and embraces. And of course Iago may also have been attracted to Desdemona and resented her preferring Othello.

But Shakespeare's impact, characteristically, is strengthened rather than weakened by the genre of the stage play. Many of his murders are experienced as more frightful because they occur offstage. Some actions may never explicitly enter the text but must be inferred. We can fairly make inferences from the gaps and silences in the strange courtship between Iago and Othello, in which an experienced and judicious leader becomes paranoically irrational. What we see is that a single cunning person, with a little help from witting and unwitting accomplices, can produce the terrifying fall of a great man. The audience is spellbound by the details of character and action, by the bringing of Othello to take leave of his judgment. The horror is all the greater because Iago's jealousies and consequent destructiveness are disproportionate to the situation(s) that appear to provoke him. We are left with only a fragmentary sense of Iago's motives, and we are told hat even despite forthcoming torture, Iago will not reveal more: "Demand me nothing. What you know, you know. / From this time forth I never will speak word."[24]

The full measure of Iago's dark horror cannot be weighed through the number of his followers; he does not have that many. Rather, his horror can best be measured by the momentousness of his effect on the apparently good (and in that sense ordinary) people close to him, turning their worlds upside down and ending their lives. As with Voldemort, the deepest and darkest horror lies not within the villain but with those who have wittingly or unwit-tingly followed and been tainted by the villain's version of reality: "Will you, I pray, demand that demi-devil / Why he hath thus ensnared my soul and body?"[25]

Why Doesn't Rowling Frighten Children? And Beyond Childhood...

Even though Voldemort is a quintessentially salable and engrossing if not engaging villain for all ages of readers, it seems that he lacks the capacity to haunt the nightmares of even young children. Every time new volumes were released (at midnight), very young children and their approving parents were in the long lines at large bookstores, many having reserved their copies. Yes, parents approve of reading, and are not always aware of the erudition that Rowling brought to her tales. The archetype of Quidditch, for example, was the Palio di Siena, an annual, originally particularly aggressive version of a horserace. But in an age of electronic distraction, to see children reading actual books warms the hearts of parents.

But why does Voldemort fascinate though not frighten children? And why have they eagerly read Aesop, Grimm, Sendak, and a host of other authors who employ beasts and monsters as devilish antagonists? Perhaps it takes an adult, a particularly aware adult, to discern that the evil entities have a reality outside the storybook. And it can take an adult to realize that the depth and power of evil stem from its empowerment through social structures. We all are fascinated by the thrills of battle between people with white hats and people with black hats, especially when we know that the white hats, however underdoggish at the start, will triumph. It takes an adult to ask who or what set up the battle, who benefits, and who is harmed.

I have argued there is another dimension of evil than that which manifests itself in individual wrongdoing. This depth or darkness, through which an evil heart attracts and affects followers and causes people to fall tragically away from their better selves, is another sort of evil entirely — and whoever understands it, however young, is no longer a child. The deepest horror of evil resides not in one particular villain but in numerous followers (possessed of varying degrees of self-awareness) and their actions.

A credible hint of the deeper, darker evil may (or may not) be beyond the imaginations of most children — but adults can know it in their own ways, sometimes by names such as original sin, or class warfare, or the concept of property as demonized by Rousseau, or institutionalized tribalism or racism, primordial chaos, a will to power, or the death instinct. Is it not frightening to believe that the foundational heart of darkness lies not only in individual hearts, but also in the communally generated (or at least transmitted) structures of our understanding and existence? Is it not frightening to believe that the darkness so often overpowers our flickering efforts at moral judgment of individuals and likewise our efforts to create good societies? Is it not frightening to believe that there is a darker, deeper struggle beyond that of the

Apollonian with the Dionysian? That Iblis and his retinue reside not only in individual hearts, but also in any society's potential for destructiveness (warfare, genocide, plague, famine, drugs, hopelessness, more) on a huge scale?

The adult-world complexity of evil goes beyond the portrayal of Aurors and the Order of the Phoenix, against Death Eaters and Dementors. John Le Carré recounts this story:

> Years ago I talked to a man who had been flogged, an English mercenary who was doing us [British Secret Intelligence Service] a few favors in Africa and needed paying off. [He had been caught and flogged, and later escaped.] What he remembered most was not the lash but the orange juice they gave him afterwards. He remembers being helped back to his hut, he remembers being laid face down on the straw. But what he really remembers is the glass of fresh orange juice that a warder set at his head, then crouched beside him, waiting patiently, till he was strong enough to drink some. Yet it was this same warder who had flogged him.[26]

Le Carré comments that this occurrence presented a "mystery of good hearts turned inside out" and was a "terror." To judge the warder's actions within the frame of reference of individual choice of good or evil increases the mystery and the terror. But within that frame of reference, analysis comes to a dead end. The evil resided foremost in the social organizations which governed the prisoner and the warder, and that is where scrutiny is needed.

In the Western tradition, through the Hebrew Bible, we repeatedly confront the limits of moral judgment of the individual, the question of whether and how morally disordered primeval chaos persists within, behind, beneath the individual in a world believed to be divinely created:

> And the Lord had regard for Abel and his offering, but for Cain and his offering he had no regard. So Cain was very angry, and his countenance fell. The Lord said to Cain, "Why are you angry, and why has your countenance fallen? If you do well, will you not be accepted? And if you do not do well, sin is lurking at the door; its desire is for you, but you must master it."[27]

I have argued that "sin is lurking at the door" not only in the obvious sense that we may be lured into murder for emotional or pecuniary gain, but in the sense that with varying degrees of awareness we may become active accomplices in evil (Death Eaters or death camp guards, Eichmann-like following orders and doing their duty). Or we may become so transformed that we mistake good for evil (Othello throttling Desdemona). I have argued that the deepest chamber of the heart of darkness is our own belief in our own ordinariness in a disordered world — whether we become accomplices or victims of an über-villain's mind-twisting.

Do Western philosophy and Judeo-Christian moral theology help us to understand and to be better moral creatures? Traditionally, philosophy and theology divide harms into natural evil (step on a snake and it bites you) and moral evil (unprovoked assault). But is there not another paradigm of evil, in which good hearts apparently acting rationally and with good intentions wreak great harm because of the institutional structure within which they act? If "sin" is persistently lurking at the door (even after Voldemort is scattered to the winds), is there not a locus of sinfulness beyond that of the individual? Hitlers and Stalins may provide direction and templates of action, but why have there been so many followers? Even with Voldemort gone, is society safe?

In several novels, Le Carré speaks of "grey men." The "grey men" who manage the bureaucratic systems on which our lives may depend, systems which treat people as things, have little need for individual passion, awareness, moral choice, or articulated principle — and systems rarely reward individuality. Whether or not Rowling ever brings Voldemort back to the page and screen, in today's world the sin lurking at the door is at least as much systemic, institutional, organizational, and implicit as it is a matter of individual moral choice.

Finally...

Is there a linkage between the chamber of the heart of darkness in which the arch-villains reign, and the chamber of danger in which most of us dwell, where the horror is that we may become followers (like many of the Death Eaters) without counting the stakes, or victims (like Othello) without adequately assessing our assumptions? Is that linkage written in our cultures and personalities?

Iago stabs Roderigo fatally, attempting to conceal his deception and use of Roderigo. At the verge of death, Roderigo cries out: "O damned Iago! O inhuman dog!"[28] That line was not throwaway Elizabethan rhetoric. Rather, it gets to the heart of the matter. Whenever we treat another person as purely a means, a utility, and engage (at most) in a monologue with that person, we are treating him or her as an "it" rather than a "thou." In an "I-Thou" relationship, on the other hand, we are listening and hearing, responding within a dialogue, seeing and valuing the other person in a direct, mutual, personal relationship.[29]

Whether one be an arch-villain such as Voldemort or Iago, a follower such as a rank-and-file Death Eater, or a victim who was too easily taken in such as Othello, the sin lurking at the door is that any of us may become an inhuman dog, following a leader, accepting a dehumanized world view, doing our jobs as grey men, and entering the darkest reaches of dehumanized heartlessness. Voldemort died rejecting an opportunity for reconsideration of the self he had made, the world which he had tainted, the grey men who so easily aligned with him. And the Harry Potter cycle closes without our knowing whether Draco Malfoy and many others would align with the next power-loving, death-dealing villainous leader.

The cycle closes, also, with our having been treated to a panoramic vision of the moral universe as created by J.K. Rowling. Biological inheritance, nurture, the power to choose within finite circumstances, and the vagaries of fortune are all operative. Moral evil very often implicates — indeed requires — groups, not villains operating in vacuums. In that sense, ethics and politics are one.

NOTES

1. Joseph Conrad, *Heart of Darkness* (London: Everyman, 1995), 85.

2. In William Shakespeare's *Othello*, Iago two-facedly plots to destroy Othello. Othello trusts Iago until the last scene. Until then he frequently addresses Iago as "honest Iago," and often the audience, knowing better, laughs. Voldemort, on the other hand, is manifestly the "Dark Lord" to both his followers and his enemies.

3. See standard editors' introductions, such as that by Wilbur L. Cross and Tucker Brooke to *The Yale Shakespeare* (New York: Barnes & Noble, 2005).

4. From the beginning to the end of the series, Voldemort and Harry have magical connections. Initially, Voldemort's failure to kill the infant Harry establishes a bond between their minds and moods. See J.K. Rowling, *Harry Potter and the Sorcerer's Stone* (New York: Scholastic, 1998). At the end, Voldemort's death curses fail to kill Harry, in large part because their wands contain empowering cores from the same sources. J.K. Rowling, *Harry Potter and the Deathly Hallows* (New York: Scholastic, 2007).

5. In like manner, Draco Malfoy even before Harry arrives at Hogwarts, and the Sorting Hat itself, offer Harry a panoply of earthly advantage if he chooses to join Draco's clique in Slytherin House (*Sorcerer's Stone*). And in the Epilogue to *Deathly Hallows*, Harry confides to his younger son that the Sorting Hat listens to choices. Rowling's moral universe, as we shall see, involves nature, nurture, and choice, with perhaps more than a small component of pre-destination or fate.

6. J.K. Rowling, *Harry Potter and the Half-Blood Prince* (New York: Scholastic, 2005), Ch. 10.

7. John Milton, *Paradise Lost*, ed. John Leonard (London: Penguin, 2003), IV.75–78.

8. Luke 23:34. All scriptural references are from the New Revised Standard Version.

9. Christopher Marlowe, *Dr. Faustus and Other Plays*, ed. David Bevington and Eric Rasmussen (New York: Oxford University Press, 2008), V.111–113.

10. *Deathly Hallows*, Ch. 25.

11. J.K. Rowling, *Harry Potter and the Goblet of Fire* (New York: Scholastic, 2000), Ch. 32.

12. Asking Lily to step aside and save herself, when Voldemort came to kill the infant Harry, is in a limited sense a moral act; Lily's death would not have served Voldemort's purpose of assuring himself a God-like immortality. But Voldemort never is said to have rebuked his followers, the Death Eaters, for random thrill-killings of "Muggles" (ordinary humans).

13. *Deathly Hallows*, Ch. 32.

14. This generalization includes accidental and judicially imposed killing. Counseling is routinely provided in those circumstances.

15. *Half-Blood Prince*, Ch. 23.

16. *Othello*, V.ii.47.
17. The aptly named Cornelius Fudge gets a good laugh from audiences if not his co-players when he finally blurts out that Voldemort has returned, rather like the laughter in some audiences when Othello addresses "honest Iago."
18. The hymn is cited in William Sloane Coffin, *Once to Every Man* (New York: Atheneum, 1977), 243.
19. Ibid.
20. The several philosophical and theological views of evil employed in this essay, and the assertion that evil is often collective even though particular arch-villains can be identified, are inspired by the life's work of Hannah Arendt. An excellent starting point for the reader is her *Eichmann in Jerusalem: A Report on the Banality of Evil* (New York: Penguin, 1994).
21. Coffin, 243.
22. See Aristotle, *Poetics*, trans. Malcolm Heath (New York: Penguin, 1997).
23. Notice that it requires eight films to depict the seven Rowling novels — and much needed to be left out.
24. *Othello* V.ii.355–6.
25. *Othello*, V.ii.353–354.
26. John Le Carré, *The Russia House* (New York: Bantam, 1990), 280.
27. Genesis 4:4–7.
28. *Othello*, V.i.74.
29. See Martin Buber, *I and Thou* (New York: Scribner, 1955).

BIBLIOGRAPHY

Arendt, Hannah. *Eichmann in Jerusalem: A Report on the Banality of Evil*. New York: Penguin, 1994.
Aristotle. *Poetics*. Trans. Malcolm Heath. New York: Penguin, 1997.
Buber, Martin. *I and Thou*. New York: Scribner, 1955.
Coffin, William Sloane. *Once to Every Man*. New York: Atheneum, 1977.
Conrad, Joseph. *Heart of Darkness*. London: Everyman, 1995.
Cross, Wilbur L., and Tucker Brooke, eds. *The Yale Shakespeare Complete Works*. 2nd ed. New York: Barnes & Noble, 2005.
Le Carré, John. *The Russia House*. New York: Bantam, 1990.
Marlowe, Christopher. *Faustus and Other Plays*. Ed. David Bevington and Eric Rasmussen. New York: Oxford University Press, 2008.
Milton, John. *Paradise Lost*. Ed. John Leonard. London: Penguin, 2003.
Rowling, J.K. *Harry Potter and the Deathly Hallows*. New York: Scholastic, 2007.
_____. *Harry Potter and the Goblet of Fire*. New York: Scholastic, 2000.
_____. *Harry Potter and the Half-Blood Prince*. New York: Scholastic, 2005.
_____. *Harry Potter and the Sorcerer's Stone*. New York: Scholastic, 1998.
Shakespeare, William. *Othello*. New York: Signet, 1998.

Epilogue

Upon accepting the Nobel Peace Prize in 1986, Elie Wiesel ushered his audience into the kind of place that evil makes possible. In the concentration camps, Wiesel explained, the pillar of what our culture holds to be good became something very different:

> Night after night, seemingly endless processions vanished into the flames, lighting up the sky. Fear dominated the universe.... Life in this accursed universe was so distorted, so unnatural that a new species had evolved. Waking among the dead, one wondered if one was still alive.[1]

These words shattered the sense of stability that the notion of good affords. Wiesel refused to let the dignitaries in the audience forget the extent to which Hitler's evil erased humanity across Europe. This evil distorted the notion of good to the point that life — that which the Judeo-Christian's good God gives — ceased to be certain.

The vast majority of the intellectual, cultural, and literary concerns that influence the examples treated throughout this book still have at their core a stable assumption that Wiesel fractures. When goodness is no longer certain, evil's effects can be felt with full force. As Wiesel makes clear, the extent to which evil can affect our world must be taken seriously. The question, then, is how we are supposed to respond to history's horrors, to the countless victims that evil has left strewn across our memories?

Though a clear answer may well be impossible, Wiesel recognizes that what matters is our willingness to enter into a place where evil has disjointed our most reliable beliefs: "No generation has had to confront this paradox with such urgency. The survivors wanted to communicate everything to the living: the victim's solitude and sorrow, the tears of mothers driven to madness, the prayers of the doomed beneath a fiery sky."[2] Those who encountered evil in its raw ability to destroy did not let go of what is (or was?) good; they still prayed into that sky.[3] What is at stake when confronting evil is our willingness to listen those voices, however faint, and therefore to admit that we cannot affirm the notion of goodness without admitting that same goodness' failure.

Wiesel knows well what it means to suffer and to look everywhere without finding the hope that good offers. "Have we failed?" he asks an audience of powerful people who uphold the good. "I often think we have."[4]

The point of this project is not to privilege the good in our culture, and it is certainly not to root for the villains that so often capture our attention. The point, which I hope has come across in the ways these essays echo one another, is that evil matters in our culture, however one chooses to define it. Though fictional, the villains treated in this project pinpoint a serious concern in our shared cultural heritage and in our shared humanity. Sometimes we cannot look away from evil. Sometimes the devil manages to trick us. Sometimes we find ourselves drawn inexplicably (or even willingly) towards an end that we know is not good. Such possibilities have proven to be capable of much damage, and it is for this reason that evil is worth thinking about.

To close, I will merely quote Wiesel's concluding paragraph, which I think speaks to what is at stake in thinking about evil:

> There may be times when we are powerless to prevent injustice, but there must never be a time when we fail to protest.... A destruction only man can provoke, only man can prevent. Mankind must remember that peace is not God's gift to his creatures, it is our gift to each other.[5]

Notes

1. Elie Wiesel, "Hope, Despair and Memory," Nobel Lecture delivered 11 December 1986, available at http://nobelprize.org/nobel_prizes/peace/laureates/1986/wiesel-lecture.html (retrieved 22 June 2010).
2. Ibid.
3. Cf. Exodus 1.
4. Wiesel.
5. Ibid.

Bibliography

Wiesel, Elie. "Hope, Despair and Memory." Nobel Lecture delivered on 11 December 1986. Available at http://nobelprize.org/nobel_prizes/peace/laureates/1986/wiesel-lecture.html. Retrieved 22 June 2010.

About the Contributors

Sarah Lynne Bowman received her Ph.D. from the University of Texas at Dallas in 2008. She is the author of *The Functions of Role-Playing Games: How Participants Create Community, Solve Problems, and Explore Identity* (McFarland, 2010). She is currently an adjunct faculty member for Brookhaven College, Richland College, UTD, and Ashford University. Her scholarly interests include, among other topics, psychoanalysis, evolutionary psychology, role-playing, and gender/sexuality, and the study of consciousness in its many forms.

Bryan Dove is a researcher at Glasgow University's Centre for Literature, Theology and the Arts. His work examines a variety of literature from an interdisciplinary perspective. His research interests range from Milton to the Victorian fantasists and from David Hume to Iris Murdoch.

Daniel A. Forbes is an assistant professor of philosophy at West Chester University of Pennsylvania. His research focus is on the history of early modern philosophy, particularly the metaphysics and epistemology of Spinoza. He also has research interests in American pragmatist philosophy and process philosophy.

E. Quinn Fox earned his Ph.D. in religion from Vanderbilt University in 1999 and is associate for theology for the Presbyterian Church (U.S.A.) in the Office of Theology and Worship. A Presbyterian minister, Quinn has taught for 12 years as adjunct professor of church history and historical and systematic theology for Fuller Theological Seminary, mainly at Fuller's Colorado campus.

A.J. Grant is a professor of English studies at Robert Morris University in Pittsburgh. Grant's research interests include writing in the academic disciplines and professions, literature, the history of communications and popular culture topics. Grant received his Ph.D. in rhetoric and English from Northern Illinois University.

After teaching philosophy at West Chester University, **Jamey Heit** is completing his Ph.D. in Glasgow University's Centre for Literature, Theology, and the Arts. His previous book, *The Springfield Reformation:* The Simpsons, *Christianity and American Culture*, was published in 2008. In addition to his critical writings on cultural media, he frequently presents work on John Donne and Emily Dickinson in a variety of academic settings.

Kelly Kelleway earned her Ph.D. in 2002 from the University of California, Riverside, and is currently an assistant professor in the Language and Literature department of Bucks County Community College. Kelly enjoys the shocked looks she receives when her students learn she has been playing video games for 30 years.

Sarah Lafferty is a cultural criminologist and media analyst, as well as an award-winning screenwriter. She holds an M.A. in popular culture studies, a B.A. in film studies, and a B.A. in criminal justice. Her research focuses on gender roles and the interplay of evil in crime genre fiction.

Kristine Larsen is a professor of physics and astronomy at Central Connecticut State University. She is the author of *Stephen Hawking: A Biography* and *Cosmology 101* as well as numerous articles and book chapters on science in the works of J.R.R. Tolkien and C.S. Lewis, the role of women in the history of science, and innovations in interdisciplinary science education. She is co-editor of the recently published book *The Mythological Dimensions of Doctor Who*.

Michael J. Lewis is a freelance writer and media analyst. He has a master's degree in popular culture studies from Bowling Green State University. While at BGSU his academic work focused on television, comics, and online communities. He has written and spoken widely on the topic of terrorism, and he blogs many diverse topics at nifftystuff.com.

Ken Rothman has accumulated five college and university degrees, practiced several professions, and recently retired from college teaching in philosophy and religious studies and in related literature and film. He is an adjunct chaplain and participant in the spirituality, religion, and health seminar at the University of Pennsylvania. For most of his working week, he provides spiritual solace and counseling as an interfaith chaplain for hospice patients.

Nathaniel Van Yperen lives in Princeton, New Jersey, where he is a Ph.D. student in religion and society at Princeton Theological Seminary. When he is not reading or writing, he enjoys spending time in the Adirondacks. His current project explores intersections between political theology and environmental ethics.

Antoinette F. Winstead received a B.F.A. in film and television production from New York University and an M.F.A. in film from Columbia University. She counts among her favorite subjects to write about demonic possession, lost souls, and haunted houses. She is currently a tenured professor of drama and English at Our Lady of the Lake University in San Antonio, Texas, where she teaches courses in screenwriting, film studies, and production.

Index